Created and Directed by Hans Höfer

INSIGHT GUIDES

FRANKFURT
& SURROUNDINGS

Edited by Wieland Giebel
Translated by Ian McMaster, Anne Midgette and
Tony Halliday
Managing Editor: Andrew Eames

HOUGHTON MIFFLIN COMPANY

FRANKFURT

First Edition (Reprint)
© 1993 APA PUBLICATIONS (HK) LTD
All Rights Reserved
Printed in Singapore by Höfer Press Pte. Ltd

Distributed in the United States by:
Houghton Mifflin Company
2 Park Street
Boston, Massachusetts 02108
ISSN: 1064-7880
ISBN: 0-395-65775-X

Distributed in Canada by:
Thomas Allen & Son
390 Steelcase Road East
Markham, Ontario L3R 1G2
ISSN: 1064-7880
ISBN: 0-395-65775-X

Distributed in the UK & Ireland by:
GeoUK **GeoCenter International UK Ltd**
The Viables Center, Harrow Way
Basingstoke, Hampshire RG22 4BJ
ISBN: 9-62421-179-5

Worldwide distribution enquiries:
Höfer Communications Pte Ltd
38 Joo Koon Road
Singapore 2262
ISBN: 9-62421-179-5

ABOUT THIS BOOK

Its name appears almost daily in international newspapers and on almost every international flight departure board in the world, yet Frankfurt's nature as a travel destination is surprisingly little-known. Goethe, Germany's great man of literature, was born here; emperors were elected here, and this is the home of some of Germany's finest arts and museums.

But modern Frankfurt's skyline seems to belong to the future rather than the past. Its contemporary life is based on commerce and banking, its streets are often corridors of glass, steel and concrete. If you know where to go, though, this is as rewarding a city as any in Germany; nuggets of the traditional and the unusual glisten side by side in those corridors of glass and steel, and the city is surrounded by some of the finest countryside in Europe.

The challenge for the authors and photographers of *Insight Cityguide: Frankfurt and Surroundings* was to bring out the best of this city, and to preserve a balanced picture of the urban area and its environs. This, of course, is where Insight Guides excel: in channelling the expertise of local authors into a format which addresses the needs of sophisticated travellers around the world.

Frankfurt is surrounded by extensive forests and castles, by non-active volcanos and river valleys famous for their wine-growing. It is strident and fast, green and gentle. The tension between tradition and high-tech, the American-style skyline and *Ebbelwoi* (apple wine) pubs is the attraction of this city.

This is the latest in a series of Insight Guides to German cities which includes books on Berlin, Munich, Hamburg, Cologne, Düsseldorf and Dresden. In addition, there are Insight Guides to *The New Germany* and *The Rhine*, and Insight Pocket Guides to Berlin and Munich.

The editor of this book, **Wieland Giebel**, has written for travel guides for many years. He has also worked for international radio stations and was consultant to the European Parliament for environmental affairs. He edited *Insight Guide: The New Germany*, and *Insight Cityguide: Dresden*.

An Expert Team

For this book, he recruited 11 journalists, all from Frankfurt or settled in the city. **Heide Platen** learned her profession in the editorial department of a local newspaper. She has lived in Frankfurt for 20 years and has been witness to its transformation through the turbulent 1960s to the financial centre of today. She has reported these changes on radio, in magazines and for the past 10 years as editor of a newspaper. For this book she wrote about the people and many of the downtown districts of the city.

His colleagues claim that **Klaus-Peter Klingelschmitt** is not a real Frankfurter. He lives in Bischofsheim, at the gates of Frankfurt, and has written about Frankfurt and Hesse for the past decade. Klingelschmitt thinks that his contribution on the city's history, particularly about Friedrich Hecker's fighting stand in the Paulskirche and the organisation of the masses to revolt, has been given too little space. He has published a book about Hecker.

The German scholar **Jasna Gerhardt** wrote about Rosmarie Nitribitt, the most-famous prostitute of the time of the economic miracle, and about the teenagers who greeted

Giebel

Platen

Klingelschmitt

Gerhardt

Elvis Presley when he was the most famous GI ever to be stationed at Frankfurt.

Arnd Wesemann, who writes for the local *Journal Frankfurt*, contributed articles about art, literature, theatre and music. He also compiled the material for the invaluable *Travel Tips* section.

You can trust **Regina Schneider's** recommendations of restaurants and pubs. She comes from the culinary triangle between France, Germany and Switzerland (Freiburg) and certainly knows what's what.

Some years ago **Christel Burghoff** chose to settle in the Vogelsberg, about which she has written for this book. In the past she has been actively critical of tourism, but now has changed her mind to support the sort of tourism that is environmentally and socially sustainable.

Kerstin Rose knows the Taunus inside out. When she was a child every second family excursion went to Frankfurt's most popular destination for day-trippers, which she has described for this Insight Guide.

Heipe Weiss studied philosophy at Frankfurt university and has worked in many fields of publishing. For these pages he wrote about Offenbach, the Spessart and the Odenwald, as well as his own work environment.

Johannes Bröckers once worked for the *Pflasterstrand*, the alternative local magazine, and now writes for the advertising industry. In these pages he covers the growth of the Frankfurt Fairs. The Book Fair, an event naturally close to Insight Guides' heart, has been assessed by **Nicholas Clee**, news editor of Britain's *Bookseller* magazine.

The historian **Wolfgang Metternich**, one of the most knowledgeable people on the development of Höchst, contributed the chapter on that district.

As with all Insight Guides, photography plays a crucial role in this book. **Jochen Keute**, whose work is extensively represented in these pages, lives in Frankfurt and believes that the attraction of the city unveils itself only on second sight. He is fascinated by modern architecture and loves the blemishes and contrasts of world cities.

His work was supported by **Erhard Pansegrau**, who has contributed to many Insight Guides, and **Jan Erik Posth**, whose visual charm and charisma have produced many lively people pictures. **Günther Pfannmüller** took the cover shot and provided a photographic essay on Frankfurt's restaurants and pubs.

An International Effort

Appropriately for such an international city, the production of the book was carried out simultaneously in Apa's London and Munich editorial offices – in London under the supervision of **Andrew Eames** and **Brian Bell** and in Munich by **Dieter Vogel**. The translation work of **Ian McMaster**, **Anne Midgette** and **Susan Sting** was supervised by **Tony Halliday**, a Yorkshireman who lived for 10 years in Germany.

Two Insight Guides stalwarts, **Lyle Lawson** and **Wilhelm Klein**, reviewed the choice of pictures, and the knowledge of **Erich Meyer**, a Frankfurter who currently works in Insight's London office, was more useful than a million street maps. Proof-reading and indexing were completed by **Mary Morton**.

Schneider

Rose

Weiss

Metternich

History

Features

Surroundings

Maps

TRAVEL TIPS

Compiled by Arnd Wesemann

**For detailed information
see page 241**

Traditionally, the Frankfurters aren't so much concerned with their city's place in the world as its place in Germany: they like to distinguish themselves from the north Germans, and retain their essentially southern German identity. As a result, the Bavarians and Hessians regard the Main as being the obvious border dividing two totally separate worlds, and have dubbed it the "Weisswurst Equator", or the white sausage equator. This is where the south begins and the Prussians have no business here.

To be suspected of belonging to Prussia is almost more frightening for the Frankfurters than it is for the Bavarians; the events of 1866, the year when the north Germans captured Frankfurt and made it into a Prussian provincial city, have not been forgotten. In the ensuing period, the refined ladies of Frankfurt used to embellish their invitations to festivals and receptions with the abbreviation "P.u" – Prussians not desired – something which only true insiders would have understood.

The true Frankfurter is a woman: There must be a reason why the Frankfurter men are so often portrayed in films and cabarets as grousing, obnoxious individuals. For example, the eternally grumbling caretaker, who begins every sentence by claiming that he's not prejudiced but…; or the somewhat stupid, fat and showy vegetable trader; or the continually carping husband. It's not surprising that the popular image of a genuine Frankfurter is usually based on a woman. A little bit plump and rosy-cheeked, blonde – or at least with bleached hair – she is resolute and has a cheeky tongue and a fair degree of coquettishness in her blue eyes. Warmhearted and totally practical, she loves cooking (and, even more, eating), is ingenious and witty. One thing that can't be said of this Frankfurter lady is that she's mean. But she

expects good value for her hard-earned money: knick-knacks are not to be found in her house. And if you're wondering why there are so few nouvelle cuisine restaurants in Frankfurt, you haven't taken this formidable lady into account. When she takes the family out to eat she wants a proper meal – and that doesn't just mean good homely quality, but also a full plate. Exorbitant prices for mini portions are anathema to her.

The Frankfurters are not mean, but rather careful. They don't speculate, they invest, and preferably in something solid like land or property. Pubs and restaurants, shops and businesses – these are their domain. And they like to look after their wealth. It is said of Baron Rothschild that he once left a coachman standing around without a tip. As the latter pulled a long face and pointed out that the Baron's son had always rewarded him handsomely, the old man remarked brusquely that his son could indeed afford to behave in this manner – after all, he had a rich father.

Money makes the blood blue: Titles count for little in the Main metropolis. Everyone knows that an individual who has risen from petty trader or publican to baron owes his or her meteoric advancement solely to money. Here, where debt-ridden emperors and kings ennobled the generous men of money *en masse*, it's better not to enquire into background too closely. The people have little respect for the nobility, knowing that the alchemy of money can quickly turn red blood blue.

In fact, most of the local families owe their position not so much to their titles – that came later – but rather to the desirability of the young Frankfurter girls. The advantages of marrying one of them was enough to attract numerous suitors from outside the boundaries of the free imperial city. As a result, the young girls were choosy and self-confident, preferring a handsome bank account to a title. A title that is only an academic one – a Doctor or a Professor – has even less weight. Admittedly the city likes to hold on to its teachers, professors, scientists, and even its philosophers, artists, actors and

Preceding pages: tradition prevails at the Römerfest; living art during the Museumsuferfest; hardware students; modelling sunglasses. Left, the Fountain of Justice on the Römerberg.

other similar types. But this is only for show, not for what really matters – wealth.

One is often reminded that the Frankfurters are not mean. A respectable tradition of charitable donation flourishes quietly in this city, which otherwise tends to display its wealth in the fashion of the *nouveaux riches*. The citizens make donations for the maintenance of many hospitals and old people's homes, as well as opening accounts for pensioners and orphans, the Senckenberg Museum and its research arm, the University.

The Old Opera House (Alte Oper), which the emperor described at its inauguration as being so splendid that he couldn't afford such a building in Berlin, was also financed by donations from the citizens of Frankfurt. The same is true of the zoo and the zoological society, membership of which is an honour. Avoiding the glare of publicity, the Society works intensively to promote nature reserve projects all over the world. And where else would you find the well-known owner of a bordello establishing an annual prize for literature, and maintaining a house (the "Roman-Fabrik") for poetry readings and other cultural events.

The city authorities are also actively involved in supporting cultural life: the annual budget of half a billion marks (£175 million/US$330 million) is the highest in Germany. Half a dozen museums have either been built from scratch or extended; works of arts and whole collections have been acquired. Over the past 20 years Frankfurters have become much more outward-looking, a rare virtue in earlier times. Now that Frankfurt has been raised to the ranks of one of the world's metropolises, it seems as though the business success needs to be legitimised. After all, Frankfurt is aiming to become the location for the future European Central Bank, despite strong competition from London.

The people on the Main have a reputation for celebrating, and the city authorities are continually forced to forbid excessive alcohol consumption and noise. Yet it's not easy: the Frankfurters are reluctant to have their fun spoiled, as former CDU Mayor Brück learned to his cost when he angered his own natural supporters – the retailers – to such an extent that he was forced to leave office in 1989. He had got so carried away in a dispute with the State Government of Hesse over the building of the U-bahn that, at short notice, he cancelled a street festival to celebrate the opening of a new line, and forbade any kind of celebration. The shop owners were as sour as the local apple wine, thousands of litres of which had been specially bought for the celebration. They proceeded to serve the wine illegally, without waiting for an official occasion.

Every city gets the scandals it deserves: The bribery scandals which were the cause of such a furore in the town hall a few years ago had their comical side. In typical Frankfurter style, only small sums were involved. It wasn't simply a handful of big sharks who profited from the affairs, as for example in Berlin, but everyone, from secretaries to heads of departments. The bribes amounted to a few lottery tickets, some gold chains, at most a Mercedes; little cash changed hands.

At the end of the affair came a typical Frankfurter statement from the offices of the mayor: in future, it said, no celebrations were to be held in the offices involving people from outside. Gone are the days when building contractors used to turn up at the town hall with baskets full of presents and bottles of wine.

Old Frankfurt habits: If it's the old, traditional Frankfurt which you are looking for, it can still be found today – for example, during a Sunday afternoon stroll in the palm gardens (Palmengarten). Here you can see elderly ladies with white perms sitting having coffee and cakes, listening to waltzes by Strauss and discussing their illnesses and their grandchildren.

Old Frankfurt can also be found in the Bornheim apple wine pub, the Solzer at the top end of Berger Strasse, where the men spend the day with warmed apple wine, which is reputed to be good for the stomach. Each of them has their own personal lid (which they leave with the publican) so that the *Micke* – Frankfurt's expression for common houseflies – don't fall into the glass whilst the men sit there gazing thoughtfully for hours on end into their drink.

Right, skateboarding on the Konstablerwache.

While the Frankfurt region was settled with farming communities of the Danubian Culture around 4,500 BC, the development of the city itself didn't really begin until the Bronze Age, which dawned some 1,000 years later. Indeed, the hill at the ford over the Main river where the cathedral now stands has been continuously occupied since the Bronze Age, which saw the emergence of the Celtic civilisation. The Celts built their towns, their *Oppidae*, in the region and defended them with hill forts. In the Frankfurt area, such settlements existed in the Taunus mountains and in the Rhön.

Roman remains: But it was with the triumphant advance of the Romans that Frankfurt began to appear in historical records, although in the 1st century AD it was little more than a transit area for the legions. As they pushed east of the Rhine, the Romans came up against stiff resistance from the Chats, an indigenous Germanic tribe from north Hesse. Fortified camps and later the *limes*, the fortified border posts of the Roman empire, were subsequently erected. They not only provided protection from marauding tribes, but also acted as bases for military operations into Germanic territory.

Only after this part of their empire was secured did the Romans proceed to build their baths and their brick kilns. They also built villas in the fertile and hospitable Frankfurt region, one on the cathedral hill, and others in Bornheim and the Holzhausen district, near the Roman trading routes. (The northern district of Bonames is said to have derived its name from the heyday of Roman settlement when it lay under the protection of the *limes*; "Bona Mansio", the good hostel.) The locals came to terms quickly with the Roman occupation. They latinised their names and worshipped Jupiter and Cybele as well as their own gods.

Preceding pages: the execution of burgher leader Wilhelm Fettmilch in 1616, when the Jews lost their civil rights. Left, Dukedoms became the backbone of the empire in the 10th century.

But Frankfurt could never have claimed to be a Roman metropolis. The Romans preferred Mainz on the Rhine. When the *limes* finally fell to the Alemanni in AD 260, the Rhine once again became the eastern border of the Roman empire. Remains of Roman settlements have been found within the city area, notably Vicus Nida in the district of Heddernheim. Today most of these ancient sites lie buried under the offices and flats of Römerstadt and Nordweststadt.

The Franks in Frankfurt: When the Alemanni drove out the Romans, they established a settlement on the cathedral hill. In 500 AD they, in turn, were conquered by Franks invading their territory from the west. The Franks took over the administrative and settlement structures left behind by the Romans, and the Frankfurt area became the heartland of their operations. In the course of time, Frankfurt was to become the royal and imperial city of the Frankish Empire.

But before this could come about, stability had to be achieved. The chaos brought about by the migrations of peoples throughout Europe resulted in constant warfare and the Franks regularly changed their allegiances. Their arch enemies were the Alemanni, and they proceeded to conquer their territory in league with the Burgundians, against whom they were later to turn. The Rhine-Main region was fiercely fought over and as was so often the case in its history, the region became a contested border area, in which peoples fought and merged.

The Frankish royal family, the Merovingians, had little decisive role to play in the fortunes of the city. Frankfurt became involved in the power struggles only after the Merovingians' major-domo, Charles Martel, made a grab for the crown. After being made duke of the Eastern Franks in 716, the founder of the Carolingian Dynasty defeated the Western Franks and in 719 became ruler of all the Frankish kingdom.

Christianity could now begin its triumphant advance through Germania. The chief protagonist in this chapter of history was the

Anglo-Saxon missionary St Boniface. In 719 he travelled northwards through Hesse and in 744 his pupils founded the monastery at Fulda. In the summer of 754, the local inhabitants lined the streets for the final homecoming of the revered Boniface, who at the age of almost 80 had been killed while attempting to convert the wild tribes of the North Sea coast. His body was brought by ship as far as Hochheim, and from there along the old Roman road to its final resting place in Fulda. Shrines, chapels and crosses were erected along the wayside, hence Frankfurt's Bonifatiusquelle (Boniface spring) and a stone cross with the year 754 inscribed on it.

the founder, patron and friend of the city. In February 794 he wrote its name on a deed of gift to the imperial city of Regensburg, "Franconouvurd". A second deed from the same year referred to "that famous place called Frankfurt". Charlemagne loved Frankfurt and he erected his palace on the walls of the Roman ruins on the Römerberg. Merchants and craftsmen settled around it and created the core of the old city.

Fourteen years after being crowned by the pope as Emperor of the Romans on Christmas Day 800, Charlemagne died and was buried at Aachen. His vast empire, which had embraced most of the former territory of

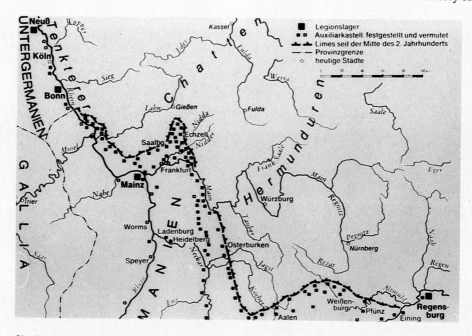

Charlemagne's legacy: In 768, on the death of Pepin the Short, the Frankish kingdom was divided between Pepin's sons, King Charles (later to be called Charlemagne) and his younger brother Carloman. That Frankfurt was soon to reach its peak of glory is due to the first of the great religious disputes that wracked Christendom at this time. Scholars and politicians, Rome and Byzantium, vied for power.

In 794 bishops, counts and kings travelled to the city to attend the Council of Frankfurt which aimed to resolve the Iconoclastic Controversy. Charlemagne was recognised as

the Roman Empire in the West, did not survive for long after his death; his sons did not possess his vision or authority and the empire soon disintegrated into a number of smaller states. This decline obviously had its effect on Frankfurt, although the city continued to grow and Charlemagne's grandson, Ludwig the German, built the first church next to the old palace. This is where the cathedral (Church of St Bartholomew) now stands. The original church on this site (St Saviour) is said to have been dedicated on 1 September 882 by the curious mystic Hrabanus Maurus. Remains of this church were discovered after the great cathedral fire in the 19th century.

Electoral city: Apart from the fact that a few imperial Diets were held here, little is known about the development of the city during the latter part of the Carolingian period. The empire's fortunes were revived by Otto the Great, the son of the founder of the Saxon dynasty, Henry the Fowler. But real glory didn't return to Frankfurt until a new palace was built here by the Hohenstaufens in 1138. The building, which was fortified by a mighty wall, is connected with another famous name: Emperor Frederick I, called Barbarossa (Redbeard). Considered to be the greatest of the

bishop of Trier entered the city with a retinue of 1,800 knights. In 1147, a bishop arrived by river with 40 ships and countless barges. That same year the Second Crusade, which was to end in disaster, set out from Frankfurt's cathedral hill under the command of Conrad III.

The Golden Bull: In 1356 Frankfurt again made a name for itself as a place where history was written. A Golden Bull was any document whose importance was stressed by authentication with the imperial seal. Specifically the term Golden Bull is used for the edict promulgated by Emperor Charles IV in 1356 to define the German constitu-

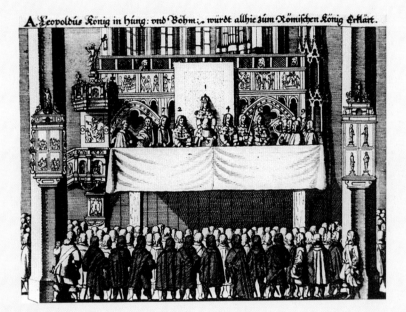

Hohenstaufen rulers, he became the first German emperor to be elected by princes and bishops in Frankfurt.

Over the next 650 years Frankfurt was to play out its role as the electoral and later the coronation city of the Holy Roman Empire of German Nations. Up to 1300, no less than 21 imperial Diets were held in the palace and eight kings were elected here. They were magnificent occasions. One time, the Arch-

Left, route of the *limes*, Roman fortifications constructed to fend off Germanic tribes. **Above**, after 1356 Frankfurt became the electoral city.

tion. It formally confirmed that the election of an emperor was by a college of seven princes and recognised them as virtually independent rulers.

The long power wrangle between the pope and the emperor was thus settled; the election of an emperor no longer needed to be confirmed by the pope, and Frankfurt duly became an electoral city "for all time".

Emperor Charles IV had an amicable relationship with Frankfurt. The city's tradesmen became the patricians and merchants that guided its fortunes. As a free imperial city, Frankfurt was answerable only to the emperor himself. In 1372, the people paid the emperor huge sums of money for the right to elect their own city captain. But it was very much a question of mutual support: the imperial treasury was in a sorry condition and that same year the Frankfurters helped out by buying the royal forest, hence the city forest of today.

Frankfurt continued to grow. Fortifications, squares and broad streets were laid out. The knights in their castles began to envy this prosperous city on the Main. They plundered the tradesmen's caravans on their way to market and stole the cattle. In fact, Frankfurt's enemies were so many that the name of

Worms were eagerly waiting for the chance to relieve Frankfurt of its status as a free imperial city.

From 1564, emperors were not only elected in Frankfurt, but crowned there as well. The trend was set by the Habsburg Maximilian II; it is said that the weather was so awful that the new emperor could not be bothered to travel all the way to Aachen to receive the crown.

While enjoying the favour of the emperor, the city council had to contend with increasing dissatisfaction among the burghers. The craftsmen and guilds united against the nobility, and Frankfurt faced its first corruption

the prevailing adversary had to be posted on the door of the town hall. The citizens of the free imperial city constantly complained to the emperor, but eventually they fell out with him as well and the tide of Protestantism that was sweeping over Europe engulfed Frankfurt too.

When in 1542 the Lutheran princes of the League of Schmalkalden pitched themselves against the Catholic emperor Charles V, the people of Frankfurt added their weight to the cause. But the turn-about lasted only five years. In 1547 the city yielded voluntarily, mainly because the cities of Mainz and

scandals. The reports on the various affairs are echoed in any number of modern-day committees of enquiry. The city council was not only accused of nepotism, but also of funding its excessive drinking binges from the city purse. The burghers demanded remission of taxes and to this end they captured the entire council and locked them in the town hall for three days. The burghers' leader was the gingerbread baker Wilhelm Fettmilch, who met his end on the scaffold in 1616. The heads of Fettmilch and three of his comrades were impaled on the tines (slender columns) of the bridge tower and left there to rot until the bridge was pulled down in 1801. But the primary victims of the council's wasteful politics were the Jews, who were robbed of all their worldly goods and chased out of town.

The depradations of the Thirty Years' War (1618–48), with all its catastrophic consequences for the general population, largely passed Frankfurt by. The city boomed. It steered a careful, zig-zag course aimed at appeasing the parties involved. In 1631 the Swede Gustav Adolf set up residence for a short while in the city (he had his soldiers build a mighty fortress with eleven bastions). But he was mortally wounded one

further catastrophe on 26 June 1719, when fire broke out in the Zum Rehbock inn and the old city burned down, the flames abating only when they reached the Jews' alley. The latter had already been destroyed by fire in 1711; now it was the turn of the property of the Christians.

Goethe is born: Local Frankfurt girls were highly sought after: marrying one meant a secure existence and guaranteed civic rights. In 1748 Johann Caspar Goethe, the son of a tailor apprentice and a publican's daughter married Elisabeth Textor, the daughter of the city captain. On 28 August 1749, the young couple proudly announced the birth of their

year later when his Protestant army defeated the forces of the Catholic Habsburgs at Lützen near Leipzig, and the Frankfurters once again made their peace with the emperor.

While the city had survived the war unscathed, it could not escape its consequences. Refugees poured in from the countryside, and hardship, depravation and disease came with them to settle within the city walls. No fewer than 7,000 people succumbed to the plague in 1635. The city was visited by a

Left, 2,000 Frankfurt men lay siege to Kronberg Castle in 1389. **Above**, the Imperial crown.

son Johann Wolfgang, who was to become Germany's foremost literary figure.

The young child's formative years coincided with the Seven Years' War (1756–63) between the French and the Prussians. By that time the Empress Maria Theresa of Austria had already visited Frankfurt. Voltaire was arrested when he passed through the city, and Schiller's reception wasn't much better. He arrived here in 1782 in rags and tatters after his escape from Mannheim, and was upset that a city that had already seen so many prominent visitors took no notice of him at all.

When the Bastille was stormed in 1789, only a few of Frankfurt's intellectuals, such as Goethe, paid any attention. But three years later, French forces came knocking on Frankfurt's door, demanding 2 million gulden in war tax. To avoid a bombardment of their city, in the dead of night the craftsmen rendered the French cannons inoperable and opened the Friedberg Gate to the troops of the allied Hessian and Prussian forces. The French soldiers subsequently fled out of the Bockenheim Gate to seek refuge from their pursuers in "French" Mainz. French forces finally succeeded in bombarding and occupying the city in 1796 under Marshal Jourdan.

Belle époque and Napoleon's downfall: The *belle époque* was an era of cultural flowering for Frankfurt. Napoleon's Continental Blockade brought substantial economic advantages to the city as a result of the elimination of British competition. The Grand Duchy of Frankfurt, created in 1810, became a cradle of the sciences and art. The accordance of equal status to the Jews provided the basic conditions for the free social and economic development of the city's Jewish community; it was while Frankfurt was a French protectorate that the Rothschilds rose to become Europe's leading banking family. The Frankfurt Chamber of Commerce was founded and the separation of the judiciary from the administration resulted in a better justice system.

On 1 November 1813, after Napoleon's defeat at the Battle of Nations near Leipzig, French rule in Frankfurt was finally over; Cossacks and Bavarian troops of the "Holy Alliance" came marching into the city.

Oppression under Metternich: At the Congress of Vienna in 1815 Frankfurt once again became a free imperial city, this time as part of the patchwork quilt of German states known as the German Confederation. The assembly of deputies from the 35 sovereign princes and four free imperial cities, the

Bundestag, met regularly in Frankfurt under the chairmanship of the Austrian Prince Metternich. However, the presence of the arch-conservative Bundestag in such a liberally-minded city as Frankfurt gave rise to repeated unrest and tension. The princes used the assembly as a means of halting any liberal aspirations on the part of the common people, so the freedoms that the city had known under the French were abolished and the Jews were robbed of their new civil liberties.

Liberally-minded citizens formed associations so that they could discuss the ever more oppressive political climate.

Moves for a new constitution: The overthrow of the French king in Paris in July 1830 led to a general outbreak of unrest throughout Europe, and the nationalist movement for the establishment of a new constitution for the whole of Germany came into being. "Get rid of tolls and customs-duties, civil servants, paramours and Jews so we can all have our daily bread!" they cried. Because political gatherings were forbidden, the protagonists struggling for Germany's "unity in free-

Left, the French army besieges Frankfurt in 1792.
Right, a firestorm ravages the city in 1867.

dom" held clandestine meetings. The first uprising was quickly put down.

In 1848, 2,000 Frankfurt citizens assembled in the Reithalle to demand freedom of the press, the right of assembly and the unification of Germany. In Baden, the revolutionaries decided on the convocation of an all-German assembly in Frankfurt – in preparation for the first German National Assembly. This pre-parliament was to set the course for establishing a new, united and democratic Germany. It was at this assembly that the fate of the German Revolution of 1848 was decided (*see facing page*).

The age of industrialisation: Two years after the bourgeois revolution, with the complete lifting of trade restrictions in 1864, industry was able to develop unhindered. Heinrich and Hector Roessler established a gold and silver refinery, the forerunner of the firm Degussa. The Fries iron foundry was contracted to build the Eiserner Steg, a footbridge over the Main which was the first suspension bridge in Germany. In 1872, Frankfurt acquired its first horse-drawn tram, which plied its way between the Hauptwache and Bockenheim. The seven carriages had special compartments for ladies and non-smokers.

Prussian Frankfurt: Bismarck annexed Frankfurt in 1866, apparently because there

the bourgeois revolution, the old Bundestag was once again opened in Frankfurt. The "ultra-royalist" Otto von Bismarck, later to become chancellor of the Empire, spent eight years as the Prussian delegate to the Bundestag. Frankfurt boomed economically in the 1850s and '60s. Joint-stock companies sprang up like mushrooms and a central bank was set up in 1854. A railway link was constructed between the city's west stations and the east station. In 1861 the Friedrichsdorf teacher Philipp Reis gave a public demonstration of his new telephone equipment to the Physics Society.

had been too much public criticism of Prussian militarism in the city. The fact that Germany became a "united fatherland" accounts for the Frankfurters' tolerance of the occupation of their city by the Prussians. The new nationalism, expressed in reverence for the Kaiser, was greater than any feeling of local patriotism. Property speculation began and it led to a staggering increase in rents. Workers' committees in the city demanded a remedy for the shortage of cheap housing.

Above, revolutionaries attacking the Hauptwache in 1833 (see opposite page).

FIRST NATIONAL ASSEMBLY

In 1815, because of its historical importance as an electoral and coronation city, Frankfurt was chosen as the seat of the Bundestag, the assembly of the German Confederation which was created at the Congress of Vienna to fill the void left by Napoleon's destruction of the Holy Roman Empire in 1806. The Bundestag, which met in the Palais Thurn und Taxis, was under Austrian presidency; the fate of the Confederation was very much governed by the conservative doctrines of monarchical absolutism that had been re-established by the Holy Alliance against Napoleon.

The Metternich system cast aside any aspirations of German nationhood, and in the ensuing years there was increasing unrest among many sections of society: from the liberals who wanted to see a united German state and who opposed internal customs within the Confederation, to left-wing radicals who resorted to violence in their pursuit of democracy and justice. When in 1833 revolutionaries attacked the Hauptwache (Guard-House) in Frankfurt, their actions received little public support and only resulted in intensification of the persecution of liberals.

In 1848, revolution spread all over Europe and the Bundestag adopted the German national colours – black, red and gold. On 31 March 1848 a pre-parliament convened in Frankfurt's Paulskirche (St Paul's Church) and resolved to summon a German National Assembly. The question was whether the French Revolution would now be repeated in Germany.

But the outcome of the pre-parliament was a major disappointment for the democrats and republicans: their revolutionary programme, which included a people's army and abolition of the hereditary monarchy, replaced with a freely-elected parliament with a federal constitution, was voted off the agenda by supporters of a constitutional monarchy. And when, before the elections to the Assembly, the republicans' bill for the suspension of Metternich's repressive Carlsbad Decrees was defeated by the conservatives, 76 republicans walked out of the Paulskirche.

On 18 May 1848 the National Assembly came together as representatives of every state in the German Confederation. Six hundred delegates arrived at the Paulskirche, including the poet Ludwig Uhland, the republican Robert Blum,

Right, the Paulskirche assembly in session.

who was later shot by counter-revolutionaries, and the linguist Jakob Grimm, better known as the collector of fairy tales.

Afraid of the radical demands of the radical left, the liberals came down firmly on the side of the nobility. The parliament ended up electing the Austrian archduke Johann as the chancellor and, in 1849, offered the imperial crown to the Prussian king Frederick William IV. The latter was not positively disposed towards the popular movement and rejected this offer from the "dirty scum", but by that time the counter-revolution was in full swing. With a series of uprisings, the republicans tried once again to save the bourgeois revolution and there was yet more bloodshed as Prussian and Austrian infantry crushed the revolt.

The Assembly, which had resisted resorting to arms, was put down by the sword.

After Prussia and Austria recalled their delegates from the Paulskirche in May 1849, and the "rump parliament" was moved to Stuttgart, the German revolution died together with the ideals which had been voiced in the Paulskirche. The princes once again took over control. The victors pulled down the black, red and gold flag from the roof of the Palais Thurn und Taxis. The "upright, orderly, political revolution" had come to an end having scarcely got off the ground.

In the following years, many, including liberals, were persecuted and killed. The outcome was a national tragedy for Germany. ∎

The authorities reacted in 1872 with the establishment of an Association for the Creation of Cheap Housing. But the general situation went from bad to worse. In 1873 there was an uprising in the city because the price of a beer was raised by half a kreuzer. Pubs and breweries were plundered.

Eleven years later, the city's workers celebrated a political breakthrough. The Social Democrats defeated the Conservatives at the ballot box and by 1910 they had become the strongest political force in the Empire. Between 1866 and 1910 the real earnings of a skilled worker rose threefold.

War and revolution: In 1914 thousands of time the Red Flag was hoisted on the Römer, Kaiser Wilhelm was already in exile in Holland and the Social Democrat Friedrich Ebert was the president of the Republic.

However, the situation did not improve very quickly. It wasn't until 1923 that conditions had stabilised enough to allow ration cards to be phased out. But in that same year inflation led to a drastic decrease in the value of people's money. In February 1923 one could travel on the tram for 200 Reichsmarks; by November, travellers had to pay the conductor the unbelievable sum of 90 billion Reichsmarks.

On 1 April 1924, Radio Frankfurt came on

Frankfurters volunteered for the front, but the euphoria soon evaporated. In 1916 there were already serious food shortages and the authorities issued vouchers for butter, milk and potatoes. That same year 20,000 people turned up at a peace rally organised by the Social Democrats and demanded a stop to the fighting. When, in 1917, the October Revolution began in Russia, demonstrators outside the factories exhorted the people to revolt. Worker and soldier committees replaced the police and by November 1918 were recognised by the city council as the "highest representatives of the city". By the air for the first time. In the following year the inaugural celebrations for the new Waldstadion (stadium) were held and the firm Hafraba, in which the city had a stake, drew up plans for the building of *autobahns*. Frankfurt grew: in 1928 Lord Mayor Ludwig Landmann succeeded in incorporating the town of Höchst into Frankfurt. Prior to that the communities of Rödelheim, Hausen, Praunheim, Heddernheim, Ginnheim, Eschersheim, Berkersheim, Niederursel, Bonames, Preungesheim and Eckenheim had all become part of the city.

By 1929 there were 70,000 unemployed in

Frankfurt. The collapse of the Frankfurter Allgemein Versicherungs AG was the German prologue to the world economic crisis of 1929–30. When the Western world was rocked by the Wall Street Crash, banks and public companies also went bankrupt in Frankfurt. The brown-uniformed SA troops of the National Socialists (NSDAP) were already marching on the city's streets.

Nazi terror, war and devastation: In 1933 the members of the Social Democratic Party (SPD) and the Communist Party (KPD) were expelled from the municipal government. SA troops were posted outside Jewish shops and banks, and even the university was occu-

night of November 1938, when Nazis burned down the synagogues in the Friedberg Park, on Börneplatz, in Börnestrasse and Liebigstrasse. Among those tortured at the Frankfurt headquarters of the Gestapo was the jazz musician Albert Mangelsdorff, on account of his "degenerate" music. Shortly before the outbreak of the war, the "Aryan city of Frankfurt am Main" bought up the land and property of the Jewish communities for the bargain price of 1.8 million Reichsmarks. In 1941 the first of the 10,000 Jews who had remained in Frankfurt were packed into trains and deported to Minsk and Riga in the "Generalgouvernement Poland". They were sub-

pied by the men in brown. Jewish and "Marxist" professors had their identification papers confiscated and had to leave their posts. Anne Frank and her family fled to Holland. The Nazi terror also forced leading scientists and artists to emigrate; among them were the heads of the Institute for Social Research and Theodor Adorno and Herbert Marcuse, members of the "Frankfurt School" movement.

The terror culminated in the pogrom on the

Left, the nobility arrive for the Paulskirche Assembly in 1848. <u>Above</u>, Nazi display of power, 1 May 1939.

sequently escorted to Auschwitz and to Theresienstadt, where most died.

The death knell for Frankfurt's old city was rung on 22 March 1944 by 816 bombers of Britain's Royal Air Force. Frankfurt was a prime target of allied bombing sorties, for a number of militarily important industries were based here. These included the headquarters of the IG Farben concern, which produced Zyklon B, the gas used to exterminate the Jews in the concentration camps. After the war the victorious Americans made the IG Farben offices on the ring road the headquarters of the US forces in Europe.

Frankfurt lay in ruins. The victorious powers set about dismantling those industries that had played a key role in Hitler's war, such as IG Farben, the Adlerwerke and VDM. Refugees from the east poured into the destroyed city. The people found shelter in bombed-out houses; any empty flats that had escaped the bombing were shared by several families. The black market flourished on the Römerberg and at the Rossmarkt. With the continuing decline in the value of gold, the unit of currency on the black market was the American cigarette. The hungry city folk got on their bikes and headed for the country to swap their silver and carpets for potatoes and mangels. In the "trizone", as the union of the American, British and French zones of occupation was called, the only way the people could keep their heads above water until the introduction of the D-mark was through bartering whatever they had.

Among all the destruction, misery and general demoralisation, the people of Frankfurt set about clearing away the rubble of the "1,000-year Reich". It was primarily the women, the *Trümmerfrauen* ("rubble women") who undertook the initial reconstruction, as many of the men died in the war or were still prisoners of war.

The foundations of the economic rejuvenation of the new Germany came with the currency reform of 20 June 1948. The establishment of the democratic Federal Republic of Germany came one year later in September 1949. The old free imperial city of Frankfurt almost became the new capital; it was only with a narrow majority that the Bundestag chose Bonn as the seat of the new German Parliament.

Reconstruction: That same year the Book Fair once again took place in Frankfurt. After the reconstruction of the Obermainbrücke, Frankfurt was finally linked to its district of Sachsenhausen once more. One

Preceding pages: war damage on the Römerberg. Left, Mayor Kolb heads the clean-up campaign. Right, in 1947 the Allies were still in control.

year later, on the eve of the Jewish new year, the chief rabbi Neuhaus consecrated the rebuilt synagogue in Freiherr-vom-Stein Strasse. A milestone in the post-war economic development of the city was the decision of the Bundestag in 1957 to locate the headquarters of the Bundesbank in Frankfurt. The city's preoccupation with rebuilding allowed little time for the populace to reflect on Germany's recent history and the role that Frankfurt had played. When in 1955

there were demonstrations against the decision of the conservative government to re-arm the country, the police used water cannon and batons to disperse the trade unionists, Social Democrats and Communists. A political dialogue did not take place. The scenes were repeated 13 years later, during the student revolts of 1968.

In the meantime, the city was completely rebuilt, although the results were not always very inspiring from an architectural point of view. Today the tenements on Berliner Strasse remain examples of the building style of the years of reconstruction, when living space had to be quickly and cheaply provided for thousands of people, particularly the refugees forced to flee from the former German-occupied territories in the East.

In the 1960s and '70s the city's political fortunes were guided by the Social Democrats. Under Lord Mayor Rudi Arndt, Frankfurt became the "capital of crime in Germany", as the tabloids wrote at the time. *Steamy Nights in Frankfurt* was the name of a film which was popular at the box office in the early 1960s. And in real life things weren't much different. The murder of the call-girl Rosmarie Nitribitt, who had been the paramour of politicians and industrial magnates

between the police and students. The latter wanted to cast aside the political fustiness of the older generation, free the workers and establish a socialist society in the Federal Republic. The "Frankfurt School" of Adorno, Marcuse and Horkheimer, whose *Critical Theory* drew on the ideas of Marx and Freud, played a large part in forming the theoretical basis of the new society that the students envisaged. Along with Berlin, Frankfurt was the major stronghold of the student revolts in Germany.

But instead of talking with the students, the government replied with force. The street battles dominated life in the city for months.

alike, was for months the number one topic of conversation in the city. The ever-increasing number of revelations about personalities who had been with Nitribitt was one of the factors that led to growing criticism from the man in the street of the whole German "economic miracle".

It was during this time that Frankfurt's station area, the Bahnhofsviertel, rose to become Germany's number two den of iniquity after Hamburg's Reeperbahn. Frankfurt was considered ungovernable.

The student protests: In 1968 and 1969 the streets of Frankfurt witnessed pitched battles

One of the agitators at the barricades inciting the students to revolt was Daniel Cohn-Bendit. Today Cohn-Bendit is the head of the Department of Multicultural Affairs. Fierce ideological battles were fought in the legendary lecture theatre 5 at the university. And outside the gates of the Adler typewriter factory and the Hoechst paint factory the students distributed leaflets exhorting "a common struggle against capitalism and the political big shots in Bonn".

Even if the students could register no immediate and obvious success, their actions did bring lasting changes to German society.

The 1968 revolts were primarily a cultural revolution – and in Frankfurt the young people acquired space in the city to practise an alternative lifestyle. Their squatting campaigns against the property speculators in the Westend saved numerous old villas from demolition. One of the activists in the squatter movement was Joschka Fischer, today the environment minister of the federal state of Hesse.

The financial heart of Europe: In the late 1970s, the image of Frankfurt changed. Although there were massive demonstrations against the planned new runway at the airport in 1981, the overall character of the city than 1,000 homeless persons living under the bridges of the Main river, in tents provided by the city.

Hotbed of corruption: Under the aegis of the Christian Democrats the city achieved more dubious fame. In the 1980s *Der Spiegel* magazine dubbed Frankfurt the "capital of corruption". Civil servants and employees of various local government departments had taken bribes when issuing contracts to private companies. "Don Alphonso" of the public gardens department was the most notorious figure of this period. In only a few years he redirected hundreds of thousands of marks to his own personal account. Officials at the

now came to be governed by its emergence as the financial capital of Europe.

The city boomed, but during the 1980s social tensions increased. While the modernisers cleared the way for the growth of banks and advertising agencies, the interests of the socially disadvantaged were seriously neglected, and thousands were forced out to the periphery as the city expanded. Rents went through the roof, and today there are more

Left, Prof. Erhard, the "father of the industrial miracle", at the car fair in 1959. **Above**, the Römerberg has hosted many celebrations.

building authorities also lined their pockets. When the SPD and "Green" coalition took over power in 1989, the new environment secretary of the Greens complained about the inefficiency of the administration: no fewer than 100 employees and civil servants were either behind bars already or were on remand pending trial.

At the end of the 1980s a special commission of enquiry discovered that the underworld had also been involved in government at city hall. The notorious "brothel kings" Hersch and Heim Beker fostered an amicable relationship with influential politicians and top administrators. The wealthy brothers thus gained first-hand information about the city's development strategies, especially pending building projects and land transactions. The police spoke of a "hotbed of corruption".

Control mechanisms have now been installed in the individual departments to ensure that no such irregularities take place. Nowadays employees are not even allowed to accept a pen as a gift.

Cosmopolitan city: Frankfurt is twinned with several other cities, including Tel Aviv in Israel, Milan in Italy and Barcelona in Spain. More than 150,000 people (about 25 percent have a special Department for Multicultural Affairs, whose aim it is to bring all the 154 different nationalities living in the city closer together. The problems are as many-sided as the interests, social origins and nationalities gathered on the Main. But in Frankfurt there are none of the ghettos to be found in Berlin, Paris or New York, in which ethnic groups live isolated from each other: even the gangs of youths are "multicultural".

Only in the area around the railway station do the international gangster syndicates – for example from Turkey, Israel, or the Andes states, and more recently a Chinese protection money racket – operate separately, on

of the population) with foreign passports live and work in Frankfurt itself. Many of them have become true "Frankfurters". The services sector is booming and badly needs personnel, skilled and unskilled. The city's hospitals would have ground to a standstill by now without the nurses from east European countries and Asia. And since many Japanese banks and trading companies have decided to move their head offices from Düsseldorf to Frankfurt, as a result of the superior transport links, Japanese restaurants and food shops have boomed too.

Frankfurt is the only city in Germany to the basis of a strict division of labour.

At a recent festival at the Konstablerwache on the Day of German Unity (3 October), traditional Turkish dance groups met African women demonstrating the painstaking plaiting of their hair; Spanish paella cooks sampled the delights of the neighbouring Vietnamese chefs; and performers such as Miriam Makeba and Udo Lindenberg sang in the Kongresshalle, an event that attracted Frankfurters in their thousands.

Above, on and off duty at Edwards Barracks. Up to 27,000 GIs have been stationed at Frankfurt.

ELVIS AND THE AMERICANS

When Elvis Presley disembarked from the transporter ship *General G.M. Randall* in October 1958, together with 1,400 other GIs, it wasn't only the youths of Bremerhaven who jumped for joy: all of Frankfurt did. The rock 'n' roll star from Memphis, Tennessee, was to serve in the military for 18 months in Bad Nauheim, in the immediate vicinity of Frankfurt. Thousands of teenagers, especially female, tried to storm the train station on his arrival, screaming hysterically for a glimpse of their idol.

The following day, the army held a press conference at the Bad Neuheim barracks to present their famous soldier. They put in special telephone lines and installed extra outlets for the cables and lights of news and television teams. No other simple US soldier had ever had such a reception in Frankfurt – or anywhere else, for that matter. And no other soldier ever had as comfortable a time in the service as Elvis did.

Although he maintained that he was "a soldier like any other", the 23-year-old former truck driver rented a huge villa, where he lived with his father, his grandmother, and a few friends. In the morning, his chauffeur would take him to the barracks in his Cadillac, to the loud jubilation of his fans. What he liked best about Germany were the blond "frolleins". Whenever a pretty blonde girl asked him for his autograph, he had his bodyguards take down her address – just in case. He's certainly reputed to have had several affairs with German fans.

Most American soldiers in Germany didn't, and don't, have it so good. The barracks around Frankfurt are like ghettos, buildings pressed close together, surrounded by barbed-wire fences 10 feet high, and patrolled by armed guards. Helicopters circle ceaselessly over the settlements of row houses in the suburbs; sometimes you can hear the noise of their rotors into the early hours of the morning. Soldiers and their families have their own supermarkets, where they can buy traditional American products – protecting them from any risk of homesickness – at bargain prices. Their children go to "American schools", and you can glimpse them, with their braces and chewing-gum, riding the bus back to their home base.

Back when the dollar was strong against the Deutschmark on the international currency exchange, American soldiers were assured of a comfortable family living. They thus played a considerable role in the local economic life, particularly in Sachsenhausen, where the apple wine flowed. Today, however, a married NCO with children earns the equivalent of about 2,000 marks a month – no more than an average German worker. Most GIs can hardly afford to go out any more. Country music clubs are closing, while new US video-rental stores make it easier for more people to stay home more of the time. Consequently encounters with German locals are rare, and scarcely encouraged. There aren't even any more of those mass fistfights in the city centre which used to bring about some kind of contact.

One great exception to this trend toward

isolationism is the German-American Volksfest. Since 1985, the Americans have celebrated their Independence Day on 4 July by inviting everyone to Ratsweg to celebrate everything which corresponds to the German cliché of "American": hot dogs, hamburgers and spare ribs prepared by soldiers and generals wearing outsized cowboy hats; American beer, square dancing, football, and – a high point for German guests – rodeo. The Americans, on the other hand, are fondest of the stall selling cuckoo clocks. What would become of the Black Forest cuckoo clock industry if the Americans pulled out?

They probably never will. The Rhine-Main air base is America's door to the world. ∎

Right, Elvis relives his army life in *GI Blues*.

The development of Frankfurt into the major financial metropolis it is today has not always met with positive reaction. The German author Günther Grass was once quoted as saying that "when God made Frankfurt-am-Main, he shat a lump of concrete". Even locals have nicknamed their city "Mainhattan" or "Bankfurt" as ever more skyscrapers have transformed the skyline. These new cathedrals of big business, primarily the banks, have become a potent symbol of the enormous financial influence that Frankfurt wields.

Not a day goes by without some reference being made to Frankfurt in the international press. And it will invariably be about money: about the Bundesbank and its interest rates affecting the whole European economy, or about exchange rates, commodities and stocks and shares. In terms of volume of financial trading, the only city in Europe that outstrips Frankfurt is London; no other German city, whether it be Berlin, Hamburg, Munich or Cologne, can hold a candle to the metropolis on the Main. No fewer than 50,000 people are directly involved in the business of dealing in money here. The pull of Frankfurt as an economic magnet within Germany is increasing, and will continue to do so even if the city is not chosen as the location for the European Central Bank.

Frankfurt is not only the stronghold of the German mark; it is also its birthplace. In June 1948 the powers that be waved goodbye to the old Reichsmark and brand new DM notes, printed in the USA, were put into circulation. The total value of the new money in those days was 10.7 billion marks, a paltry sum when one considers that this is precisely the amount that now changes hands here in the form of securities during a single average day.

Over 700 advertising agencies are either based or represented here, as well as 400 publishing companies and 150 insurance companies. Frankfurt's industry has a gross annual turnover of 200 billion marks, of which electronics and chemicals account for half.

There are still more people living in the city than working here, but only just – a total of 635,000 people to fill 580,000 jobs. The queues on the motorways provide ample indication of where people prefer to live. Over 1½ million people live within the city's immediate catchment area.

The city's international status is confirmed by its airport which, coping as it does with some 27 million passengers a year, is the largest in Central Europe. The main railway station is still the busiest in Europe, moving a total of 255,000 passengers on 1,640 trains every day.

Preceding pages: Frankfurt skyline with the Römerberg and the Paulskirche in the front; modern Frankfurt represented in the Purpur Designer Gallery. Left, the German eagle marches from strength to strength.

In the heavens over Frankfurt, all hell is breaking loose. In the early 1990s the Rhein-Main Airport serviced 310,000 flights a year – and the number is expected to increase. On top of their flight time, airlines have to allow 15 minutes more for circling over the runways waiting for permission to land, especially in the early evening. Every 1½ minutes, a plane swoops into Rhein-Main or takes off from one of the two parallel runways or Runway 18 West. Nearly 100 Frank-

McDonald's. A high-class British department store introduced the idea of a food hall to Rhein-Main; night owls draped in gold chains meet up at the super-disco Dorian Grey; and an airport chapel is available to everyone, regardless of religious affiliation. There is also an airport clinic, complete with operating theatres.

Even local residents think it worthwhile to travel out to the airport occasionally. The observation deck at the airport's highest level

furt-based airlines and an additional 80 charter lines disgorge 27 million passengers a year into the customs halls.

A small city: With 53,000 employees, Frankfurt airport is a miniature copy of the city of Frankfurt itself. Here the red-light district is mirrored by two sex shops; bank employees have locked themselves into boxes of bulletproof glass; and the city's numerous restaurants, both local and international, are well reflected in the selection of eating and drinking outlets at the airport, which ranges from fine Italian and Chinese restaurants to apple wine pubs and – of course – an underground

is the most-visited place in Germany after Mad King Ludwig's castle Neuschwanstein. There, you can watch the air traffic or view relics of aviation history in a permanent exhibition. In front of the airport, one of Lufthansa's first propeller planes is on display. The observation deck is also the departure point for one-hour tours of the airport, which begin at 11am and 2pm (on weekends, also at 1pm and 3pm).

Family groups also flock to the West runway's observation deck, situated just at the point where jumbo jets lift off. Years ago, opponents of this runway left their own critical appraisal of this facility spray-painted on the concrete: *"Gaffer, haut ab!"* (Spectators, clear out!) because its construction more than 10 years ago had incited strong opposition among the local population. The construction work and the ensuing increase of aeroplane noise destroyed the peace of the nearby nature recreation area of Mönchbruchwald, used by the 500,000 inhabitants of the surrounding communities.

Pilot memorial: At the entrance to the adja-

Getting out: After clearing passports and customs in the arrivals hall, passengers are ferried along conveyor belts. Rhein-Main boasts the rare convenience of a train station directly in the airport. If you're planning to take a train elsewhere, or the U-bahn (underground) into Frankfurt, you'll have to descend into the catacombs beneath the airport. An express train, which you can take only if you show an airline ticket, links Frankfurt with Cologne and Bonn, passing the pictur-

cent US airbase British and American visitors may be interested to see the memorial to the flyers who died breaking the Soviet blockade of Berlin in 1948–49 and bringing in supplies for millions of people. Today, this airbase is the central airport for US troops throughout the world. The airport authority would be only too happy to use the area for its own expansion plans, but Washington's signals are clear: the US won't be pulling out in the foreseeable future.

Left, Frankfurt Rhein-Main is the base airport for Lufthansa. **Above**, checking in.

esque castles along the Rhine. It takes the U-bahn (underground) only 10 minutes to get to the central railway station; compare this to a taxi, which takes at least half an hour to get into the city.

Rhein-Main's future: The airport, owned equally by the Federal Government, the state of Hesse, and the city of Frankfurt, has big plans for the future. The new East Terminal will mean the processing of some 35 million air passengers a year – a victory over London-Heathrow, which, in the secret contest for the title of biggest European airport, has hitherto led by a nose.

The most impressive view of the Main metropolis is from the Frankfurt-Kassel motorway. Just beyond the junction to Bad Homburg the skyscrapers of the large banks and towers appear on the horizon: welcome to so-called "Mainhattan". Frankfurt has the highest buildings in Germany, including the 257-metre (843-ft) Messeturm tower, the highest office block in Europe. Two more such monsters are planned – even though, as this book went to press, only half the Messeturm had been let.

Hardly surprisingly, Frankfurt has the reputation of being the most American of all the large European cities. Some 426 credit institutions, with 280 from foreign countries, have offices here, employing more than 50,000 people (9 percent of the city's working population). They work either in the smart 19th-century villas in Westend or in the sky-scraping towers of the Rhine-Main industrial area. From these premises they handle a quarter of all German capital transfers and about half of all transactions with foreign countries. Furthermore, more than two-thirds of the nation's share transactions take place in the stock exchange, as does 70 percent of trade in pension funds.

Federal Bank, not federal capital: The largest German banks have their homes in the tallest skyscrapers: Deutsche Bank, Commerzbank, Dresdner Bank and the Bank für Gemeinwirtschaft. Once you get above the 15th floor the weather and the view improve dramatically, even when there is a real pea-souper down below.

At the top of the Mainzer Landstrasse are the glistening 500-ft (155-metre) high twin towers of the Deutsche Bank, standing for credit and debit. They symbolise the strength of the largest of all German banks. Cameras in front of the main entrance give the impression of guarding the supple, entwined granite of Max Bill's sculpture. The DM 400 billion (£140 billion) turnover of the Deutsche

Left, the Deutsche Bank, Germany's largest.
Right, the foreign exchange market.

Bank in 1990 was equivalent to the size of the total federal budget in Germany.

Following German unification in 1989, the Frankfurters showed little interest in the debate about whether Bonn or Berlin should be the new capital: their main concern was that the money should remain in their city. Ironically, Frankfurt was just a hair's breadth away from becoming the capital in 1948: in the end Konrad Adenauer, who found Bonn more agreeable, got his way.

As a form of compensation, the Bundesbank (the Federal Bank, a national establishment of a kind that is rare in the world because of its independence from the government) came to Frankfurt, paving the way for the city's transformation into a financial metropolis. According to the Bundesbank's charter, it should have moved to Berlin after unification but, in the ensuing euphoria, Paragraph 1 of the charter was amended almost without anybody noticing: the Bundesbank was to remain in Frankfurt. After all, what is the transfer of the Parliament and Government to Berlin compared with moving Frankfurt's skyline? By the year 2000 it is estimated that more people will be working in Frankfurt than actually live within the official city borders. By then Frankfurt hopes to have become the home of the first European Central Bank. It won't do so without some argument, however, because London's institutions have a far greater capacity and turnover than Frankfurt's.

The Bundesbank building – closed to normal mortals – is known as the German Fort Knox. But, in fact, all that is stored in the Bundesbank, say the bankers, are securities and civil servants. To be on the safe side, the German gold and currency reserves are dis-

had previously been responsible for supplying the Royal Families of half of Europe with gold. In his review of the history of Frankfurt in 1960, the chronicler Walter Gerteis noted that two world powers had emerged from the city: Johann Wolfgang von Goethe and the legendary banking family Rothschild.

Mayer Amschel Rothschild was the founding father of a financial empire of hitherto unprecedented scale. In 1780 the Rothschild family moved into their house at 148 Judengasse: just 50 years later they had become the most influential banking family in Europe. They owed their rapid rise from humble origins to two war-related factors.

tributed amongst the cellars of the various state banks. A fantastic view over the premises of the Bundesbank is to be had from the "Ginnheimer Asparagus", the television tower in the north of Frankfurt.

The rise of the Rothschilds: The political decision to set up the Bundesbank in the Frankfurt district of Ginnheim after the war was a tribute to the historical role that the Main area had played in trade and finance. Although both national and foreign banks moved to the imperial capital of Berlin following the establishment of the Second German Empire in 1870, it was Frankfurt which

The first was that their founding father, Mayer Amschel, was responsible for administering the estates of the landgrave of Hessen-Kassel, who had made his wealth by selling farmers' sons from Hesse to the English. With the help of these Hesse boys, the English fought their war against the rebellious colonies in North America. The second factor was the extent of the Rothschild family's connections, particularly in England, which meant that they were the largest financiers during the Napoleonic Wars. Following the Congress of Vienna in 1815, one of the Rothschilds was a permanent visitor to the French

King, another was banker to the Pope, Nathan Rothschild was taking care of the family business in London, and Mayer Amschel's eldest son, Anselm, administered the parent company in Frankfurt.

Apart from a street named after them and a park where they owned a small mansion, little remains of the Rothschild legacy in Frankfurt. Their domestic and business premises were destroyed by the Nazis during the war. There is a marble family gravestone at the Jewish Cemetery in Rat-Beil-Strasse.

From Landstrasse to Wall Street: Stretching between the Messe and the Alte Oper, the rather impersonal Mainzer Landstrasse,

has modestly rented the second floor of an office block in Brönnerstasse in the city centre, next to the editorial office of the satirical magazine *Titanic*. In 1990 the turnover of the Ökobank was just DM 100 million (£35 million), but growing faster than average. Its funds are used to support socially and ecologically useful projects. The Ökobank is the only one which allows its investors to have a say in how their money should be used: arms manufacture, nuclear power and apartheid links are forbidden.

Hitting back at the bourgeoisie: The desperate desire of the banks to find new premises knows no taboos. Negotiators for the

where several new buildings are planned, hopes one day to become the Wall Street of Frankfurt. Its link to the Messe is symbolic, because the latter has a turnover of 250 million DM and attracts over a million business visitors to the city: all these executives – most of whom have come to do large international deals in the Messe halls – need to have banking facilities close at hand.

In contrast to the towers of Mainzer Landstrasse the Ökobank (ecological bank)

Left, a glimpse of German gold reserves, and, **above**, the latest in dealer technology.

Commerzbank even set up a deal with ex-Maoists. The bank was keen to get hold of a complex at number 147 in the Mainzer Landstrasse, which was being administered by the successor organisation to the Maoist Communist Federation (KBW), which had disbanded in 1985. The KBW had called upon the Party stalwarts in the 1970s to collect their inheritances early, and attack the bourgeoisie with their own weapons. Some DM 2.7 million (£1 million) was collected and the complex purchased on what, at that time, was the edge of the banking area. Even after the KBW had disbanded, bankers were met by the "Workers of the World Unite" motto in large letters as they entered the "communist bunker". But within 10 years the ex-Maoists were able to increase the value of their investments more than tenfold.

Ridiculed at first by their banking colleagues, the Commerzbank built an Öko-House (ecology office building) for some DM 30 million (£10.5 million), with toilets which flushed with rain water, heating provided by the waste heat from their own printing works, and plenty of greenery to provide a pleasant working atmosphere. The editorial offices of the *Tageszeitung* and *Ökotest* were allowed to move in; doctors and lawyers followed. In return for this investment, the Commerzbank was given permission to demolish the former KBW bunker and build afresh. Although the board members of the Commerzbank still behave as though this deal was an embarrassment, their colleagues no longer laugh: the project has proved a useful public relations exercise, in tune with the times.

The bankers – Frankfurt's yuppies?: The common image of bankers is that they spend their meal-times in the salad bars and restaurants around the Stock Exchange, ordering Perrier or San Pellegrino and raw fruit and vegetables or pink-roasted chicken. In the boutiques that they frequent, the shirts, blouses and suits are more expensive than anywhere else in the city. They buy Italian shoes and eschew German coffee in German cafés in favour of a double espresso at one of the Italian bars, where their highly polished shoes and half boots can be seen lined up in neat rows (as for example at Leiter in Kleine Hochstrasse).

The bankers vigorously dispute such stereotyping, claiming it describes the money-brokers from the Stock Exchange rather than them. Of course there are similarities between all financial executives: the *Handelsblatt* and the economics section of the *FAZ* are compulsory reading for both the bankers and brokers, as are *Wirtschaftswoche* and *Manager* magazine. Be that as it may, the bankers regard themselves as belonging to the "white-wine faction", a term to describe the new burghers in the enlightened larger cities of the republic ruled by red-green coalitions, such as Munich and Frankfurt.

In contrast to many of their American counterparts, Frankfurt's bankers do at least have a proper training behind them. Yet, because they are the only people who can still afford to have a flat in the city and at the same time drive a Golf GTI or S-class Daimler, they are written off as yuppies. In fact, most of their possessions are bought on credit, albeit on preferential terms.

Taken as an average their salaries are not enormous: 50,000 bankers earn roughly DM 5,000 (£1,750) net per month. Of course, such an average is misleading: bank apprentices earn around DM 1,000 (£350) net a month, office workers some DM 3,000 (£1,050). For the rest, the increments can be as high as the skyscrapers.

The Stock Exchange: Two enormous bronze animals keep guard over the entrance to the Stock Exchange (*Börse*) at Börsenplatz, holiest of holies in the city; the bull as a symbol of financial booms and the bear symbolising the slumps. The Stock Exchange, workplace for 3,169 dealers, ranks after London and Paris as the third most important trading centre for securities, fixed interest-bonds and real estate investments. Around 500 German and 390 foreign share holdings are traded here, together with 6,500 loans.

The Frankfurt securities and currency markets can be visited in the morning: those who take advantage of the organised tours will immediately understand why the supporters of Chaos Theory are becoming ever more numerous. To the uninitiated it is a madhouse; but for the economic politicians this madness is an indicator of the health of the national economy. Even when an arson attack led to the intervention of the police and fire brigade in April 1989, life at the Stock Exchange continued as normal after a break of less than an hour. Extinguishing the fire, and the subsequent inquiries, proved to be more of an obstacle to business than the molotov cocktails which the militant young "anti-imperialists" had thrown into the foyer: unfortunately the fire brigade had flooded the exchange's computer system.

Right, bull and bear, symbolising boom and slump, outside the Frankfurt Stock Exchange.

The Messe Frankfurt GmbH, the Frankfurt trade fair centre, owes its existence to Frankfurt's geographical position at the centre of Europe, at the hub of European transport routes. It is fitting, then, that the unassailable high-point of the exhibition calendar is the International Motor Show held every two years in September. Over a period of 12 days more than one million automobile buffs assemble here to see all the latest wonders of engineering and design displayed in the 10 halls. Unfortunately the high-tech pilgrimage invariably gets bogged down in the traffic jams at the Wiesbadner Kreuz, a major interchange on the A3 autobahn.

The oldest German fair: Hardly had the first bridge been constructed over the Main river in the 13th century than "Franconouvurd" began to boom. It was around this time that farming became more than just a matter of subsistence, and the farmers from the area came to town to barter their surplus.

The fair began in Frankfurt on 11 July 1240 when Frederick II, the grandson of Frederick Barbarossa, conferred trade fair privileges on the city, the first such privileges to be granted in the Empire. But soon the harvest, or autumn, fair could no longer satisfy demand. From 1330 a second fair was held shortly before Easter because this was the best time for wine and wool and goods produced in the wintertime.

This pattern has remained the same ever since with the International Frankfurt Autumn Fair and the Spring Fair, which has recently been divided into two.

The influx of these early traders produced the other Frankfurt industry: banking. Because of the general scarcity of money, the first credit agreements came into being. The first bank was founded here in 1402, and regular meetings of the Stock Exchange have taken place since 1585. Today the Messe has a turnover of about 250 million Deutschmarks, netted from 23 different trade fairs

Left, the Messeturm is the tallest office block in Europe. **Right**, walking made easy in the Messe.

with 31,000 exhibitors and 1.1 million visitors. The Messe also organises fairs in other parts of the world.

In the Middle Ages, fairs were established at all junctions of the main trade routes through Europe. Alongside Frankfurt, there was Leipzig, Brunswick, Antwerp, Bruges, Lyon and Milan. With the development of these transport routes, Frankfurt developed from a primarily regional to an international trade fair centre. Cloth came from England,

oil and spices from the East, furs from Russia and Poland. By the mid-16th century everything that the heart could possibly desire could be had in the "greatest commercial city in the world", as Francis I of France called it.

The department store of the world: From the mid-16th century onwards trade fair activities were centred around the Römerberg, the Neue Kräme and the Liebfrauenberg. Visitors lodged in cramped conditions in the houses and front rooms of the burghers; the population of the city more than doubled at the time of the fair. Until the 19th century merchants came to these fairs with their entire annual production. With increasing industrialisation, however, sample fairs emerged at which products were only presented and ordered later. The city of Leipzig led the way in this development, and because of developments in the east eventually took over as the leading German trade fair centre. Along with many other fairs, the Book Fair, which had been based in Frankfurt since 1580, moved to Leipzig. It was really only after World War II that the Frankfurt fair managed to re-establish its supremacy.

A milestone in the history of the Frankfurt fair was the opening of the Festhalle in 1909, at that time the largest domed structure in the

Mobile, the moving walkways, transport visitors from one hall to the other.

The model for the post-modern Galleria, designed by Professor O.M. Ungers, was the Galleria Vitterio in Milan. The Torhaus, opened in 1985, is also Ungers' work. This is where the fair's Service Center is housed. The Messe has to be relatively self-contained: located to the north of the railway station, it is not within easy walking distance of any of the tradition recreational areas.

The average consumer can't actually buy anything in this world department store, whether it be the Book Fair (the largest in the world), the Music Fair, the International

world. It was around the Festhalle that today's trade fair centre grew. The hall is now used for exhibitions as well as sports events such as the Six-day Cycle Race and rock festivals. In the 10 new exhibition halls, covering a total area of 260,000 sq. metres (10 sq. miles), 32,000 exhibitors annually display their wares. Entering the fair for the first time via the Galleria entrance, the visitor – greeted by a 120-metre (390-ft) long vaulted space of glass – might think that he has landed in a city of the future. There is air conditioning in all streets, restaurants and shops. Nobody walks. Buses and the Via

Butchers' Fair or the International Motor Show (most fairs open to the general public later in their run). For most people these products are as unattainable as the pinnacle of the 257-metre (843-ft) high Messeturm, but at least one dream is fulfilled: when fairs are in progress the closing times of pubs and restaurants in the city are extended for a full four hours, allowing Frankfurt, at least for a few days in the year, to live up to its reputation as a late-night cosmopolitan city.

Above, aerial view of the Messeturm, Messe halls and Festhalle (with dome).

THE BOOK FAIR

For a week each autumn, over 200,000 visitors descend on Frankfurt for the world's biggest book fair. They are there to buy books and sell books, and sometimes to buy and sell companies that publish books. For many of those involved in the publishing business, the Frankfurt Book Fair is by far the single most important event of the year.

For German visitors, the fair provides an opportunity to browse among the wealth of titles produced by the country's publishers. Booksellers get an advance look at the titles they will be selling in their shops. For overseas publishers, Frankfurt is the forum in which to buy and sell titles around the world. Some years ago, for example, an American publisher signed up the autobiography of Muhammad Ali, and brought him to the fair. Publishers from other countries, fired with enthusiasm as a result of meeting the former world heavyweight boxing champion, forked out huge sums to buy the rights.

When the Frankfurt Book Fair was re-established in 1949, the aim was simply to create a centrepiece for the German book trade. But, just as Frankfurt airport has become the busiest in Europe for international connections, so the city's book fair has become the place where the worldwide publishing community meets. In 1950, representatives from seven foreign countries took part. In 1971, the number had gone up to 59. By the 1990s, more than 90 countries were represented and there were nearly 8,500 exhibitors.

In 1949, much of Frankfurt was still in ruins following the war. There was one exhibition hall, and overseas exhibitors were housed in makeshift buildings like Nissen huts. Now, the principal international hall is a purpose-built, glass fronted structure that is a village by itself: it contains nine restaurants, two banks, bars, kiosks and frankfurter stalls, as well as meeting and conference rooms. To walk from one side of the fairground to another takes a good 20 minutes; visitors who wish to save their legs may be transported on a series of moving walkways, or they can take advantage of the free buses.

In the aisles of the various halls is the constant noise of, as one cynical observer suggests, thousands of people saying "How interesting". At one stand, a publisher of illustrated books is showing off a "dummy" – a mock-up designed to show what a potential book might look like. If enough foreign publishers show interest, the publisher can afford to go ahead and produce what will be a lavish adornment for coffee tables next Christmas. Next door, a rights director is showing off her list to an Italian publisher, who wants to know if the Italian rights to a promising first novel are available; he might offer the equivalent of £3,000, some of which will go to the publisher, the rest to the author. At the next stand, a publisher who produces three books a year from his kitchen table is arranging a deal to get his list distributed in New Zealand. Other publishers are prowling the aisles, on the look-out either for books to buy or for ideas to copy.

The impact of 200,000 visitors on a city of 625,000 inhabitants can easily be imagined. Space

is at a premium, and smart hotels like the Hessischer Hof and the Frankfurter Hof can be booked up a year in advance. One believable tale has it that, when a German publisher died in his sleep at the Hessischer Hof, 17 people had inquired by the following lunchtime about the availability of his room.

At such a large international gathering, there is plenty of scope for the eccentric. A popular competition each year offers a prize for the oddest title on display at the fair. Entries have included *Big and Very Big Hole Drilling*, *Proceedings of the Second International Conference on Nude Mice*, and *The Madam as Entrepreneur: Career Management in House Prostitution*. ∎

Frankfurt's international reputation as a centre of literature is undoubtedly based on the annual Book Fair. The Fair – held each year in October – is primarily concerned with selling world-wide translation rights and bringing South-American, Asian and African works to the notice of Europe. Politics is never far from the surface: following the Gulf War in 1991 Iraqi literature was banned and the Iranians were re-invited, despite the death threats against Salman Rushdie.

The literary scene: For visitors to Frankfurt who miss the Book Fair there is still a huge and well publicised collection of literary events and venues.

The Literaturhaus (House of Literature) in the Westend is an open institution which hosts readings by translators and authors independent of the current market situation, whilst the bookshops hold regular readings of new publications.

The main pillar of the public literary scene in Frankfurt is the Hessische Literaturbüro, on the third floor of the Mouson Tower (Mousonturm) in Waldschmidt Strasse in Bornheim. This centre not only serves to promote literature but also has an editorial office which is open to the public. Here aspiring authors can receive advice on their manuscripts from established writers, who will comment more thoroughly than publishing companies.

Another private initiative is the Roman-Fabrik, a pub in Uhlandstrasse, which, in addition to staging concerts, offers a platform for authors. The importance of the Roman-Fabrik declined when it lost its patron, a Frankfurt bordello owner, who had been prepared to give authors free lodging.

Renowned publishing companies: It is no accident that the Literaturhaus (see above) is located in the Westend, because this area of smart villas is also the home of some of Germany's most famous publishing companies. Also here is the entrance to Frankfurt's university campus, a now somewhat shabby legacy of Frankfurt's Institute for Social Research. In the 1960s the philosophical

ideas of Adorno and Horkheimer attracted students to the city. These were philosophy combined with literary ambition and a fundamental critique of society, which was sometimes bigoted, sometimes trenchant, but always aimed at being a literary challenge – you have to read Adorno to appreciate this.

It was in Frankfurt that the first translations of foreign authors such as Samuel Beckett or James Joyce were produced. Within Germany Frankfurt acquired the reputation of being the home of the written sciences and of literature, thanks in particular to the efforts of Peter Suhrkamp. After the war the large literature publishing company, Samuel Fischer, moved from Berlin to Frankfurt, producing among other things the *Neue Rundschau* newspaper. In 1950 its publisher, Peter Suhrkamp, left Fischer and set up the Suhrkamp company.

These two companies, now equally strong, spawned yet another publishing venture in the wake of the 1968 student revolts. The Verlag der Autoren (Authors' publishing company), with former Suhrkamp editor Karlheinz Braun at the helm, has developed into one of the best theatre publishing companies in Germany without ever deviating from the maxim of 1968 that the company belongs to the authors.

A further publishing company, the Luchterhand, has since been established. It was the first to publish in the West authors from the former East Germany and such "trouble makers" as Günter Grass. Luchterhand, however, represented the most glaring example of the conflict between money and intellectual pursuits. The Dutch owner is an extremely business-minded woman and, as the number of disputes rose, the company moved to Hamburg, leaving just an editorial office behind. Frankfurt may be fertile ground for intellectual pursuits, but the real publishing money is to be found in Hamburg.

Critique of money: Frankfurt's publishing scene fears this constant conflict between intellectual ideas and financial considerations just as the devil fears the holy water.

The patron Siegfried Unseld, successor to Peter Suhrkamp, is regarded as a hard judge by authors and editors alike, but he always takes care of those whom he favours. Meanwhile the Eichborn company sells millions of copies of cartoon books just in order to be able to publish the more demanding works of authors such as Albert Sellner or Hans-Magnus Enzenberger.

The simple gives birth to the sublime. The ultimate satirical magazine *Titanic*, with au-

furt's cultural avant-garde. In addition, the Café Voltaire serves as a communal debating forum, and each year in summer the Römerberg Discussions take place in the city parliament. This is an open symposium attracting famous names. Academics take the place of politicians and a dream comes true – cant and political point scoring is replaced by reason. This is probably the most remarkable legacy of the Frankfurt School.

Newspapers: Sixty-nine newspapers and

thors such as Robert Gernhardt, Chlodwig Poth and F.K. Wächter, also has its home in Frankfurt. These gentlemen of the self-proclaimed "New Frankfurt School" lampoon the contradictions and hypocrisies of modern society.

Intellectual debate: Particularly popular in Frankfurt are the debating establishments, such as Kultur in III in the Mouson Tower next to the Hessische Literaturbüro, which acts as a cultural-political forum for Frank-

Thanks to the Book Fair, Frankfurt has become a major publishing centre.

magazines are listed in Frankfurt's yellow pages, including such giants as the *Financial Times* and the *Asian Wall Street Journal*. Local names are the *Handelsblatt, Frankfurter Rundschau, Frankfurter Neue Presse* and last and most importantly the *Frankfurter Allgemeine Zeitung* (*FAZ*). The latter is the flagship paper for the financial world, controlled by five equally-ranked publishers. It is much praised by its 400,000 readership. However, its rather reactionary commentary column, usually on the front page, regularly manages to bring the blood of the intelligentsia to boiling point and beyond.

Frankfurt without its museums would be just as difficult to imagine as Frankfurt without its Book Fair, its banks or its apple wine. Historically, however Frankfurt is not so much a city of museums as a city of patrons. The private patrons of the past century collected art treasures: not as a means of subsidising art, but as hard-nosed business transactions. This led to extensive collections, the most famous of all being the Ströher Collection of Modern Art. These collections naturally required museums of equal standing: when, in 1978, the villas of the former patrons were deemed too small and out of sync with the modern *Zeitgeist*, new museums were developed on the banks of the Main.

Breaking new ground: The museum developments have been aided by the fact that, thanks to the tradition of patronage, Frankfurt has the highest cultural budget of any city in Europe. This is now topped up to a considerable extent by private sponsorship. Yet Frankfurt is still not able to rival Cologne or Basle. To suggest that the work of every Frankfurt artist can be found hanging in the Museum of Modern Art would be a gross exaggeration. There have also been disappointments: from time to time gallery owners and artists threaten to turn their backs on Frankfurt altogether. Museum life in the city can have a suffocating effect on the artists; with everyone knowing each other so intimately, creative freedom can be stifled.

As one response, Frankfurt's sculptors have turned to new art forms, radically different from the sort of exhibits which can be admired in the Liebieghaus (Museum alter Plastik). Frankfurt's famous "art in open places" is one example: taking turns each year, the artists display their new creations in the area around the Römer, works which neither fit the description of sculpture nor that of museum pieces. Frankfurt's museums have created the art of the counterpoint:

Preceding pages: Goethe as depicted in the Städel Museum. Left, outside the Alte Oper during the Frankfurt Festival. Right, mixed media.

whatever styles are currently on display in even the most modern museums are soon overtaken by the creative ideas outside.

Outsiders: Indeed, some artists would rather not have their works displayed in a museum at all, like the artists of Neue Medien, who have their own institute under the direction of the Viennese art philosopher Peter Weibel. What, they ask, is a picture? Likewise Frankfurt's designers, such as those in the Ginbande group, are not anxious to be included in the

Frankfurt Museum of Arts and Crafts. Instead they concentrate on bringing internationally acclaimed trends to the annual Design Horizonte show in late summer (admittedly the Museum of Arts and Crafts is its central forum).

The advertising industry, which has caused a major sensation in Frankfurt, is similarly concerned about its work being turned into museum pieces: the building of a German advertising museum in Frankfurt is being planned and exhibitions have already been held in other premises in the city. All the same, most Frankfurt artists would not be averse to seeing their work displayed in the Museum of Modern Art in their lifetimes.

Nonetheless, the schizophrenic relationship of Frankfurt's artists to the museums has a positive influence, helping to make Frankfurt a centre for art forms which break down the normal barriers. Groups such as Formalhaut, for example – comprising artists and architects – are carrying out pioneering work on new ways of incorporating art into building design. One example is the new Finanzamt, the city's tax office which is being developed by Formalhaut into a multimedia venue, where video artists, radio play producers and photographers will be able to

several influential institutions on the way.

The Holbeinsteg bridge leads over the Main to Frankfurt's oldest and most famous art museum, the Städel. This is the largest art house from the Frankfurter patron tradition, with Tischbein's famous painting of *Goethe in the Roman Campagna* and highly acclaimed exhibitions on the ground floor. At the back of the Städel is the smallest German art academy, the Städelschule, with Kaspar König, the principal and well-known exhibitor, and such controversial figures as the artist Hermann Nitsch among its teachers. Frankfurt's most progressive form of art appreciation is taught here. A few steps fur-

present their work via permanently installed electronic media. The high standard of the two newest museums – the Museum for Modern Art, and the Postmuseum, which presents media art among other things – has had a positive impact on contemporary art.

A tour of the Museumsufer: The Frankfurter Museumsufer (literally "museums bank"), the collection of museums along the south bank of the river Main, forms a cultured promenade. Visitors can walk from the Liebieghaus, with its sculptures ranging from the ancient world to the baroque, all the way to the Museum for Arts and Crafts, passing

ther is the Deutsches Postmuseum, in the shape of an igloo or a ship, which despite its name is a celebration of telecommunications rather than stamps. In this transparent glass building – created by the architect Behnisch, who also designed the roof of the Olympic stadium in Munich and the new German Parliament in Bonn – are exhibitions of works by modern media artists. A real eye-catcher in the entrance is a sculpture by the "originator" of video art, Nam June Paik.

The Architectural Museum, which concentrates on building history in the 20th century (particularly post-modernist designs).

The "house within a house" here, built by Oswald Mathias Ungers in 1984, has been highly praised.

Under the direction of Vittorio Lampugnani, the Architectural Museum is regarded as one of the most important centres of architectural thought and of research into city building, and has a splendid collection of model buildings ranging from the German *Bauhaus* school to the post-structuralist architecture of Daniel Libeskind, who presented a spectacular but neglected design proposal for the development of the Potsdam Square in Berlin.

Next door is the Film Museum, with im-

Across the Untermainbrücke on the northern side is the Jewish Museum in the Rothschild-Palais, with its unpretentious portrayal of Jewish history. On the north end of the Eiserner Steg is the city's Museum of History (entrance from the Römer). On the way to the Cathedral from the Römerberg is the Schirn Kunsthalle, with its international exhibitions of artists such as Picasso, Chagall, or German Expressionists.

The pièce de résistance: Heading left from the cathedral, on Domstrasse, is the much celebrated new Museum for Modern Art, focal point of the contemporary Frankfurt art scene, designed by the Viennese architect

portant exhibits from the history of film, and the oldest German Communal Cinema which shows three film rarities daily.

Moving on you first come to the Ethnological Museum (Museum für Völkerkunde) and then, located in a park, the Museum of Arts and Crafts, with exhibits from all over the world, spaciously displayed in the cubic construction of the American architect Richard Meier. It also has a fine café.

Left, dinosaurs at the Senckenberg museum.
Above, the owner of Germany's only advertising museum, in Frankfurt.

Hans Hollein. Nicknamed the "piece of pie" on account of its ground plan, it is a temple of modern art and has just as much tourist appeal in its building as in the works it contains. The museum opened in 1991. Along with the art fair, "Art Frankfurt", which was initiated two years previously, it has raised hopes that the collector and patron city of Frankfurt will become a modern city of art.

In the district of the university around the Senckenberganlage is the Naturhistorisches Museum Senckenberg, famous for its dinosaurs (for details, see page 154 of the chapter "From the Station to the University").

Music in Frankfurt currently means new music instead of classical: world-famous techno and hip-hop instead of rock bands up on stage. Theatre is new, as is the post-structuralist ballet with performances which break down all previous barriers; here dancing stage sets, not dying swans, are the fashion. Frankfurt's live scene adds that touch of the electronic, the intellectual and the innovative into the city's culture.

Main stages: The theatre in Frankfurt has long been highly successful. It is fortunate in that it has had very few financial restrictions. Frankfurt has the most modern opera house in the world, one of the best ballet troupes and Europe's number one house of avant-garde theatre in the form of the Theatre am Turm (TAT).

The TAT is where such film and theatre stars as Rainer-Werner Fassbinder and Claus Peyman, or the author Peter Handke, rose to fame. Five years ago the TAT, together with the Wuppertal ensemble of Pina Bausch, was the main stage for European dance theatre. Now it has become the undisputed centre of European avant-garde theatre. Even though it doesn't have its own ensemble, productions have been developed in Frankfurt which have played throughout the world – for example, the work of the well-known stage designer Michael Simon and the musician Heiner Goebbels.

New theatre concepts are developed into international successes at the TAT and the theatre unites what would appear to defy unification – musicians, painters, writers and artists have more influence than the actors, directors and literary managers in determining the aesthetic form of drama which is breaking new ground in the artistic world.

The Opera House (Opernhaus), not to be confused with the Alte Oper even though it is, confusingly, closer to Frankfurt's historic centre, is famous well beyond the city boundaries. Destroyed by fire in 1987, it has since

been lavishly renovated. The stage equipment is amongst the most modern anywhere in the world.

In the 1980s the Frankfurt opera was famous for such productions as the Wagner Cycle by Ruth Berghaus along with her grand-scale operas, including Berlioz's *Les Troyens*, as well as for the intellectually impressive productions by Michael Gielens. Following a turbulent period presided over by several interim directors, Sylvain Cam-

breling has now taken charge.

Also housed in the same building is the Ballet Frankfurt under the choreographical direction of William Forsythe. He has not only blown away the cobwebs from ballet but has taken its dance steps to the point of abstraction and even parody. Every Forsythe première is a major European event. Critics from all over the world wait in line for tickets, with the second première regularly taking place in the Théâtre de Chatelet in Paris. Deep respect for Forsythe's choreography has grown with his discovery of such architectural talents as Daniel Libeskind and the latter's passionate conveyance of the American art theory of post-structuralism, which Forsythe exemplifies in his extraordinary choreographical interpretations. The close relationship between Ballet Frankfurt and the Frankfurt art scene speaks volumes: where else, except in New York or London, could you find a dance company providing the impulse for the art world? With Forsythe, fellow choreographer Amanda Miller, and such high-quality dancers as Stephen Galloway, the Ballet Frankfurt is currently regarded by the critics as being the number one ballet group of its kind in the world.

Then there is the Schauspielhaus, or municipal theatre. Its first venue is the studio theatre at the back of the main auditorium, which has aroused particular attention through its schools theatre under the direction of Alexander Brill. Its second venue is the Bockenheimer Depot, a former tram depot which is being used as alternative quarters whilst the main theatre is being renovated. The Bockenheimer Depot became a talking point in the town as a result of Peter Brook's production of *Mahabharata*, and is generally regarded as an outstanding venue. With theatrically exciting choral productions by the author and director Einar Schleef,

the Depot has also achieved a degree of fame outside Frankfurt.

In the slip-stream of the large theatres are the fringe groups. Their venues are the Mouson Tower (Mousonturm), a former soap factory also noted for its literary connections, the Frei Theaterhaus and the Gallus Theater. Each has its own particular significance. The Mouson Tower has rendered particularly outstanding services to European dance theatre, although it attracts its largest audiences to its Summer Festival, and to the performances of outstanding cabaret artists. The newest theatre of them all, the Frei Theaterhaus, houses not only various re-

gional theatre companies but also Frankfurt's children's theatre. The Gallus Theater continues its long-established tradition of being the most important stage for the local fringe scene.

A modern ensemble: If you asked the citizens of Frankfurt to direct you to the heart of the city's more traditional culture they would probably suggest the Alte Oper, which stages the Frankfurt Festival every summer. The Festival specialises not only in classical music but also in more modern forms. Such established artists as Claudio Abbado, Mauricio Kagel and Hans Werner Henze alternate with new discoveries and re-discoveries including compositions from Russian futurists. The Festival is the three-month-long climax to Frankfurt's musical year, and the symbol of its importance as a city of representative modern music. Performers include the internationally recognised Ensemble Modern, who are regarded as "anti-authoritarian": rather than being directed by any one particular conductor, the musicians are allowed to choose the conductor themselves for each particular piece.

The only other group of equal status is the Kammeroper Frankfurt, a private ensemble producing excellent modern interpretations

music and popular entertainment are held neatly in balance. There is, for example, no exclusively classical music crowd: even the Alte Oper has given equal rank to all the various different musical forms. From musicals to jazz, from new music to symposiums, from Ute Lemper to Chick Corea – the Alte Oper has a large and faithful audience despite its catholic tastes, and is thus open to the widest possible cross-section of society. Popular music, which also attracts mass audiences to the Alte Oper, has a second large venue at the exhibition centre (Festhalle): despite its enormous size, the Festhalle is often sold out.

of opera, despite their modest financial circumstances. Their audience tends to be the genuine opera fans rather than the gala crowd. Their venue, the Finkenhof, once almost unknown, has become the centre of Frankfurt's chamber music. Not far from this lodge house in Finkenhofstrasse is the Frankfurter Musikhochschule, which regularly invites guests to respectable concert evenings of a very high standard.

Frankfurt's music scene is characterised by the fact that the borders between classical

Left, glass musicians. **Above**, fringe production.

The jazz scene: One of Frankfurt's real institutions is the Jazzkeller, Germany's longest running active jazz club. Every Wednesday, large crowds – not only of jazz freaks – gather in the cellar rooms near the Alte Oper, to hear Eugen Hahn's famous Jazz Disco get the feet tapping. Nowadays jazz giants are less likely to be found guesting in this traditional cellar, where the jazz brothers Albert and Emil Mangelsdorff rose to fame, and which can look back on such distinguished guests as Louis Armstrong and Miles Davis. Nevertheless, every now and again there are still some real gems – often rising stars from the American jazz scene who make their European debuts in the Jazzkeller, before becoming world-famous and prohibitively expensive. The Frankfurter Jazz Festival is also worth mentioning, and the initiative of a small, dedicated club, Jazz und Maus, created by Michael Damm, which causes a great furore each year in February at the Heddernheim Carnival. His Ford Transit has been converted into a giant mouse, from the top of which the new jazz-session season is opened with the first performance, before it moves on to various small pubs.

Included amongst the latter is the little Jazzkneipe in Berliner Strasse, a comical

where such shooting stars can often be seen for the last time at close quarters, before they hit the charts or disappear for ever. The Omen and the Techno-Club don't have live performances in the strict sense. Instead, the 27-year-old self-proclaimed Pope of Techno music, Andreas Thomalla – alias Talla II XCL – exports his artificially produced techno-music as far as America.

Thus Frankfurt's most indigenous musical direction is generated directly under the airport terminal every Friday night, and exported round the world. In the city-centre dance temple, Omen, Sven Väth determines the hit-list of German dancefloor music, test-

half-timbered pavilion in which Frankfurter jazz musicians meet every evening for a cosy, informal session.

Discotheques: Three discos share the limelight as ultra-fashionable music venues: Batschkapp in Escherheim, which planned to move to the City-West in 1992, Omen in the banking district and, on Fridays, the Techno Club in the Dorian Gray discotheque under the airport.

Batschkapp – known as "the Kapp" for short – has established a reputation for having one of the best noses for bands from the underground rock scene. This is the place

ing the music which will be played over the next weeks in German discotheques. Some become world-wide hits, such as *You've got the Power*, a disco-hit produced on the edge of Frankfurt in 1990 by Luca Anzilotti and Omen co-owner Michael Münzing, which also seemed to serve as a Frankfurter synonym for eternal subversiveness.

The Omen, converted from a rather plush and conservative dancing venue called Vogue, can justifiably describe itself as being Frankfurt's number one discotheque – the place to get high at the weekend, with leading dancers who display enormous stamina, as well as the most formidable light and sound equipment in the city.

As in every large city, the rest of the music clubs can be divided into those where the crowds go and those where the "in" people go. For years now the crowds have been going to Cooky's near the Hauptwache, the dance-hall for locals, who are presented with avant-garde music live every Monday night. Plastik is another possibility if you want to meet up with the city's yuppies. Or Hans Romanov's EX K 17 near the station, where you can find students, pimps, Greens and shift workers, romping around until the early hours, united by music across the whole

Ballroom" on Fridays and Saturdays in Batschkapp, a dance which looks exactly like its name.

A third scene, ranging from Creole to black music, American to Jamaican, can be found at Funkadelic in the Zeil, with Frankfurt's most famous female disc jockey, Lady D, and a consistent jovial cellar party atmosphere, open to all skin colours. Another venue, albeit not a disco but nevertheless a loud and essential part of Frankfurt's music culture, is the Dreikönigskeller, where the city's musicians meet to listen both to their own new singles and to their mainly British inspirations.

range of compact disc and long-playing record production.

The more intimate "in" discos of the local scene are located as far away from each other as are the sub-cultures which they represent. Negativ is a "Gruftie" disco – its customers doll themselves up in black with totally pale faces – with droll and sometimes deliberately bad bands from Germany, England and America. Those who find this scene too limited, but don't want to renounce the underground scene altogether, dance the "Idiot

Europe's highest disco is 222 metres (728 ft) above the ground in the television tower, nicknamed the "Ginnheim Asparagus". The Sky Fantasy, like the Dorian Gray, belongs to Gerd Schület and Michael Presinger, who have over 50 venues all over Germany. From the top, the view is magnificent, the desire to dance not exactly excessive and the optical stimulation from Tele 5 cable-TV somewhat less than inspiring. Yet the view over Frankfurt lit up at night makes the experience worthwhile, as does the Wednesday night "everyone can be a star" entertainment provided by karaoke singing.

<u>Left</u>, jazz on stage. <u>Above</u>, creative space.

Frankfurt is an eldorado for those of catholic culinary taste. The delights of more than a dozen nationalities are represented in the metropolis: French, Italian, Greek, Spanish and Portuguese specialities can all be sampled here. Homely kitchens offer up juicy Polish roasts or crispy duck; a fiery goulash or an ice-cold vodka can be had in **Scarlet Pimpernell** (Krögerstrasse 7, Tel: 29 21 38, reservation necessary); or mince, boiled pork and the newest wines in **Erzherzog Johann** (Schloßstrasse 92, Tel: 57 38 00).

The delights of Asian cooking, consisting mainly of lightly cooked vegetables, rice and fish, are presented delicately here. This is the cuisine for vegetarians and those who generally prefer to do without meat. The best Chinese restaurants, **Tse Yang** (Kaiserstrasse 67, Tel: 23 25 41) and **Regent** (Kaiserstrasse, Tel: 23 12 73), are in the area around the railway station. The English, Thais and Vietnamese eat their "rice and curry" in Polynesian style at **Lord Jim** (Bockenheimer Landstr. 92, Tel: 74 64 64) in Westend.

The Frankfurters have also recently discovered their passion for chopsticks and raw fish: Thai and Japanese food is now considered trendy, as healthy, light and well-spiced dishes are well suited to the low-calorie programmes of the health-conscious. Food aesthetes and the culinarily adventurous spend their lunch-times and evenings in a sushi bar. World-beating Japanese dishes are created here by hand: appetizingly decorated, rice balls with raw fish filling are at the top of the culinary charts. Connoisseurs enthuse about such delights, claiming them to be an edible art form. For newcomers, **Sushimoto** (Konrad-Adenauer-Strasse 7, Tel: 28 00 45) is a good bet, whilst a good value lunch can also be had at **Juchheim's** (Am Salzhaus 1, Tel: 28 02 62/63).

Preceding pages: the Eulenberg apple wine pub in Bornheim; a quiet drink; local specialities Rippchen und Kraut (left) and Handkäs' mit Mussig (right); testing the new apple wine. <u>Left</u>, the Rosa restaurant. <u>Right</u>, foreign specialities.

If your palate craves for more than cooked beansprouts, raw sea-urchins on sour rice and water-chestnut puree, try Middle Eastern and Arab food. **L'Emir** (Baseler Platz 2, Tel: 23 01 23) near the station offers Lebanese delights; traditional Lebanese starters, along with piquantly prepared offal dishes and sweet desserts, are all served on sparkling white tableclothes. Here you can leave your knife and fork on the table: all you need to eat with are your fingers and unleavened bread.

Thai restaurants are also shooting up like thickets of bamboo, the boom having produced a wide range of quality. Excellent food can usually be recognised by the variety of aromatic spices: the best is at **Tamnak Thai** (Berliner Str. 64, Tel: 28 78 33) and **Suvadee** (Baumweg 19, Tel: 49 40 764).

Multicultural food: Local cooks have long been praised for one ability above all others: that of producing excellent reproductions of the cuisines of the city's many foreigners. International cooking has a long tradition in Frankfurt, without ever having lost its genuine Frankfurter quality. Although the proverb says that too many cooks spoil the broth, Frankfurt proves that the opposite can also be true. Cooks from up to three different nationalities are often to be found together in the same kitchen.

Frankfurt's best Turkish food is served on wooden tables in an old Bornheim pub. To accompany delicious kebabs and legs of lamb the guests drink Irish stout and delight in evergreen stories from the 1960s. The regulars swear by the combination of a devilishly hot "Chicken Saag" and a juicy schnitzel. The German-Indian alliance in the **Wilder Kegler** is also regarded as being a great success.

ter **Ernst** (Alte Rothofstrasse, Tel: 28 38 22) in the city. Among the specialities of this simply-decorated pub are smoked pork chops with sauerkraut and pork sausages. The Schlund family runs Mutter Ernst, Frankfurt's most successful gourmet address for good plain food. The head of the family, busy at the stove, has a whole repertoire of regional German dishes. From ox-tail ragout to potato fritters, the food is always fresh and of a consistently high standard.

Pasta prego!: The current pasta boom represents the second great Mediterranean culinary offensive to reach Frankfurt following the pizza wave. Discovered some 30 years

A rock amongst the waves: Despite the various culinary fashions and exotic trends, the classical German combination of meat, potatoes and vegetables is in season all year round. The best bet for a sumptuous cutlet in cream sauce with vegetables is the cosy **Wielandstubb** (Wielandstrasse 1, Tel: 55 85 51). University professors, families, respectable middle class citizens and students are all to be found in this typical German pub, sitting over generous portions both at midday and in the evening.

Bankers, brokers and craftsmen in search of that home-made taste go regularly to **Mut-**

ago as filling and easily prepared, cheap food under Italian direction became a delicacy on the Main. Frankfurt's "Little Italy" lies in the university district of Bockenheim; all lovers of Neapolitan cooking have their own Italian somewhere here. The best pizzas are served at **Da Cimino** (Adalbertstrasse 29, Tel: 77 11 42). On the other hand, those who end up at **Basalteck** (Basaltstrasse 35, Tel: 70 08 68), a typically German establishment, shouldn't be surprised to find a colourful mixture of guests sitting over steaming pasta dishes. Lina from Italy is the cook, and the *pasta diabolo* is freshly prepared and truly devilish. The more refined Italian restaurants are to be found in Westend and the city centre. The pasta portions are less ample, the sauces less fatty, but the bills are correspondingly higher. Try **Incontro** and **Florian** (both in Kettenhofweg) or **Da Enzo** and **Isoletta** (both in Feldbergstrasse).

A difficult choice: The palate of the true Frankfurter is divided. On the one hand it loves the refined and international dishes which are a part of the city's history. This is all the more understandable as half a dozen of the much-desired "stars" awarded for culinary expertise in just such cuisine twinkle in the Frankfurter sky. On the other hand the

to Hamburg. The green sauce happily combines tradition and recent trends. Said to have been Goethe's favourite dish, it has long enjoyed the reputation of being healthy, and is a particularly fortifying meal for Maundy Thursday. Complementing the salad and herb boom of recent years, the grass-green sauce is in season the whole year round. Together with new potatoes and a portion of ox-breast, the spring-fresh dish has numerous varieties.

The classical way to prepare it is as follows: seven herbs – cheril, pimpernel, sorrel, borage, parsley, chives and cress – are chopped very finely by hand. The white of

local gourmet is also attracted to popular traditional dishes.

Frankfurt's most original dish is centred around apple wine, based in the district of Sachsenhausen (see page 143, "Apple Wine"), and is said to offer a good solid base for a long drinking session. Green sauce, smoked pork chop with sauerkraut and *Handkäs'* or curd cheese – the culinary Holy Trinity – are to Frankfurt what Weisswurst is to Munich, rye bread to Cologne and eel soup

Left, chefs take their break. **Above**, coffee-drinking has always been a serious business.

hard-boiled eggs is cut into small pieces and the yolks strained and made into a mayonnaise with vinegar, oil, mustard, pepper and salt. Then mix everything together. For a change, yoghurt, sour cream or crème fraîche can be used.

The time taken preparing the sauce is made up for by the other ingredient, *Handkäs'*. This curd cheese can be quickly dressed with vinegar and oil and, according to taste, mixed with *Mussig* (finely chopped onions). This quick dish is regarded as an essential accompaniment to apple wine. Substantial portions of pork with sauerkraut, lentil soup and juicy beef sausages – the Frankfurters prefer the latter to the small Frankfurter sausages – are served in every apple wine pub in Sachsenhausen, south of the river, with little difference in quality.

Frankfurt is a place for gourmets, as witnessed by the international cookery exhibition which is held here, along with cookery's Olympics, every four years.

The cooks: The city has been showered with cookery awards. A huge number of chefs, both men and women, are making names for themselves with creative and varied dishes which bear their unmistakable trademarks. Willi Tetz from **Humperdinck** (Grüneburg-

biological farms; white flour and refined sugar are frowned upon. Gourmets will enjoy themselves at **Hessler** (Am Bootshafen 4, Tel: 06181 49 29 51).

The numerous red piglets hanging on the wall of Frankfurt's most original bistro are misleading: you won't find pork on the plates. Juliane Oehler, chef in the **Rosa** restaurant (Grüneburgweg 25, Tel: 72 13 80), specialises in much lighter dishes. Her fish dishes are excellent, the delicate turbot with spinach and lobster sauce being one of the most popular choices.

Klaus Trebes, master of every style of international cookery, doesn't believe in

weg 95, Tel: 72 21 22) describes his refined cooking as classical. This likeable one-star cook, a student of Lévy and Witzigman, puts the emphasis on technical skills. In his opinion, fish should be somewhat pink on the bone, and not over-cooked. Green beans must still be crunchy when they are served, and pasta should also have a bit of bite.

The dynamic Katherina Hessler is regarded as the professor of wholemeal cookery. Her high-quality food represents a daily campaign for healthy eating, her efforts having been rewarded as early as 1979 with the award of a star. She prefers products from

keeping his philosophy to himself. He's convinced that a voyage through the various culinary landscapes of the world has never done any of his colleagues any harm; in his **Gargantua** bistro (Friesengasse 3, Tel: 77 64 42), for example, he offers his own creation of lobster couscous.

Guy Bastian, the young chef from **Erno's Bistro** (Liebigstrasse 15, Tel: 72 19 97, reservation necessary), who comes from between Strasbourg and Colmar, is master of two styles of cooking: the good solid variety from the Alsace region and the haute-cuisine which bears his own special mark. He demonstrates that good solid food needn't necessarily be simple: on red and white checked tablecloths he presents perfect French dishes. Blood sausages, liver sausages and pike-perch with pickled cabbage have an equal place on the menu with home-made liver pâté. The choice of wines is the sign of a connoisseur and Guy Bastian is a collector of good wines.

French is also the style of the Mosbach brothers: in their **Bistro 77** (Ziegelhüttenweg 1, Tel: 61 40 40) in Sachsenhausen – also awarded a star – brother Dominique is at the stove, whilst Guy takes care of the service. In the ornate Côte d'Azur ambience, the chef

off in matters of architecture and design is impressive. Big names from the international design scene are here, and the new architecture has permanently altered the face of the city, with the development of a lively "designer scene".

This move to become a designer city has not, however, been without controversy. Golden chairs, neo-Baroque sofas and decorative armchairs had no sooner been installed in the café of the post-modernist **Kunsthalle Schirn** (Römerberg 6a) when they became the object of vicious quarrelling. Dismissed from on high as being nouveau riche, the décor was seen by the

shows how God eats in France: the food is simply classical. The desserts in particular are uniquely delicious.

Sachsenhausen also boasts a large number of eating places of differing qualities and prices; walk the narrow streets around the Grosse Rittergasse and take your pick. Recommended are **Maaschanz** (Färberstrasse 75, Tel: 62 28 86) and the **Tannenbaum** (Brückenstrasse 19, Tel: 61 13 04).

A change of scene: Frankfurt's vertical take-

café's management as a progressive statement in terms of style. Once the conflict was resolved, the café began to enjoy great popularity. And no wonder; this stylish "in" venue wouldn't be out of place in London, Paris or New York.

According to connoisseurs, the best places to meet are the bars of the new Frankfurter museums: the **Café in Kunsthandwerkmuseum** (Schaumainkai 17) is ranked as being the best of the bunch. Here you can brunch and lunch to your heart's content, sitting on replicas of Otto Wagner's post savings bank chair from 1902. In summer the

<u>Left</u>, a more traditional menu. <u>Above</u>, Frankfurt has many jazz bars.

terrace is open, facing towards the splendid Park am Main.

The guests in the **Buchcafé of the Jewish Museum** (Untermainkai 14–5) can also sit in style. Wire chairs by Eames, lamps from da Costa/Wolff and glass tables provide the metropolitan ambience. Journalists, theatre people and other artists make up the regulars. Meanwhile the **Café in the Museum for Modern Art** (Domstrasse 10) has been the cause of scandal since its opening. This ground floor venue, in the famous Hollein building, bears the name Sacco and Vanzetti, which large sections of the city's population under no circumstances wanted to see associated with eating and drinking.

Designer meeting points: Places where the guests have the feeling of being welcomed as a part of the overall ambience are in high demand. They are where the city's creative artists prefer to meet and the various scenes mix together. In contrast to Hamburg or Munich, however, there is less segregation between such people and the general public, and the meeting places are well-known. In Sachsenhausen, for example, there is the **Schwarze Café** (Schweizer Strasse), designed in severe black by the architect Dudler, members of the art and architecture scenes gather every evening for light Italian dishes.

Herr Lampugnani, director of the architectural museum around the corner, also drinks his *cappuccino* here during creative breaks. **Hildebrandt's** (Untermainanlage 8), Dudler's second venue, is regarded as Frankfurt's most imposing design address.

The bar, brasserie and restaurant at the **Schauspielhaus** (Hofstrasse 2) all offer business lunches at midday, and house a substantial "Who's Who" of the scene in the evening. In Lux, it is not so much the lights as the light chairs of the star designer Jasper Morrison which are the attraction. Young regulars gather before lunch for black coffee in this peaceful little venue made entirely of high-grade steel.

Night style: The ideal designer bar should have sparse walls, high stools, little space and endless cool drinks. The **Bar Oppenheimer** (Oppenheimer Strasse 41, Tel: 62 66 74) in the heart of Sachsenhausen fits the bill perfectly, an oasis for late evening conversations. After the trials of the working day, advertising executives, authors and publishers relax here until the early hours of the morning. If you are looking for something to eat during the small hours, there is an establishment which has devoted itself both to variety shows and good food. Whilst the artists are performing above, down below in the cellar of the **Tigerpalast** (Heiligkreuzgasse 16–20, Tel: 28 96 91) you can feast in style. In this melting-pot of the local scene, lawyers, politicians, business people and lovers are all mixed together.

The **Orfeo** (Hamburger Allee 45, Tel: 70 91 18), located in a former foundry, is regarded as a Frankfurt institution. At midday it is a high-class canteen for advertising executives, film people and graphic artists; in the evening a market for the gossip from the art, cultural and political scenes.

The best way to end the evening is under the moon. Small hungers and large thirsts can be satisfied until 4am in **Nachtcafé** (Taubenstrasse 7, Tel: 28 94 21), Frankfurt's most cosmopolitan night-life address. The beautifully painted walls encourage guests to reach for the stars.

PLACES

There is a great deal more to Frankfurt than banking and c
On a tour of the city the visitor will be confronted not
present, but also by its rich and varied past. Extensive v
has created long corridors of glass and steel, but these corridors leau
to preserved pockets of the old city.

Most of the sights are located within walking distance of each
other in the historic centre, clustered around the famous Römerberg
Square, where the original Frankfurt fair was held, and where,
inside the Imperial Hall, the emperors were once crowned. Nearby
is the Church of St Bartholomew, Frankfurt's "cathedral" and main
landmark – at least until the banks started building their skyscrapers. Here also is the venerable St Paul's Church, the venue of the first
German parliament back in 1848, and the distinctive Rententurm on
the embankment of the Main, a river that was traditionally one of the
primary sources of the city's prosperity. Not far away is the house
where Goethe was born and grew up.

Once visitors have looked inside the Stock Exchange to see how
the Deutschmark makes the world go round, they can go along the
"Fressgass", Frankfurt's street of self-indulgence, diving in and out
of pubs, cafés and restaurants. Beyond the Hauptwache, the Zeil,
Frankfurt's major shopping street with its own streetlife, begins.
Streetlife of a rather more sordid nature can be found in the red-light
area in front of the station (here too is probably the most visible
drugs scene of any European city); real "alternatives" are still to be
found in and around the university.

The city's various districts include Sachsenhausen on the south
side of the river, which regards itself as being virtually independent
from the rest of the city. This is the place for culture, because the
city's most important museums and galleries are strung out along
the south bank of the river. Thanks to the wealth generated by the
banking sector, the city is particularly generous with arts, museum
and gallery funding, and with free festival events. Sachsenhausen is
also the place for a taste of Frankfurt's own special brand of
sustenance, its apple wine – not to be confused with cider and
generally a lot more potent.

Apple wine also flows freely in Bornheim, probably the most
traditional of all Frankfurt's districts. The visitor can then doze off
its effects in one of the city's many parks, or even spend an
afternoon at the zoo, before heading off to more distant pastures
such as Höchst, an attractive medieval town bordered by a massive
modern monster – the multinational chemical and pharmaceutical
combine Hoechst AG. All of these places are fully covered in the
pages that follow.

Preceding pages: Frankfurt skyline at dawn; steel and glass; there's
always parking space for the directors; river restaurant on the
Sachsenhausen bank of the river Main. **Left**, the Römerberg Fountain of
Justice during the 1990 World Championship football celebrations.

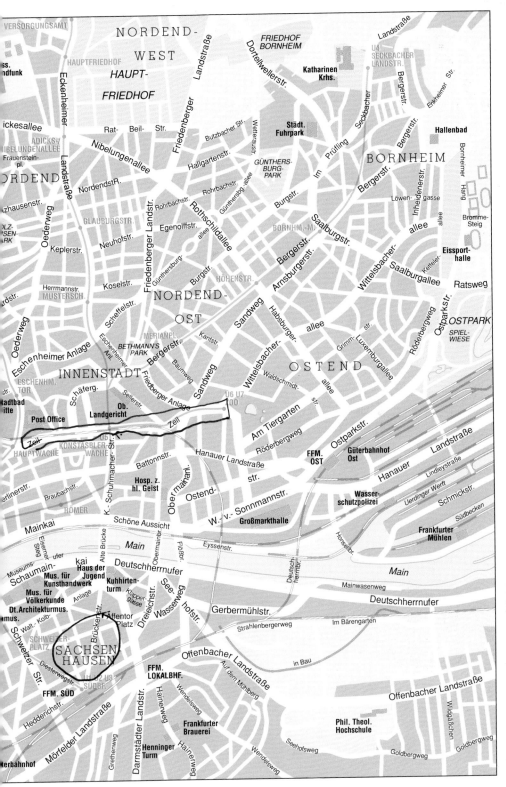

THE HISTORIC CENTRE

Just about all the main sites are situated in the centre of the city, clustered around the Römerberg, the ancient square which the Frankfurters affectionately call their "Gut Stubb" ("front room"). In view of the continuous state of traffic congestion in the city, it is best to try and do without a car.

If you get off the U-bahn line 4 at the Römer and take the exit to the cathedral, you will emerge at the site of an archaeological excavation, the **Historical Gardens**. Here in the oldest part of Frankfurt the various layers of the city's history have been laid bare: here are the remains of the Roman baths, the foundations of the Carolingian Kings' Hall, once part of Charlemagne's royal palace, and here also are the foundation stones of Gothic houses and offices. The architectural compactness of the city, which the inhabitants repeatedly built anew on top of the buildings of their forefathers, is still evident today.

The site lies sandwiched between the walls of the recently-developed Kulturschirn on the one side, and the grey concrete walls of the Technical Town Hall, built in the 1970s, on the other. There has always been a shortage of building land in the city centre.

The cathedral and its martyr: On the occasion of elections and coronations, the emperors and electors would walk at the head of the splendid procession which made its way from the royal palace to the crowning ceremony in the **Church of St Bartholomew** (undergoing renovation). The Frankfurters rather generously call this building their cathedral. This is not strictly correct, however, because Frankfurt was never a bishop's see. With its single spire, the cathedral isn't exactly awe-inspiring in its dimensions either; Frankfurters were never given to excessive grandeur. The narrow alleys and market stalls which crowded against the cathedral walls for hundreds of years were simply the domain of the common butcher and grocer. The cathedral was built upon the foundations of the old Church of St Saviour which is said to have been built in the days of Charlemagne. The tower was only completed after the cathedral fire in 1867, according to the original plans of the Gothic master builder Madern Gerthener. Until then, the building had had to make do with a temporary cupola. It is possible to climb up the tower from the south entrance. The steps leading up its tower were rediscovered only in 1950 when the new organ was being installed.

Two men are venerated in the cathedral: Charlemagne, the city's first benefactor, and St Bartholomew. Tradition has it that Bartholomew died a martyr's death while working as a missionary in Armenia. It is said that he was skinned alive, which is exactly how his statue in the cathedral depicts him. There are in fact two statues: one in the recently renovated high choir and the other in the

cathedral museum in the covered cloister. The saint, with his wild curly beard, has a slight smile. His eyes are closed. At first sight he appears to be carrying his robe over his left arm, but closer examination reveals that this is in fact his own skin.

Kneeling place of kings: On the right side of the choir a small door leads through into the small chapel in which from 1356 the German emperors and kings were elected. There, where the small altar now stands, knelt the king, the first of whom was Frederick Barbarossa, and the seven electors decided on the fate of the Holy Roman Empire of German Nations. The room was actually originally built in 1425 as a library for liturgical books, but its primary historical significance is its other role as the **Election Chapel**. It is simple but harmonious and, although it possesses nothing of the upwardly-striving Gothic, it nevertheless exudes an atmosphere of dignity and calm.

High up on the left wall of the cathedral's nave there is a magnificently framed *Descent from the Cross*. It is the work of the Flemish painter Sir Anthony Van Dyck, one of the great 17th-century masters of portraiture. Commissioned by the Prince Bishop of Mainz at the beginning of the 17th century, the picture is colossal by Frankfurt standards. It is said that, because the bishop either couldn't or wouldn't pay the final asking price, the painter donated it to the Franciscans in return for a bowl of soup. The fate of the painting immediately thereafter is unknown; suffice it to say that 200 years later it turned up in Vienna, the property of the Birkenstock family, and then duly arrived in Frankfurt by virtue of the fact that Antonie von Birkenstock married the Frankfurt merchant Franz Brentano. In their last will and testament, the couple bequeathed the painting to the cathedral.

In the first chapel on the northern side of the high choir, stands the late-Gothic *Death of the Virgin* altarpiece, the work of an unknown Rhenish master. It is the

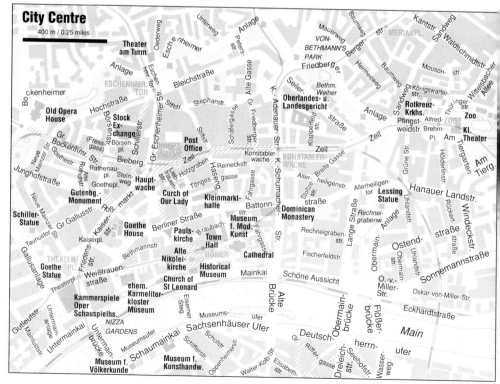

only original altarpiece in the cathedral to have survived. The body of the virgin lies on its death-bed, surrounded by the mourning disciples, while her soul in the form of a tiny figure of a child is carried by the angels to God in Heaven. Astonishing for this 15th-century work are the lifelike individual gestures of the mourners.

The chimes of Frankfurt: The only reason the cathedral bells survived the destruction of the bombing raids of World War II is because they had been taken away by the Wehrmacht to a central depot in Hamburg, only to be brought back to the city after hostilities had ended. Most of the other church bells were melted down and used for making heavy artillery, but their destruction was made good by the people of Frankfurt.

The old cathedral bells and the new bells from a further 10 churches have been harmoniously synchronised. They ring out on the afternoons of the Saturday before Easter, the day before the first day of Advent and Christmas Eve, as well as ringing in the New Year. Visitors come from all over the world to hear the chimes of Frankfurt.

The Römerberg: From the cathedral hill it is only a short walk to the Römerberg, Frankfurt's beautiful market square. Medieval bustle is still in the air here, most noticeably at the Main Fair in summer and particularly the traditional Christmas Market in December. In former times the wine merchants held their market in front of the **Römer**, the old house on the western side of the square which since 1405 has been combined with other houses to form Frankfurt's Town Hall. Tradesmen and craftsmen of all guilds came together at the Frankfurt Fair. They stored their goods in warehousing provided in the surrounding houses.

The gold- and silversmiths resided in the **Römerhallen**. These five houses, whose fronts make up the classic facades of the Römer ensemble, gradually became the property of the city. They are, from left to right, **Alt Limpurg**, the

The Ostzeile on the Römerberg.

Römer, **Haus Löwenstein**, **Haus Frauenstein** and the **Salzhaus** (salt house). Until the 19th century the facades were actually much more typically Frankfurt, and much less ornate, than they are now. The balcony and the figures of the emperors and sundry decorations were added in 1896. The mosaics date from the 1950s and at first created a public outcry. When it was decided to remove them, there was more opposition. The conservationists put their foot down, claiming that these were now history and so, even if they were detested, they were still worth preserving.

Information about the Römer, the city, city tours and events can be obtained at the **information office** in Haus Frauenstein. The emperors did not enter this building through the main portal, but through the much more modest little door to the left. They first had to negotiate a narrow staircase before entering the **Imperial Hall**. Today newly-weds have to take the same route, as it leads directly to the registry office. But the Imperial Hall itself now has to be approached from the back, past the Römer and into the Römer courtyard and up the steps. The Imperial Hall is an airy architectural flirtation that originally came into being during the Thirty Years' War, when most of Germany was suffering appalling hardship and deprivation, but Frankfurt was booming. It was so prosperous that the city council even had to forcibly impose a limit on the consumption of sweet wine and confectionery.

Portraits of the German emperors hang in the hall, each painting in its own niche. During World War II the pictures were packed in crates and moved out to the comparative safety of the countryside. This was a wise decision because, after the bombs had stopped falling, the hall had to be rebuilt. Nevertheless, it is still possible to imagine the coronation banquets and binges that went on in this hallowed place.

The open space between the Römer and the facades on the other side, with the **Fountain of Justice** in the middle

Concert in the Imperial Hall (Kaisersaal) in the Römer.

and the **Minerva** statue behind, has seen everything. The Romans, the emperors, ox roasting on spits and wine gushing from the fountains the French and the Prussians and the demonstrations of the 1960s and '70s. Football world champions have waved from the balcony here and squatters have set up camp around the fountain. John F. Kennedy was a guest here, as was Margaret Thatcher. The square was never built upon, apparently because the ground was too unstable. It got its name Römerberg only after the acquisition of the Römer, the old house which was the original Town Hall. Previously the square had simply been called "Auf dem Berge" (on the hill).

With its half-timbered facades, the **Ostzeile** of the square is a reconstruction; an attempt to recreate the old city and with it a bit of the "good old days". The houses are imitations of medieval buildings. They are called, from the left, **Grosser Engel**, **Goldener Greif**, **Wilder Mann**, **Klein Dachsberg-** **Schlüssel**, **Grosser und Kleiner Laubenberg** and the **Schwarze Stern**. Their design was based on old pictures and engravings and, seen from behind, they don't attempt to conceal their concrete cores. Frankfurt is at least honest.

If you continue in the direction of the Church of St Nicholas towards the River Main, you will reach a metal plaque that has been mounted at the northwest corner, known as the four tower point. From here it is possible to see the spires of the cathedral and the churches of St Nicholas, St Paul's and Our Dear Lady all at once. In the cul-de-sac between the church and the **Historical Museum** are the "town houses" where architects have experimented with new styles and mixed them with old.

Where the Römerberg opens to the Main stands the only preserved Gothic half-timbered building in the city centre: **Haus Wertheym** was built around 1600. If you can get a seat outside, a good place to enjoy coffee and cake is the Café Hollhorst from where you can

gaze at the river or the **Rententurm** at the same time. In medieval times the Rententurm, with its distinctive pyramidal roof, was a defensive tower designed to protect the Fahrtor, the main entrance to the town, from any assault launched from the Main.

The tower adjoins the western end of the **Saalhof**, now the home of Frankfurt's **Historical Museum**. The building itself goes back a long way; it is the site of the palace that Ludwig the Pious had built on the city's original Merovingian stronghold. During the Staufen era, Frederick Barbarossa converted it into a moated stronghold. In the 18th century it was sold and converted into a lodging place and warehouse for merchants dealing at the Frankfurt Fair.

The legend of the ford: In medieval times the river was shallow at this point and an arm actually flowed behind the hill on which the cathedral now stands. The old bridge which was built across the former ford (Franconouvurd) no longer stands today. In its place is a new construction upstream from the pedestrian bridge **Eiserner Steg** (under renovation). But it is still possible to appreciate the strategic importance of the location, and understand why Charlemagne chose to settle on that well-known ford across the river; legend has it that when he was fleeing before the Saxons, a white hind showed him the place to cross. At all events, the ford could be easily controlled from the palace and the cathedral hill.

The town had to be established on a hill because in those days the river was much wilder and prone to flooding. The highwater mark on the Eiserner Steg indicates that in the year 1312 the river rose to 4 metres (13 ft) above the present street level. Today the Eiserner Steg is where the Main pleasure cruisers start from, and from here it is possible to take trips on the river. The **Harbour Railway**, with its steam engine and buffet car, leaves every hour from noon on Saturday to Sunday evening.

A little way to the right along the

The Eiserner Steg links the centre with Sachsenhause

embankment from Café Hollhorst is the late-Romanesque **Church of St Leonard**. It is one of the most beautiful churches in the city and was founded in 1219 as a chapel to Saints Mary and George, built on a site presented to the town by Emperor Frederick II. Behind the entrance is the richly decorated late-Romanesque main doorway (built in 1220). The mason responsible was so proud of his creation that contrary to the custom of the time he signed it with his name, *Engelbertus F (ecit)*.

The fact that the floor of the church was once one metre lower than it is today is clearly shown by the illuminated excavation at the **St James's Door**, through which pilgrims would continue on their long journey to the tomb of St James the Apostle in Santiago de Compostela in Spain.

The *Last Supper* painted for the Dominicans in 1501 by Hans Holbein the Elder and donated to the church is a copy. The original hangs in the Städel Museum. The life-sized figure of Christ which lies under the Altar of the Cross was sculpted around 1500 from one single slab of stone. At one time it was thought that this work was lost, but then miraculously it turned up during excavation work being carried out on the outer sacristy in 1927.

Stark contrasts: The **Nizza Gardens** extend in a thin strip for about half a mile along the Lower Main Embankment. They were named after the French resort of Nice ("Nizza" in German) because of their profusion of Mediterranean vegetation. In times gone by the city's green heart still beat on the banks of the Main. This was where families took their Sunday strolls. All that is left of the former elegance is the **sundial**, which took 6,000 hours to construct. The city has recognised what it has lost and is trying to breath new life into the stretch of riverbank between East and West Harbours. "Live on the river," it exhorts its citizens.

Those who want to stroll shielded from the hustle and bustle of the city can

The Nizza Gardens.

do so by crossing the road and entering the **Rampart Park** (Wallanlagen) which encircles the whole of the Old City. Laid out at the beginning of the 19th century along the lines of the old fortifications, this ring of green is divided into a number of gardens. In the Eschenheim Gardens is the **Reis Monument**, erected in honour of Philipp Reis who demonstrated his telephone to the Physics Society in 1861. The work is unwittingly comical; the two men who telephone with such concentration are stark naked!

It is in the Rampart Park that one comes face to face with another reality of Frankfurt, namely drug addicts and junkies. If you sit on the terrace facing the tall bank building opposite the large new theatre and opera house, you'll get a good impression of the scale of drug dealing and drug use in the city. The shrubs are littered with used needles.

The contrast between the two faces of the city becomes even more apparent in the **Taunus Gardens**, where from the glass facades of the twin-towered **Deutsche Bank** building, with its marble foyer, come groups of bankers in their dark tailored suits to mingle with the drug addicts in the park. The Taunus Gardens also contain the statues of great Germans – Goethe, Schiller, Beethoven and Heine. They look distinctly out of place in this environment, overshadowed as they are by the tall offices of the German banks: a symbolism which reflects the development of this free city of the Empire into present-day "Mainhattan".

Birthplace of German democracy: If you cross back over the Römerberg to the next square to the north, you will reach the next major attraction of the city, the **Paulskirche** or Church of St Paul. The round shape of this building of red sandstone, which was the favourite material of Frankfurt architects, makes this "House of the Germans" appear strangely modern for its era (the first plans were drawn up in 1786). Goethe criticised the building, not, it seems, on account of its plainness, which he secretly liked, but

Downtown bar.

because of its location; he simply felt that the edifice didn't blend in with the city. But despite the disapproval of the famous privy councillor, the building became the cradle of the first, albeit shortlived, democracy on German soil.

It was here on 18 May 1848 that the National Assembly came together to establish the "constitutional rights of the German people" (*see page 35*). It produced some 59 articles, many of whose paragraphs remain enshrined in the constitution of today. The meeting produced a lot of heated debate. The painter Johannes Grützke has depicted what the proceedings might have looked like in a massive fresco adorning the wall of the Paulskirche's entrance hall.

Like many other buildings in Frankfurt, the church did not survive the devastation of World War II intact; it burned to the ground. Lord Mayor Kolb appealed for help from other German cities in the reconstruction of this national monument, and he received an overwhelming response. Even poor communities sent donations. The steel bells, for example, were provided by the state of Thuringia. It was reopened in May 1948 and, apart from the flatter domed roof, the exterior remained almost unchanged from the original. Inside, however, the church was greatly altered and is now a well-lit hall, enabling it to be used for exhibitions and ceremonial occasions, including the presentation of the Goethe Prize and the Peace Prize of the German book trade.

A visit to Frau Aja: From Paulsplatz a road leads through the Kornmarkt to the **Goethe House** in the Grosser Hirschgraben, which is where the dry moat surrounding the city's Staufen walls used to run. At one time, as its name suggests, this was used as an enclosure for deer (Hirsch). The house in which Goethe was born gives an insight into the lifestyle of well-to-do citizens of Frankfurt in the late Baroque period. Completely destroyed during World War II, it was rebuilt in its original form between 1946 and 1951. When Goethe departed for

Friedrich Schiller statue in the Taunusanlagen.

Weimar in 1775, his mother, Frau Rat Goethe, who was known in the family as Frau Aja, sold the house with its furniture and furnishings and the building was subsequently used for industrial purposes. In the 19th century it was acquired by the Free German Foundation and restored to its former condition.

And this is how it is today, with all the furnishings and household implements back in their original position. There is the playroom, the music room and the state room as well as the study of the young Johann Wolfgang von Goethe. It was here that he captured the thwarted spirit of German nationalism in that early turn-of-the-century "Sound and Fury" masterpiece *Götz von Berlichingen*. He also began his "main work" *Faust* and mirrored his own hopeless affair with Charlotte Buff in *The Sorrows of the Young Werther*.

One of the main attractions of the house is Frau Aja's kitchen, equipped with all the requisite utensils, including a copper cake tin and an old wooden spoon. Attached to the house is the **Goethe Museum** which displays documents and other material relating to Goethe's life and activities.

To conclude your explorations into Frankfurt's past, pause at the Liebfrauenberg, an attractive small square in Frankfurt's old town to the north of the Römerberg. In medieval times this was the site of both a horse market and a cattle market, and at one time the municipal council sought to transfer some of the Frankfurt fair to the site, but were unsuccessful.

In the shadow of the **Church of Our Lady** you can relax in the **Caféhaus** or have a stand-up snack in the Heininger butcher's where, experts maintain, the best blood- and liver-sausage in the city can be purchased. Only a few paces to the east of the square is another attraction that will make anybody's mouth water: the **Kleinmarkthalle** (little market hall). Its two floors contain delicacies from all over the world in a stunningly colourful display.

Fruit and veg in the Kleinmarkthalle.

GOETHE

To Goethe, Frankfurt was the place of his childhood and youth, a period of "sound and fury", both in the sense of his lifestyle and also of the literary epoch at the start of the classical German period. Goethe spent the first 26 years of his life in Frankfurt, interrupted by periods of studying in Leipzig and Strasbourg and employment at the imperial court in Wetzlar.

Johann Wolfgang Goethe was born in 1749 in his parents' house in Großer Hirschgraben, and raised to the rank of the nobility 33 years later. His paternal grandfather had come to Frankfurt from Thüringen as a travelling journeyman, married the daughter of a Frankfurt inn owner and made his fortune within a generation. His son became a lawyer and an honorary councillor. Wolfgang's mother, Katharina Elisabeth, known as Aja, came from the respected Textor family. Her father was a mayor. In his memoirs *Poetry and Truth* Goethe wrote of his parents: "From my father I inherited a certain didactic talkativeness, from my mother the ability to take everything which the powers of imagination can conjure up, and to portray it with energy and clarity; to take well-known fairy tales and rejuvenate them, to make up new ones and tell them, indeed to make tales up as I was telling them."

Wolfgang and his younger sister by one year, Cornelia, were taught Greek, Latin, French and English by their father, and occasionally by a private tutor. Wolfgang mastered both spoken and written Yiddish, and could also read Hebrew. Not that he neglected the natural sciences, an interest which was to remain with him for the rest of his life: in 1784 he discovered the intermaxillary bone and formulated a theory of colours. His father tried to instil discipline in him – something which can't have been easy – and taught him always to finish any task he had started. His inspirations were the Bible, adventure stories and traditional stories including Dr Faustus and those by Klopstock.

Goethe's first girlfriend, a milliner's assistant, came from Offenbach, and was known as "the beautiful Gretchen". With her he experienced the election and coronation of Joseph II in 1764. But their relationship drew him into strange company: a number of her acquaintances were accused of falsifying documents and convicted. Wolfgang admitted that on some evenings he spent his time with "people of lower standing and suspicious appearance". He was put under house arrest and later found out from his warder that Gretchen had regarded him as naive, and had described her relationship with him as "sisterly". This was so painful to Goethe than it spoiled Frankfurt for him. His began to study law in Leipzig.

By the time he accepted a princely invitation to go to Weimar in 1775, he was already a famous author. The drama *Götz von Berlichingen* and the epistolary novel *The Sorrows of the Young Werther* were both great public successes, despite – or maybe because of – their mixed reception by the critics. Both of these works from the "Frankfurt period of genius" were aimed against the Enlightenment, putting energy, feeling and spirit in place of understanding and criticism. He also wrote his *Urfaust*, the first version of his main work, which he only finished shortly before his death. ∎

Goethe statue in the Taunusanlagen.

DOWNTOWN

This second chapter on the city puts less emphasis on historical sites and more on shopping. It begins at the **Old Opera House** (Alte Oper), which is best reached via the U-Bahn lines 6 and 7.

This venerable old building in an equally fine square has been returned to its former splendour after being destroyed in March 1944 and spending years as a roofless ruin inhabited only by pigeons. For the socialist Lord Mayor Rudi Arndt, the decaying pile of stones was nothing but a nuisance and he resolved to have the remains demolished. His plan prompted storms of protest and the Lord Mayor acquired the nickname "Dynamite Rudi".

The reconstruction of the Old Opera House activated the Frankfurt spirit like no other project. Appeals were launched and received a massive response. But the plans didn't go ahead without criticism. The Jewish community protested that the Opera House, which was founded in 1873, had been largely funded by donations from Jews, and that the Jews had been excluded from the opening ceremony attended by the Emperor William I. They wanted the ruin to be left as it was, as a reminder of the Third Reich and the senselessness of war. But restoration went ahead despite their protests and the building was ceremonially reopened as a concert hall and congress centre in 1981.

Along the Fressgass: From Opernplatz, Frankfurt's famous pedestrian precinct, the Fressgass runs in an easterly direction through to Goetheplatz. It gets its (unofficial) name from the multitude of delicatessens and restaurants strung out along its length (*fressen* = to eat). Few people realise that its real name is Grosse Bockenheimer Strasse, and that this was the road along which the farmers from the village of Bockenheim once led their pigs and cattle to market in the city.

The narrow streets and alleys around the Fressgass form a unique district. All of Frankfurt meets here; the beautiful and the rich, the obese and the jolly. Haute cuisine harmoniously coexists with the *bratwurst* culture; shops selling haute couture mingle with more traditional establishments. On the left-hand side, just beyond Pizza Hut, the **Konditorei Kofler** advertises its creations with certificates for the best layer cake in town. Just next door is the entrance to one of those new covered arcades which are intended to help rid Frankfurt of the concrete-block image that it acquired during the 1970s.

The incomparable **Schwille**, a few metres further, is the oldest-preserved and nicest café in the city centre. Whether you're sitting outside or on the first floor, the service is always extremely friendly, regardless of how busy the place is. And the *Baumkuchentorte*, not to be confused with the standard layer cake (*baumkuchen*), provides a temptation that is hard to resist.

A stark contrast is the **Club Voltaire**

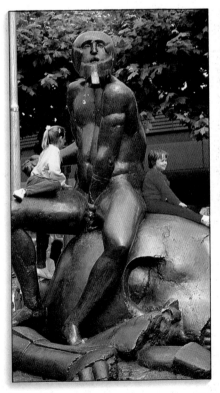

Preceding pages: orchestra of senior citizens. **Left**, all the fun of the fair. **Right**, David and Goliath statue on the Zeil.

just round the corner in the Kleine Hochstrasse. This is where the students met to plan their revolt of 1968. The apple wine still flows in copious quantities and accompanies the evening fare and discussion. Next door the **Vinum** serves excellent Rheingau wine, and in the **Bankhof** the wine is also sold to take home. The **Volkswirt** is a popular drinking haunt for people working in the Stock Exchange. The fence of the concealed bower outside is smothered in creeping vines.

Jazz in the back yard: Anyone who doesn't get stuck at the Volkswirt will probably want to continue along the Fressgass. Intriguing is the colourful life-sized figure of the Red Indian which stands chained to the **Arizona Gallery**, a shop selling Indian silver and turquoise jewellery. Continuing from **Alexandro's**, the sumptuous grocers selling rare mushrooms and strawberries past the **Schlemmermeyer** *bratwurst* stand and the **Sphinx Café**, which is open until four in the morning, you

cross the road to arrive at the **Plöger** delicatessen with its delicious salads and other tasty morsels and Tuscanstyle chicken which is best consumed on the seats around the fountain.

The above outlet can only be mentioned with the warning that even in the Fressgass establishments regularly change hands. The rents are getting ever more expensive and old-established proprietors are having to make way for more solvent retail chains. But Plöger will hopefully stick around; it belongs to Frankfurt and its Fressgass just as the cathedral belongs to Cologne.

In Kaiserhofstrasse, to the left of Plöger, you can eat good Italian food, either reasonable or expensive, with a view of the display windows of Yves Saint Laurent. Those who prefer steak should go one alley further on to **Maredo**. Frankfurt ambience is provided by the **Gaststätte Klaus** which offers a rustic apple wine. But anyone who wants just to see and be seen simply sits down in the middle of the Fressgass, inside or

The inscription on the Alte Oper reads: "To Truth, Beauty and the Good".

EM WAHREN SCHOENEN GUTEN

outside of the pseudo-rustic **tomate**.

Shortly before the latter establishment, a fork to the right leads through to the **Alte Rothofstrasse**. If your feet are not sore, you can browse through the posh second-hand shop **Carpe Diem**. Continuing along the Alte Rothofstrasse you will come to Goethestrasse, Frankfurt's noble boulevard, unless of course you choose to stay around in the old city atmosphere provided by Kleine Bockenheimer Strasse which runs parallel to the Fressgass. This is the home of Frankfurt's jazz scene. The **Jazz Haus** and **Jazzkeller** have gained reputations as venues for jazz musicians far beyond Frankfurt itself. In the summer you can relax in front of the **Pinte**, away from the hustle and bustle of the city.

With its heavy steel door and its "Nr 20", **Tiffany**'s looks decidedly modest when compared to other establishments in the vicinity; this is where the branches of Guy Laroche, Hermès Paris and Gianni Versace are to be found, as well as Bogner, Cartier with its heavy bracelets and rings – dripping with gold – and the posh furniture shops. Here also is the **Vonderbank Art Gallery**, which apart from paintings offers a large choice of art postcards and prints.

If all this is too much, too luxurious, then you can simply go back and continue along the Alte Rothofstrasse to **Mutter Ernst**, a somewhat dilapidated-looking pub offering cheap and homey cuisine such as brawn with roast potatoes for a few Deutschmarks and a plate of cheese for even fewer.

A fine platz: Goethestrasse opens out – how could it be otherwise? – into the broad **Goetheplatz**. A boulevard of shrubs and wild flowers leads from the fountain with its curious time and sun symbols to the **Gutenberg Monument** on the Rossmarkt at the southern end, a tribute to the inventor of printing with moveable letters, Johannes Gutenberg. With him on the plinth are his assistants Fust and Schäffer, commonly referred to by the Frankfurters as "*die zwaa anneren*" (the other two).

On the Opernplatz.

To the east of the centre of of Goethe-platz, there is direct access to the Haupt-wache. Here a branch of the booksellers **Hugendubel** has installed itself in a former cinema. It is said to be the largest such shop in the country. A plaque reminds visitors of the fact that this is where the Swan Hotel once stood, in which Bismarck and Jules Favre signed the Treaty of Frankfurt which ended the Franco-German war in 1871.

Despite the damage inflicted by war on this district, the planners have tried to preserve as much as possible of its former flavour. As in the Fressgass area, if you look above the shops' display windows and examine the facades around Goethe-platz, you will see how often owners have attempted to blend old and modern building styles. In many cases surviving parts of facades of ruined buildings have been incorporated into the new structures. From here you will emerge into the **Hauptwache**, at the very heart of the city.

Big-city realism: The architecture on the B-levels and on the concourses leading to the U- and S-bahns is the result of the concrete mania that overtook the city in the 1960s. In those days German planners saw the use of concrete as being the symbol of big-city functionalism and realism. But as was the case elsewhere, it only provoked aggression. The post-modern livening-up of the grey passages and halls is an attempt to make good, though this seems to have had only limited success. The only use that people have for this underground complex is to get through it as fast as possible during the rush hour. People prefer to be above ground, and that's where the action is to be found around the Haupt-wache, particularly on days when the sun is shining.

Despite the *verboten* signs, skate-boarders dart around the square, which is just as much a meeting-place for tramps as it is for bikers, buskers and rap groups. In the middle of the square by the standard clock is the **Hauptwache**, now a café and a meeting place for

Outdoor restaurant on the Fressgasse.

young lovers. Fruit sellers vie for the attentions of passers-by and the pretzel man tries his best to compete. Street vendors, sects, what you will; the whole world and its children come together at the Hauptwache.

A fortress and a prison: In centuries gone by, the Hauptwache (not to be confused with the much larger St Katharinen Church behind) served as both a base for the city's defence force and as a prison. The leaders of the storming of the Hauptwache did time here in 1833, having attempted to set the democratic torch alight. Another inmate was the legendary robber Schinderhannes who spent one day behind bars. Rebellious 18th-century councillor Johann Erasmus Senckenburg, who repeatedly accused the magistrates of corrupt dealings, was given a much tougher sentence. He was held prisoner in the attic under the roof without trial or sentence for 26 years until his death in 1795. When the U-bahn was built at the end of the 1960s, the Hauptwache was dis-

mantled stone by stone, carried off and stored before being rebuilt, its position shifted a couple of metres. This did at least enable its roof, destroyed in the war, to be replaced, but at the same time it acquired disproportionately high chimneys: these serve as ventilation shafts for the U-bahn tunnel.

Goethe's mother, Frau Aja, lived at the Hauptwache, having sold the family property in the Hirschgraben which is now a museum. In a letter she sent to her son in distant Weimar she described the view she could see from the window, of noble ladies with their sun umbrellas strolling past.

In former times, the view south along the Rossmarkt must also have been familiar to those about to meet their executioner. The scaffold was erected here, and among those beheaded were the rebel leader Wilhelm Fettmilch and his accomplices in 1616. When Goethe was a young man he witnessed the execution here of the maid Susanne Margarethe Brandt, the child murderer who pro-

Frankfurt characters.

vided him with the character of Gretchen for *Faust*.

Just to the north, on Börsenplatz, is the Frankfurt **Stock Exchange**, with the symbols of credit and debit: the bull and the bear. Trading begins at 10.30am and finishes at 1.30pm and the mood of the bankers and brokers is directly linked to the rise and fall of the dollar. But the imposing neo classical building has also witnessed performances of a different kind; until 1963 the building provided shelter for the city's theatres that had been destroyed in the war. Now they deal in billions behind the facade with its angels and sculptures of Greek gods. Dealing is an art that the winged ambassador of the gods Hermes, who looks down from the roof, understood well, for he was also associated with commerce and thieving.

To the right of the Stock Exchange the **Lorey Passage** parade of shops branches off **Schillerstrasse**. Lorey itself is well worth seeing. Since 1796 the firm has expanded its business over several floors

to become a veritable palace of porcelain and crystal. Fine cutlery, cut crystal and porcelain from the world's top manufacturers are displayed almost as if in an exhibition. Just 200 metres (650 ft) to the north, Schillerstrasse converges on the 47-metre high (150 ft) **Eschenheim Tower**, built around 1400 as part of the city's medieval defences.

On the other side of the Lorey Passage, on the **Gr. Eschenheimer Strasse**, there is a piece of history in the shape of the two entrance lodges of the former Baroque palace of the Bavarian Thurn and Taxis family, which served as the Bundestag from 1815. They are all that remains of the Red House, which was considered an architectural masterpiece. Travellers used to wait for the mailcoaches just around the corner, where the main post office now stands.

On the site of the present-day **Kaufhof** department store there used to be a pub called the Weidenhof, and the publican's daughter was none other than Goethe's grandmother.

Buskers by the Kaufhof store on the Zeil.

Record turnover: At this point the famous **Zeil** begins with its smart department stores. In amongst the small trees is a statue of David and Goliath. The pedestrian precinct between the Hauptwache and Konstablerwache achieves the highest retail turnover of any such shopping mile in the whole of Germany. It is possible to buy just about anything here, and the street life is interesting in summer. You can get oysters in the snack bar at **Hertie** and try on all the latest fashion on the upper floors.

Along this part of the Zeil it is well worth exploring some of the side streets; browsing in the Hellberger furniture shop in the **Grosser Friedberger Strasse**, for example, or giving the kids a treat in the **Spielwaren Behle** toy shop. Or you might even continue into **Vilbeler Gasse**, Frankfurt's number one address for gays. The **Konstablerwache** hasn't managed to rid itself of its reputation as the ugliest square in the city, for which the Swiss sculptor Tinguely is said to have refused a commission to design a fountain. It isn't really a square at all, rather just a patch of ground with no houses, where the dealers hang out. It is better to try to avoid coming here at night. The Konstablerwache only really comes to life on Saturday mornings when the excellent **Bauernmarkt** (Farmers' Market) is held. Here you can get herbs, bio-sausage, cheese and flowers straight from the country.

Behind the Konstablerwache, the **Staufenmauer** is the oldest surviving section of Frankfurt's city wall, dating from the 12th century. The Jews living in the ghetto behind it had to rebuild the wall after a fire, so what you see today isn't even the original. Beyond the square and to the left of the Zeil are all the city's legal institutions, a collection of imposing old and new buildings. The **Klapperfeld**, now a rather uninteresting street, has a history all of its own. Back in the Middle Ages there was a hospice here for those suffering from the plague and other terminal ailments. The dead were simply thrown into the adjacent slough,

me for freshment.

which is now the duck pond in the park on the Friedberger Anlage. If that doesn't put you off, you can seek night time entertainment in the **Diskothek Plastik** situated in the park. But the most popular nightspot at the moment seems to be the **Varieté Tigerpalast** in the Heiligkreuzgasse. Following on the the traditions of Frankfurt's variety entertainment in the 1920s, the ex-hippy Johnny Klinke brought acrobats, snake-dancers and magicians to the city. Before or after the performance visitors can dine in the excellent restaurant which is part of the establishment.

To the south of the Ostzeil, around **Breite Gasse**, the visitor will find himself in the midst of another red-light district, although the brothels here are much less conspicuous than in the Bahnhofsviertel. The continuation of the Breite Gasse, Stoltzestrasse, leads to the **Jewish Cemetery** (not to be confused with the Old Jewish Cemetery) and the site of the last ghetto that was pulled down in 1885 and which included the house in which the poet and revolutionary Ludwig Börne was born. The most dominant features in the area today are the new municipal services buildings next to the (usually locked) cemetery.

On the corner of Kurt Schumacher Strasse are the covered remains of a Jewish **Mikva**, or female baths, in the **Judengasse Museum**. Their discovery sparked off a bitter campaign against the new building, but the protests in the end were fruitless. Only the Mikva was preserved and everything else was simply built upon.

A famous painting by Max Beckmann gives an idea of how Frankfurt's Jewish quarter must once have looked. The Rothschild family, which helped to create the city's prosperity, also once lived here. The spot where their home once stood is now occupied by an escalator running down underneath the Konstablerwache. From here it's a short walk past the **Dominican Monastery** and past all the antique shops in the Fahrgasse before winding up back at the Römer.

Ball in the Alte Oper.

THE ZOO

Like everything else in Frankfurt, the city zoo (U-bahn lines U5 and U6) has to be economical with its space at the eastern end of town. You can see the first animals from the ticket counter at the main entrance; flamingos stand on one leg in their little pond. In the building behind, the Fritz Raimond Theatre presents popular dramas. The building is also home to the Frankfurt Zoological Society, a citizens' foundation which created the zoo, and which continues to give massive support to projects devoted to saving species threatened with extinction.

The first zoo, opened in the summer of 1858, was located in Westend. People crowded in to see monkey and bear cages, deer preserves and the ostrich house. In 1874 the zoo moved to its present home, the former exercise grounds on Pfingst Meadow. Income was brought in by events ranging from balloon flights to performances by "24 Amazon Warriors", and the dancing bears and giraffes were exhibited side-by-side with Siamese twins and midgets.

In World War II, the zoo was almost completely destroyed. Bernhard Grzimek rebuilt it, and earned it an international reputation. As the starving post-war city had nothing to offer in the way of money, he fell back on the spectacular fund-raising ideas of his predecessors. A giant ferris wheel attracted American GIs; the 5-mark ticket price included a glass of whisky. Old-timers can still tell you about the time Grzimek led an albino elephant through the city as a publicity stunt – although it was whispered that the animal was only *painted* white.

Equally famous, and certifiably real, were endeavours to breed the shy African okapi, which succeeded for the first time in 1957. The breeding of the great apes has recently achieved new success with the gorilla family, who are being allowed to rear one of their own babies themselves: this experiment is being followed with bated breath – proof, perhaps, that apes can maintain their natural social structure even in captivity.

Grzimek helped to make nature conservancy an international issue through film and television reports. He died of a heart attack while visiting a circus. After his death, schoolchildren brought flowers to the "Villa Okapi", his house behind the zoo. Protection of endangered species and breeding under the most natural conditions possible are also goals of his successor, Richard Faust. For this reason, every birth at the zoo is extensively featured in the local press.

In the Edelstein House, hummingbirds flit to and fro. You have to buy a special ticket to get into the Exotarium, where the piranhas look like large, attractive silver carp. This house is divided into salt-water, fresh-water and reptile departments. Here, you can watch the leaf-cutter ants at work; these insects have been known to take unauthorized excursions beyond the glass walls of their home. However, the penguins remain the undisputed stars of the show.

In the night house, called the Grzimek House, everything is topsy-turvy. At night, bright lights send the animals to their burrows to sleep; by day, the night lighting makes them lively. Desert foxes prick up their big ears, while the South American armadillo roots through the leaves with his long, pointed nose. There's only one problem with the night house; a sign recommends that you keep an eye on your wallet. ■

Zoo resident.

SACHSENHAUSEN

Sachsenhausen is unique. It is a square kilometre of Frankfurt packed with pubs, restaurants and music clubs, an entertainment area without a red-light district and a sea of half-timbered houses in a city of skyscrapers. In this neighbourhood, which Frankfurt citizens call *"dribb de Bach"* (the other side of the stream) because it's on the south side of the river, the *ebbelwoi* (apple wine) flows freely from 5pm to the early hours of the morning.

This is reason enough to take the "Ebbelwoi Express" from the central railway station to Sachsenhausen. In this local train, the "stuff", as locals term their *ebbelwoi*, is poured out for passengers on the **Friedensbrücke** (Peace Bridge) which crosses the Main between the railway-station district and Sachsenhausen. And the pretzels sit ready and waiting on the little tables. No visit to Frankfurt is complete without some time spent in Sachsenhausen.

Every Sachsenhausener is still a resident of Frankfurt, but not every Frankfurt citizen is a Sachsenhausener, commented the Frankfurt folk poet Stolze. Stolze reckoned he could distinguish "sachsenhausenic" from "frankfurtic" with the sharp scalpel of a born humorist. In the **Gemaltes Haus** (Schweizer Str. 67) or at the **Drei Steubern** (Klappergasse), you can find Sachsenhausen specialities: ribs and mixed grills to raise your cholesterol level, as well as the infamous *Handkäs'* (curd cheese) with *mussig*. "Mussig" is a marinade of oil, vinegar, onion and caraway, in which the *Handkäs'* spends its life before it is devoured.

Local traditions: There are still men and women in Sachsenhausen who move through the pubs with their baskets of pretzels. And fresh fruit is still sold in the district's narrow alleys. But these last vestiges of tradition are few now; one can't expect the success-oriented pretzel and vegetable salesmen of today to bring back the good old days. There remains that Sachsenhausen specialty *Hardekuche*, lying in the baskets of the pretzel-sellers. Critics maintain that this is a sort of elevated dog biscuit which no one would dream of buying, much less of eating, outside Sachsenhausen itself. It's said that this "hard cake" works as a counterbalance to *ebbelwoi* by soaking up its acid in the stomach.

As well as such typical edibles, international fast food has taken over the neighbourhood. Kebabs and hamburgers, paella and pizza satisfy the appetites of a very mixed public. To drink, there's Guinness on tap, Pilsner Urquel, and wine from the Rhineland or from Tuscany. Nearly 100 pubs, discos and live-music clubs in the pedestrian-only streets around **Klappergasse** and **Affentor Platz** attract a mixed, international crowd. "Action" is the order of the day—especially after midnight, when fists fly in the streets after the apple wine has gone to peoples' heads, or the

Preceding pages: flower lady Hilde. Left, the Bembel jug is a genuine Sachsenhausen souvenir. Right, ask Frau Zensi for a Bratwurst.

gallon of bourbon which the GIs smuggled into the disco has been emptied. By then, Sachsenhausener have long since gone to bed. Most old-time locals clear the field by 8pm, after they've had their third or fourth drink and the noise has begun to rise outside. Only a few half-timbered houses still sport the fir wreath, symbol of the typical *ebbelwoi* pub with its long wooden benches. But most establishments still serve the wine in the traditional manner (*see panel on page 143*). If you want to meet some real Frankfurters and get into the swing of things, these are the places to go.

Take a hint from the locals. A last refuge of *ebbelwoi* tradition is **uf der Insel**. This "insel" (island) was formed some 200 years ago, when two popular pubs in the countryside, the Germania auf der Insel and the Kanonensteppel, attracted plenty of business. Both of these apple wine pubs still exist today; but the "island" has long since been incorporated into the city and stands in the middle of Sachsenhausen, towards the east end of Textorstrasse. In **Germania auf der Insel**, where they've been dispensing apple wine since 1806, nostalgia sets the tone. By contrast, **Adolf Wagner**, Schweizer Strasse 71, is more a place where yuppies feel at home. There, you're likely to run into a real live football player from the Frankfurt team, or a bookie from the Niederrad race track.

Proud towers: Sachsenhausen isn't only a pleasure quarter. This district on the other side of the Main has its own history; since the Middle Ages, Sachsenhausener haven't had much in common with their Frankfurt neighbours. For much of its history Sachsenhausen has been inhabited by small businessmen and fishermen.

The watchtowers at the edge of the city were torn down under the French. Only the two on **Affentor Platz**, at the heart of the quarter, have survived to the present day. Of the nine turrets which once crowned the fortifications around Sachsenhausen, there remains only the

Time for an exquisite lunch and a fine flirt.

so-called **Kuhhirtenturm** (Cowherd Tower), just behind the Haus der Jugend (one of Germany's largest youth hostels, with an extensive programme of activities).

The tower stands alone at the top of Paradiesgasse, on the edge of the pedestrian-only pub and restaurant district. It was known as "the elephant" in the Middle Ages because of its massive appearance, and only survived French rule because the members of both of Frankfurt's historical societies joined residents of the quarter to form a citizens' action committee for its preservation. Even the French Ambassador, Count Hedouville, put in a word with the magistrate to save the Kuhhirten and Eschenheim Towers.

It's thanks to this tower that Frankfurt can count the composer Paul Hindemith a member of its "Hall of Fame". In the Golden Twenties, the musician felt so at home in the Kuhhirtenturm that he lived there for nearly a decade – one of his most productive periods, during which

he wrote, among other things, the opera *Cadillac*.

Museum Embankment: Most of the cultural institutions which enable Frankfurt residents to consider themselves citizens of one of Germany's cultural capitals are in Sachsenhausen. Art galleries and museums are lined up along **Schaumain Embankment** (see also the Museumsufer in *Art and Museums, pages 70–71*), from the famous Städel to the Postmuseum, from the Film Museum to the Museum of Ethnology.

The rather forbidding-looking **Städel Museum**, with its independent history, is the one most closely allied with the privately-sponsored material and cultural riches of the city of Frankfurt. This gallery of paintings was begun by the Frankfurt citizen and businessman Johann Friedrich Städel. Over the past 150 years, the museum has purchased exemplary paintings in every style from every epoch from Gothic to modern – all to the renown of the city and of Städel's foundation.

Fast food comes in all forms.

Städel himself had amassed a magnificent collection in his private home by the beginning of the 19th century. Goethe was one of the first admirers of the fruits of the businessman's passion for art.

Today, works of the early Dutch School (such as Jan van Eyck) hang in the museum next to those of masters such as Dürer, Cranach and Holbein. In the Italian room, one can marvel at Giovanni Bellini's famous *Madonna*, or Botticelli's 1480 *Portrait of a Lady*. Anyone interested in 19th- and 20th-century painting should spend his time on the upper storey, where he or she can see paintings by Tischbein, Monet, Renoir, the German Impressionists Kirchner and Beckmann, and the modern master Pablo Picasso, who is represented by his *Portrait of Fernande Olivier* from 1909.

The Film Museum: One of the most unusual museums on Sachsenhausen's "museum mile" is the **German Film Museum**, which strives to be "a house for film and at the same time a house for everyone" – including film buffs, researchers and interested laymen. In the museum wing of the building, virtually everything imaginable to do with the history of film or film-making is on display: posters, programmes, cameras (including the famous *laterna magica*), studio equipment and film props. The cinema on the ground floor presents retrospectives of famous directors or actors and actresses. The museum screens films from many different countries, introduces avant-garde films and documentaries, and organises special children's programmes. Events such as the open-air cinema in summer or silent film screenings with live piano accompaniment are further events which round out the programme.

As far as its permanent exhibition goes, the film museum encourages participation. Historical film equipment can be "tested"; visitors look through the viewfinders, fiddle with the buttons on the cameras, adjust lights and strobo-

The Saturday Frankfurt flea market is one of the largest in Germany.

scopes and – the culmination of a museum visit – enact the entire process of shooting a film. Every visitor can be Howard Hawks or Eisenstein, Humphrey Bogart or Bette Davis, depending on his mood and inclination: looking through the lens makes everything possible, and friends can be brought into the picture as "actors". Meanwhile, the museum's library makes some 50,000 books about film available to the public.

Over a cappuccino and croissant in the building's comfortable **Film Café**, you can look through the schedule of events at your leisure, or talk shop with some of the other film experts who are hanging around.

A neighbourhood in transition: Once a year, in the first week of September, the **Frankfurt Museum Embankment Festival** is held. At this time, the streets along the river bank are closed to traffic, and shipping is suspended on the Main. Artificial islands provide stages for theatre groups and magicians, jazz bands and hard rockers. Local residents stroll over the bridges and buy skewers of scampi or lox on toast at the numerous gourmet food stands, while champagne flows like water over the counters.

The Museum Festival is proof that there's "modern living" in Sachsenhausen – that there's more to this part of the city, in other words, than *ebbelwoi*. For a closer look at the brilliant display of fireworks, ascend to the revolving restaurant atop the **Henninger Tower** from where the river seems to be on fire. Meanwhile, jumbo jets pass close by the tower windows, bound for Rhine-Main Airport.

Sachsenhausen's main drag is **Schweizer Strasse**. Here, one boutique follows another, while people sitting in the numerous street cafés are watching streetlife "along the Schweizer".

Sachsenhausen is a neighbourhood in transition. As Frankfurt is bursting at the seams, and rents for living and office space are soaring, more and more offices, especially advertising agencies and property agencies, are moving over

"across the river". Administrators' plans to restructure the area around the stockyards will certainly result in social tensions and changes once they're carried out, for residents of the old Sachsenhausen will have a new environment to deal with – and will be hard-pressed to pay the inflated rents.

Like the Docklands area of London, the riverbank area on either side of the Main is supposed to become an economic and social hub of the city, with prosperous small and medium-sized businesses and living space for their employees. The archaic stockyards, a giant, walled-in complex which stands in the way of these plans, will be banished to the northern edge of the city, at Niedereschbach. "Live on the river" is the slogan of the new concept.

Architects' designs demonstrate that "Futureworld" is no longer an abstract Utopia in Frankfurt. Ultimately, the city wants to be able to compete on all levels with European metropolises such as Milan, Paris and London.

Haggling allowed: In the past few years neighbourhood groups have formed to deal with issues relating to the future of Sachsenhausen all over the quarter, and – often with the cooperation of elected officials – these groups regularly draw up plans of defence against the trend toward modernisation. A few years ago these groups, who are "conservative" in the best sense of the word, managed at least to convince the magistrate to allow the renowned **flea market** back from its long exile at the inhospitable stockyards to its former place on the bank of the river Main.

From sunrise to 1pm every Saturday, masses of people shove past the vendors' stands, where you can buy everything from grandpa's radio to a complete stamp collection, from an antique chamberpot to a racing bicycle. Haggling is the order of the day. And anyone who manages to snare a real bargain is sure to be back the next Saturday, standing on the Schaumain Embankment or the Deutschherren Embankment.

Matters can always be discussed over a glass (or two) of _ebbelwoi_.

APPLE WINE

Unless you rigorously avoid all contact with the people of Frankfurt, it won't be long before someone insists that you sample the local apple wine.

The tradition of drinking apple wine is a venerable one, born of necessity: a change in climate in the middle of the 18th century made tending vineyards in the Frankfurt area unprofitable, as yields constantly decreased. Innkeepers were prompted to come up with an alternative beverage to sell in their establishments and thus the apple wine bars were born. The authorities issued licences for innkeepers to press and brew their own apple wine and, just as in former centuries, a garland of fir branches hung outside a bar still indicates that the apple wine was produced on the premises.

Apple wine bars are automatically associated with the district of Sachsenhausen, although they are also to be found in the city centre and in many of the outer districts. The apple wine is traditionally served from a blue-grey clay pitcher called a *Bembel* and drunk from a special ribbed glass. In the summertime, apple wine drinkers like to drink out of doors at long tables under shady trees, chatting with their friends or with anyone else with whom they can start a conversation. Apple wine is great for breaking down the barriers.

Apple wine in Frankfurt, known variously as *Äpfelwein, Ebbelwoi, Äppler, Äppelwoi* or *Stöffche*, is not the same as cider in England, or *cidre* in France. A distinction is made between the different types produced at different times of year. Only at the beginning of autumn, when the young wine flows from the presses, is it non-alcoholic.

After this *Süsser* (sweet drink) is put into barrels, fermentation sets in quickly and the beverage becomes known as *Rauscher* (rush) – an all-too-appropriate name since some people use this half-fermented brew as a laxative. In Klappergass' in Sachsenhausen, the locals have erected a monument to Dame Rauscher: "Dame Rauscher from the Klappergass', she has a blackened eye; from Rauscher, or from her old man? Police will tell us why."

If *Rauscher* is left to ferment throughout the autumn, it comes to be regarded as highly dangerous. From this time on, the alcoholic *Stöffche* develops its malicious nature: intoxication occurs more quickly, and, unfortunately, in its wake come numerous headaches and stomach problems.

The "new light" drink (*Heller*) matures around Christmas time, and finally there is the *Alter* (old apple wine). If it is too bitter, experienced old hands simply leave it on the counter and go in search of another pub: after all, the quality of this aromatic drink is to be judged by its taste. The addition of crab-apples into the brew produces the so-called *Speierling*.

Today, apple wine producers prefer types of apples which are not the most visually appealing, but have a full, rounded flavour; many of these were planted in the Main valley between Frankfurt and Hanau at the turn of the century. The art of pressing apple wine consists chiefly of getting the right mixture of sweet and sour apple types. You can test the results in the beautiful gardens of one of the many traditional bars in Sachsenhausen, Bornheim or Seckbach. Try the Germania or Kanonensteppel on Textorstrasse, Sachsenhausen. ■

Sachsen-
hausen
Bembel.

FROM THE STATION
TO THE UNIVERSITY

High above the the station forecourt, almost unnoticed by travellers, stands the copper **Atlas group**, with its layer of green patina, carrying the world on its shoulders. With the mid-day sun in its back, the group gazes from the roof of the **Main Station** down onto the Bahnhofsviertel (the station quarter), a relatively recent part of town. It was built by the Prussians in the 19th century according to a rigid grid plan; from here, broad boulevards lead directly towards the city centre.

A symbol of progress: The monumental 210-metre (690-ft) wide facade gives more the impression of a *Gründerzeit* (late 19th century) palace than a functional building. In 1880 the Prussians had a competition for the best designs and subsequently commissioned the winner, the Berlin inspector of buildings Eggert, to build the Main Station as a fitting entry point to the city in typical imperial style.

When it was built, the station was the largest in Europe; it was only in 1915 that it had to give up this position to Leipzig. Now extended to 25 platforms, the station today is a major rail junction connecting Frankfurt to all the other major cities in Germany and Europe.

A century ago, after the inauguration in 1888, the scene in and around the station must have been rather different than it is today; as they strolled through the 30-metre (100-ft) high entrance hall, the city's wealthier citizens, dressed in their Sunday best, were rather more solicitous in matters of dress than their hurried, hectic great-grandchildren. This is where they all came to meet, and to celebrate, in the luxuriously appointed restaurants and salons and to admire the unusual architecture and the trains on the platforms.

The progress that the station represents is symbolised by the Prussian statues inside and outside the building. The

clock, the first ever electrically operated station clock, is flanked by figures representing Morning and Evening; there are also allegorical representations of commerce and transport and a series of figures depicting different types of passenger, from the honeymooner to the student. The Prince and Princess of Wales of the time came to marvel at the building after their health cure in Bad Homburg. There is even an anecdote about Kaiser Wilhelm setting his watch by the station clock.

The new Main Station was necessary because the original terminus stations of the various railway lines serving the town – the Main-Neckar-Bahn, the Main-Weser-Bahn and the Taunusbahn – could no longer cope with the enormous increases in both passenger and freight traffic. The station was built exactly on the curve where the lines leading to the three original stations converged. Only after the completion of the terminus building were the old tracks taken up and replaced by road. Nowa-

Preceding pages: more than a quarter of Frankfurt's citizens are of foreign origin. Left, a parade in the Bahnhofsviertel. Right, an Eritrean immigrant mastering the German language.

days this forecourt is congested with traffic and pedestrians therefore gain access to the city by crossing the road underground. It is impossible not to notice that the station forecourt has now become a meeting place of various fringe groups. Fixers and prostitutes stand at the escalators leading up to Kaiser Strasse and in summer they crawl out above ground to beg and offer their services.

The Bahnhofsviertel was intended to be the entry point into the town, with dozens of luxury hotels for rich travellers and visitors to the fairs and congresses. Some of these splendid buildings still stand today, for example around the small Wiesenhüttenplatz to the right of Kaiser Strasse. Opposite the noble **Parkhotel** is the headquarters of the 4th police district. The Parkhotel is the first of an ensemble of seven top-class hotels in this area.

Down-and-outs: The shifts are hard in the 4th police district. The officers are responsible for just about everything here; from petty theft to social work, from the fight against the crooked racketeers to the drugs mafia and the registration of heroin deaths. A policeman recently published a book with a selection of photographs he had taken on duty. They show the loneliness and anxieties of the people who have become stranded in the Bahnhofsviertel: the tramps, the prostitutes and the junkies.

However, the Bahnhofsviertel remains what it always was – the entertainment part of town. Even at the turn of the century this was not the domain of high culture, more a mixture of high-spirited vaudeville and colourful ballyhoo. Smart entrepreneurs brought everything to the Main that was new and spectacular. The owner of the circus built the most famous establishment in the district, Schumann's Theatre, to seat 5,000 with an arena in the middle. Karl Liebknecht gave a speech here and avant-garde works by Berthold Brecht were performed along with operetta and silent movies were screened. Kläre

Proud display of national identity.

Waldoff came and sang "His name was Hermann" and Anna Pavlova danced *The Dying Swan*. The last curtain finally fell in 1944, but the building itself was not destroyed by the bombs of World War II; it fell victim to the city's demolition and redevelopment policy in 1961.

Younger citizens become nostalgic when they stand before **Kaiserstrasse 52**. It was here in the K 52, the first large post-war discotheque, that the pop-group The Lords came and played rock 'n' roll. Today the building houses the **English Theatre** and the headquarters of the Frankfurt Tourist Board.

Back in 1891, at the point where the present-day red-light streets of Elbe- and Moselstrasse cross Kaiserstrasse, the Frankfurters had a completely different sensation to marvel at: the first "Electro-technical Exhibition". It was intended to provide the city with an entrée to the world exhibitions of centres like Paris and London and it extended all the way to the Main Kai. You can still see some of the exhibits in the Historical Museum by the Römerberg.

If you gaze up at the facades of the houses to the south of Kaiserstrasse, you'll see the ornate towers with open arches and wrought-iron railings. Looking rather out of place, these appendages are copies of Prussian style elements. Their inhabitants made them into roof gardens for the summer, and there sat whole families on hot summer days drinking coffee and exchanging pleasantries with their neighbours.

The Bahnhofsviertel is bordered in the south by the **Main Kai**. Right next door to the **Intercontinental Hotel** on the Untermainkai is the oldest house in the district, the "Villa Bonn". It was the summerhouse of a wealthy Frankfurt family who wanted an escape from the congestion of the old city. The Intercontinental, for which two other villas had to be demolished, is much higher than the neighbouring **Trades Union House**, although the latter resulted in the first popular campaign against the construction of a tall building in Frankfurt. The

nine-storey building was erected in 1929 in Bauhaus style and faced with simple limestone slabs. Local residents claimed it destroyed the harmony of the Main Kai and took the matter to court, but lost. It was the first step in the transformation of this once-so-noble part of town. Today the Trades Union House is a protected building.

The Grindbrunnen, the last of the springs whose sulphur content almost once made Frankfurt a health resort, is now hidden behind glass in the niche of a Chinese restaurant on the Untermainkai. The spring had to be capped because it contaminated the ground water, or so it was claimed.

Away from the main roads in the **Gutleut** district at the Westhafen is a new housing project of particular interest. Under the motto "living by the river", the city is busy developing the area between **Rottweiler Strasse** and the Westhafen as a residential district. In the tradition of the Bauhaus settlements in the Gallus district, Westhausen and Praunheim, architects have developed a much-acclaimed municipal housing scheme. The flats have bay windows, balconies, colourful facades and the interiors are well designed for families. In the courtyard there stands a coloured glass pavilion for performances and public meetings; there are playgrounds and vegetable gardens. The old warehouses in the harbour basin are also destined to be turned into living spaces.

On **Gutleutstrasse** between the river and the station the old Prussian "fortress" still stands. From 1879, the Gutleut barracks housed the occupying Prussian soldiers; today it is the police headquarters. The red bricks of varying tones were intended to give the facade the appearance of a medieval castle. A few steps behind, the car park at the southern entrance to the station was supposed to be the site of a new skyscraper, the "Campanile". This part of the ambitious project never got off the ground because of local protest. The heroine of the protest campaign was the owner of a block

The Bahnhofsviertel is the second-largest red-light district in Germany.

ROSMARIE NITRIBITT

Look at a photograph of her now and it's difficult to imagine that back in the 1950s blonde Rosie drove men wild. In her open-topped Mercedes 190 SL with white wheel trimmings and leather seats, she cruised the city centre in search of clients. She wasn't one for keeping a low profile. Stylishly groomed and always in the company of her white poodle, she offered her services openly. Wherever secretaries and sales girls met for lunch, wherever financiers and civil servants shared a bottle of wine, there was one topic of conversation: Rosie.

Rosie Nitribitt had instinctively understood the needs of the booming economy and had spotted a yawning gap in the market. Becoming market leader in any field is every businessman's dream. And Rosie was her own product. She wore the most expensive fur coats and had Chippendale furniture in her apartment. She could match anything that the cliché of a high-class whore demanded. For the managers of the economic miracle, only the best would do. Nitribitt's Mercedes shone.

Barely 10 years after the end of World War II it was the age of the *Fräuleinwunder*, petticoats and soppy films, an age in which Rosmarie Nitribitt knew how to exploit the pretentious morals of a society still so dominated by the church. As far as breaking taboos was concerned, she was way ahead of her time. What's more, she has had no worthy successor. In England there were good-time girls like Christine Keeler, and Italy's La Cicciolina has forged a European career. But they weren't in the same class.

When Rosie Nitribitt was found murdered in her apartment in November 1957, the police, the Director of Public Prosecutions and the journalists knew that her clientele had been made up of politicians and captains of industry. There was a great deal of speculation both in public and in private as to whom the culprit might have been. But he hasn't been found to this day. Rosie's popularity was so great that her death eclipsed news of the dog Leica that had just been launched into space by the Soviets in Sputnik II.

The author Erich Kuby wrote a novel about this story of sex and crime entitled "Rosmarie, the darling child of the German Miracle". He also wrote the screenplay to the film *Das Mädchen Rosmarie* with Nadja Tiller in the title role. When the film was shown at the Venice Film Festival, the German foreign office, the influential Catholic critics who also awarded points for quality and the voluntary self-assessment organs of the film industry all protested; nobody wanted people to get the wrong idea about German managers. Kuby justified his film by its critical approach. "That which calls itself society today is hollow and empty. With our criticism we hope to strike at all those who made up Rosmarie's clientele."

The main suspect was her boyfriend, Heinz Pohlmann. But he managed to convince the Director of Public Prosecutions Bauer that the 50,000 marks he had received in hush money from a client of his murdered girlfriend was a perfectly legal transaction. After all, the reputation of the Federal Republic and the interests of the German export industry were at stake. Pohlmann died in Munich in 1990 at the age of 69. The names of the politicians and managers involved have never come to light. ∎

Rosmarie Nitribitt.

of flats who resisted all offers of money from the contractors and finally won the battle in court.

There are still around 4,000 residents in the Bahnhofsviertel, elderly people, socially disadvantaged and a large proportion of foreigners, who form an especially closely-knit community. With the support of the parishes, they defend themselves again and again against invasion from both the red-light entrepreneurs and property speculators, demolition and luxury renovation projects.

From the planned site of the Campanile it is only a stone's throw to the station's south entrance. It was from here, from the platform on Mannheimer Strasse, that the Nazis deported people to the concentration camps. Before they were loaded onto the trains, they were herded to Gutleutstrasse 29–31 and tortured. This is where the Gestapo had its headquarters from 1933 to 1945, until the whole apparatus was moved to Lindenstrasse in the Westend.

The Westend: To the north of the Bahnhofsviertel, the **Bockenheimer Landstrasse** runs in a westerly direction from Opernplatz. In the 1960s and '70s this boulevard experienced a number of demonstrations and there were even a few pitched battles between demonstrators and police. It was in the elegant Gründerzeit villas lining both sides of the road that the people fighting to save the character of the Westend took refuge and squatted. They draped red and black flags from the windows and banners with such slogans as "tenants unite, in the end we'll win the fight". This all provided an added curiosity value for tourists to the city.

The street battles have long since been forgotten. The character of the Westend is now determined by a mix of private apartments, offices, banks and posh restaurants. The fine villas that remain are now protected buildings – the Westend was indeed saved by the actions of the squatters. The skyscrapers to which Frankfurt owes its nick-name "Mainhattan" are mostly concentrated in the

The Schach-Café in the Bahnhofs-viertel.

eastern side of the district, ranged along the rather forbidding **Mainzer Landstrasse**. In their shadow, the Westend remains a highly desirable residential and business address.

The old-established publishing house **Suhrkamp Verlag** is located in Lindenstrasse, and just round the corner is the venerable **Café Laumer** where the authors always met up. This is also where the philosopher and social theorist Max Horkheimer of the Frankfurt School came and drank coffee with his friends Adorno and Marcuse, back in the 1920s, before he emigrated to America. Together these three men founded the *Institut für Sozialforschung* (Institute for Social Research), but then moved with the Frankfurt School to New York City when the Nazis came to power in 1933. But the Café Laumer has also known wilder days; when in the long hot summer of 1968 the proprietor refused to serve bare-footed hippies, he provoked a cake battle on the steps leading up to the entrance. The Café is still a good meeting and eating place.

To the Eppensteineck: From the Café Laumer it isn't far to Eppsteiner Strasse 47, the first house in the Westend to be occupied by squatters. In 1970, students and Italian, Turkish and Greek families moved in to the vacant flats, barricaded the house and declared it to be occupied. But there are no more squats in the Westend today, although the squatters' local pub, the **Eppensteineck**, is still there. It is now a bistro kind of pub, where the only argument is likely to be one with the neighbours about how long customers can go on talking on summer evenings at the tables in the beer garden. In the good old days, this is where taxi drivers, drop-outs, trainee lawyers and book-sellers came together to discuss strategy for the occupation of Bockenheimer Landstrasse 93, for example. The next day those sympathetic to the squatters' cause stood armed with helmets and clubs as a living protective shield in the front garden of "93".

From squatter to businessman: Nowadays "93" is a number one business address; the nameplates identify consultancy firms, bank contacts and other affiliates from all over the world. The squatters of yesterday now occupy an equally beautiful villa on the other side of the road, let out by the city as the **Literaturhaus** ("house of literature"). But those squatters are writers, publishers, book-sellers, editors, journalists and critics.

The posh villas, as well as creating space in the area's prestigious office blocks, are also occupied by the high-flying world of advertising. International companies settled in this part of the town for its image, and made Frankfurt Germany's number one city for the advertising business, with an annual turnover of 3 billion marks. Of late, however, the spiralling rents have tempted young advertising businesses to search for new pastures; the Hanauer Landstrasse in the East End is now emerging as the creative centre of the future.

Bockenheim: Continuing along the

Café Laumer is a popular meeting point in Bockenheim.

Bockenheimer Landstrasse, you'll eventually arrive at an open space to the south of which is the **Johann Wolfgang von Goethe University**. The university's largely undistinguished buildings are clustered together in the Senckenberganlage on the edge of the Westend. The **Institute for Social Research**, the headquarters of the Frankfurt School, is right on the corner of Bockenheimer Landstrasse and Senckenberganlage. The latter road leads down to the Festhalle, the Messe and the heart of the trade fair area.

It is thanks to its reputation that the number of students attending the university has doubled since 1968. That year "Sixty-eight" is closely linked with the founding fathers of the Frankfurt School, Messrs Horkheimer and Adorno. Their *Critical Theory* became a *leitmotiv* for rebellious students who were out to change the world.

The University Tower was built in 1969 and was the first skyscraper in the city; now it is barely visible on the skyline. Next door is the venerable **Senckenberg Museum** in a fine old building. Famous for its collection of animals, it is one of Europe's most innovative museums of natural history. The institution was the brainchild of the Frankfurt doctor Johann Christian Senckenberg who founded the Bürgerhospital in 1763 and at the same time had the idea of a "temple of science". This was not realised until after his death; following a call by Goethe in 1815, the Senckenberg Society for the Study of Nature was established and moved into the Eschenheim tower in 1821. The new museum was built in 1904 and is modelled on the palaces of the Baroque period. It contains everything a natural history enthusiast could possibly desire: dinosaurs and and mastodons and extinct marine vertebrates; a department on the ancestry of man and other large living mammals. On the second floor there is a special exhibition dealing with fishes in the Main river.

The **Bockenheimer Warte** is the an-

Fans of the Eintracht Frankfurt football team

cient tower in the middle of the crossroads immediately to the north of the university which is often surrounded by market stalls. Dating from 1434, it is one of the four watchtowers built to reinforce Frankfurt's medieval defences.

Green oasis: Parks in Frankfurt are often named for their former owners, who built their summer residences in them. Largest of these is the **Grüneburgpark** to the northwest of the university. To the west, it borders on the **Palm Garden** (famous for orchids) and **Botanical Gardens**. Here, you can find miniature landscapes from every region from the Alps to the moors, with the characteristic flora of every area from America to Asia. Mischievous youths secretly pilfer from the poisonous plants section, experimenting with "natural drugs"; most of them simply become ill. In the park, American GIs play frisbee, joggers chug along the paths and bands play in the summer for the festival "Songs in the Park". Behind the Botanical Gardens, a pedestrian bridge leads over the ring road to another small park, backed by the Fernmeldeturm tower opposite the Bundesbank.

Leipzigerstrasse, affectionately called "The Leipziger", runs west from the Bockenheimer Warte. It is one of Frankfurt's most popular shopping streets, more colourful and downmarket than the Zeil. In 1975, this is where students proclaimed the "free state of Bockenheim". For those who feel a bit peckish, the **Gargantua** restaurant is a good bet, serving exquisite haute cuisine, although it is often very busy. If you don't get a place, don't despair: in the side streets off the Leipziger are a number of more down-to-earth Greek, Italian, Spanish or Turkish restaurants.

Even if all these restaurants are full, you can still try the **Restaurant am Schönhof** which you reach from the end of the **Friesengasse** (the continuation of the Leipziger). You're bound to find a seat in this Greek garden restaurant. Whether or not you'll find a waiter so easily is another question.

The main entrance to Frankfurt's university.

BORNHEIM AND THE NORTH END

Situated to the northeast of the city centre, Bornheim is today Frankfurt's most populous district. From 1475 to 1866 it was nothing more than a village and was for centuries a favourite destination for a day out. There was great excitement here in 1785 when the French pioneer François Blanchard chose the Bornheim Heath for his first hot-air balloon flight in Germany.

But the usual attractions for visitors in those days were Bornheim's dance halls and pubs, where even 200 years ago guests were waited on by ladies. Many found this licentious, and indeed truly Baroque customs must have prevailed here. Such was the reputation of the place that the locals were forbidden from holding their much-loved parish fair, the "Bernemer Kerb" for several years. When in 1776 the old parish Church of St John was destroyed by lightning, many took this to be a warning from God. They acted quickly to make amends, chopped down the local oak forest and proceeded to build a baroque edifice in its place. The new Johanniskirche, or Church of St John, with its onion-domed tower, is still there and marks the nucleus of the old village. When Bornheim was incorporated into Frankfurt in 1877, the city not only earned itself an extra 300,000 *gulden*, but also acquired two dozen brothels.

Bornheim and the Nordend meet the city centre at the small triangular **Von Bethmann Park**, with its attractive **Chinese Garden** and people playing open-air chess. Chinese gardeners designed a miniature garden replete with stone lions, waterfalls, a lake and bridge, painted railings and meditative groups of trees and shrubs. The park, which is protected by a wall from the rougher side of Frankfurt life that inhabits the other parks, used to be part of the grounds of the former summer house of the Bethmann banking family, which is

tucked away behind the wall on the other side of the busy **Friedberger Landstrasse**.

The **Hessian Memorial** used to stand at the Friedberg Gate. Now it is separated from the park by the main road. Covered in green patina, the lion on its basalt pedestal looks decidedly tame. The monument was presented to the city by the Prussian king Frederick William III, as thanks to the craftsmen of the city for opening the gate to Prussian and Hessian troops in 1792. The Prussians could only hold the city for four years until it was taken by the French in 1796.

Be that as it may, in Frankfurt the monarch fell head over heels in love with a beautiful burgher's daughter, and even offered her his hand in matrimony. She had a hard time fending him off, but eventually succeeded and married a wealthy banker. Perhaps she didn't like the king's taste in monuments.

Cafés, pubs and more apple wine: From the other side of the park, **Berger**

Strasse, also known locally as the "shopping street of the poor man", is Bornheim's main street. Right at the beginning of the street, trendy cliques of freaks and yuppies meet in the **Café Gegenwart**. As the evening draws on they move on to the old Odeon which houses the youth disco **Plastik** in the Friedberg Park. There are numerous pubs and cafés along the "Berger". Those who need intellectual stimulation with their coffee can sit outside the **Café Ypsilon** next to the bookshop of the same name. The biggest department store for anything electronic in the Federal Republic, the Cologne firm **Saturn-Hansa**, has established a branch on Berger Strasse beyond the Hühenstrasse underground station.

There is a lively market held on Wednesdays and Saturdays around the base of the Clock Tower at **Bornheim Mitte**. Despite having an unusually high proportion of foreign people living in their midst, the people of Bornheim remain very conscious of their traditions. The bookshop **Schutt** behind the market has already published two books about Bornheim past and present and organises regular discussions and poetry readings. The SPD (Social Democratic Party) also has a long tradition in this part of town. As long ago as 1894, the young party convened in one of the most popular inns in the city, the **Schützenhof** in Old Bornheim. The "White Lily", as the Schützenhof is still called, had a popular dancefloor where, to the horror of the general population, young people danced cheek to cheek.

Old Bornheim begins around the **Church of St John** above Rendeler Strasse where Berger Strasse gets narrower. The **Solzer**, the half-timbered **Sonne** with its shady garden of chestnut trees in which you can get the very best blood and liver sausages, the **Schmärrnche** and the **Eulenburg** in the Grosse Spillingsgasse are just some of the best apple wine pubs in the area. But if you want to sample all culinary delights in one place, then go a little bit further The Ratskeller in Bornheim.

160

around the corner of Berger Strasse, through Buchwaldstrasse to the **Ratskeller** in the Kettelerallee am Bornheimer Hang. In the restaurant you get nouvelle cuisine served up in generous Frankfurt-sized portions. More basic food is grilled and cooked outside in the courtyard, accompanied by the ubiquitous apple wine. This is the nicest pub garden in all of Bornheim. The decrepit grey house at Berger Strasse 265 is the city's most famous wine cellars, **Dünker**. The white wine here might almost seem too sweet for those who have developed a taste for apple wine.

One of the few old factories in the craftsmen's and workers' quarter was the firm Mouson in Waldschmidtstrasse. It manufactured soaps and creams and provided 300 jobs until it was forced to go into liquidation in the 1970s. All that is left is the main building, now a trendy art gallery and theatre.

Frankfurt's first pirate radio station used the building's tower to transmit a programme campaigning against the construction of the controversial western runway at the airport. An action committee fought against the demolition of the building and won. Today, the intellectuals of the area meet in the café on the ground floor.

At the edge of Bornheim to the northwest stands one of Frankfurt's four remaining medieval watchtowers, the **Friedberger Warte**. It was built on the road to Friedberg in 1478 within Frankfurt's outer defensive system. The local population was forced to help build it and contribute towards the cost. After being destroyed by fire in 1634, it was promptly rebuilt. Today it stands on a traffic island next to some American army barracks. But it is still quite peaceful in the shady garden restaurant in the courtyard.

South of the tower, **Günthersberg Park** is popular among children, who can play in the many fountains and wading pools. If you're good on your feet, take a long, green hike through Günthersberg, diagonally across the

Watching the world go by.

Friedhof Bornheim cemetery and the allotments, through gigantic Huth Park and up to **Lohrpark**. Here, Frankfurt children fly their kites in the autumn, and go sledding in winter. The café still serves home-made berry cake, and the waiters seem sometimes to indulge in the apple wine even more than the customers. On the south slope there is, incredibly, a vineyard – the only one in all of Frankfurt. The (small) vintage produced here is called *Lohrberger Hang* (Lohrberg Slope), and distributed by the city of Frankfurt; you can get it, for example, at the Town Hall.

At the bottom of the hill, in the district of **Seckbach**, you can find plenty of apple wine. Nature conservationists and, more recently, the authorities in charge have placed the apple orchards here under their protection. They're again cultivating old types such as the "sheep's nose" – small, hard apples which are hardly edible, but which are digestible (to a degree) when fermented.

The Nordend: Traditional and cosy Bornheim is separated from the more avant-garde Nordend by the ring road. The Nordend is where the trendy lefties, the punks and the Greens come together. This fact becomes apparent as soon as you walk into a café or pub, if not before. There is the **Café Rotlint** in the unofficial "main street" of the same name, as well as the **Paulaner**, and the **Horizont**, a trendy coiffeur **Indiskret** and **Cillys** healthfood store for kids. Everything close together just like one big happy family.

On the western side of the Friedberger Landstrasse, the main arterial road running through the Nordend, life is also a touch bohemian. Take as an example the **Grossenwahn** on the corner of Nordendstrasse and Lenaustrasse, where gays and non-gays crowd around the bar, or the **Weinstube** opposite, where feminists flirt with green politicians and university lecturers attempt to put the world to rights amid discussions about where to go for their next holiday. The **Gasthaus Zum Peter** is a legend. This

The drink kiosk is a typical Frankfurt feature.

is where the brave men of the satirical magazine *Titanic* first sat and joked about the end of the world.

An excellent drop of apple wine can be had in the rustic garden of the venerable **Stahlburg** in Glauburgstrasse, just before the Oeder Weg. The interior of the establishment reeks of nostalgia, with the all-pervading smell of apple wine, old wood and beeswax. On the other side of the Oeder Weg, **Holzhausen Park**, with its moated mansion was the property of an old-established family. The estate was first mentioned as early as 1398. Holzhausen Park is a gathering place for families right in the middle of the city.

New life: In recent times the city planners have turned a lot of their attention to the eastern districts of **Ostend** and **Gallus**. The old workers' districts with their industry and warehouses were in decay, but they have been rediscovered. Painters, musicians and furniture designers have moved in to the roomy factory floors on the **Hanauer Land-strasse** and converted them into studios and flats à la New York. The depressing industrial area around the **Osthafen** (Eastern Harbour) will be the site of an ambitious new housing project. Building work and renovations are also changing the face of the Gallus district to the west. Flats are now being built where the factories once stood.

The famous **Hellerhof Housing Estate** here is no longer in danger of demolition. Built between 1929 and 1931 by the Bauhaus architect Ernst May, it is a striking example of the functional architecture of the *Neue Sachlichkeit* school promoted by the Bauhaus. It was designed to produce dwellings with the lowest possible rent but without sacrificing essential housing standards. Each of the 800 houses was equipped with a kitchen with built-in cupboards, a bathroom and a balcony. Some of the houses have now been restored and are protected, but despite protests part of the complex was demolished in 1976 to make way for houses for old people.

Playing cards in the Von Bethmann Park.

HÖCHST

For over 100 years the name of the district of Höchst has been associated with the world-famous chemical concern Hoechst AG, whose name can be seen on pharmaceutical products worldwide. But **Höchst** is a lively, independent community within the metropolis which has retained the charm of a medieval town, despite lying almost in the shadow of the office blocks of Frankfurt city and directly adjacent to one of the largest chemical concerns in the world.

A long history: The hill on which the old town on the Main is situated has a long history of settlement. Even in the Stone Age, people saw the advantage of settling here on this patch of high ground above the Main, for here they were safe from the floods. The Romans built a trading settlement here at the confluence of the Main and Nidda rivers, and during the time of Augustus they erected a fort on the steep river bank. Opposite they built a large brickworks. But it was only in 790 that the place first appeared in the records, under the name of Hostat.

Even today the old town of Höchst is dominated by its mighty columned basilica built in Carolingian times, the remains of the 13th-century keep and its 16th-century Renaissance castle. In 1368 the town set about the construction of fortifications which were extended in the ensuing centuries and which still remain largely intact. Within, the unique collection of half-timbered houses built between the 15th and 19th centuries can still be admired. During this period Höchst was used by the powerful bishops of Mainz as a base against the free imperial city of Frankfurt.

A new era began with the Baroque age. In 1746 the third-oldest porcelain manufactory in Germany was founded within the old walls. Having resumed production in 1965 (it was closed for 150 years), its products are still exported all over the world. In 1768, work began on the building of the Neustadt, the new town, and industry began to settle. It was during this time that the **Bolongaro Palace**, the largest bourgeois residence in Germany, was built.

The industrial revolution arrived in Höchst during the second half of the last century. In 1863 today's Hoechst AG was founded as a small dye company. The subsequent settlement of chemical, metal and woodworking factories assured Höchst a period of economic prosperity, right up until 1928 when the town was incorporated into Frankfurt.

Medieval jewel: While the medieval core of Frankfurt has changed radically, and not only since the destruction of World War II, Höchst's medieval character has remained almost completely intact. Frankfurt's oldest surviving building, **St Justin's Church** which was erected between AD 830 and 850, stands by the waterfront. The Carolingian nave, with its unique columns and exquisite leaf-capitals and imposts, has survived the centuries unscathed.

The three original apses in the east were replaced in the 15th century by a late-Gothic choir. Renovation completed in 1988 returned all the interior features to their original splendour. Especially worth closer inspection are the **Altar of the Cross** and the **Statue of St Antony** from 1485 as well as the High Altar and the 18th-century organ. St Justin's Church, which for centuries served as the parish church and the monastery church for the nearby Antonine friary, perfectly represents the development of Middle-Rhenish art.

The main landmark of Höchst is the almost 50-metre high (150-ft) **Castle Keep**, dating from the 13th century. The castle itself was burned down by the men of Frankfurt in 1397 because the levying of tolls at Höchst hampered trade at the Frankfurt Fair. Its successor, a Renaissance castle built on the same site, suffered a similar fate in 1635, during the Thirty Years' War. It was during the subsequent reconstruction of the remains that the keep was topped off with a gallery and roof. Today the castle, with its fine grounds sloping to the river, contains the Museum for Höchst History with its collection of porcelain, and the museum of Hoechst AG.

The picturesque **Castle Square** lies between St Justin's Church and the castle. Its is surrounded by half-timbered buildings from three centuries and on the Main river side is the **Maintor** (Main Gate) and the **Toll Tower**. The medieval character is further enhanced by the 500-metre-long (1,640-ft) town wall on either side of the gate.

The oldest houses date from the 15th century. Apart from the buildings around the castle square, the **Gasthaus zum Anker** (Anchor Inn) in Bolongarostrasse is also particularly worthy of mention. Having survived the great fire of 1586, in which half the town was destroyed, it finally succumbed to a blaze in 1973, but was rebuilt using surviving fragments. The upper storeys were built in a transitional style between the Middle Ages and the Renaissance. Another fine

half-timbered building is at Bolongarostrasse 143. Built in 1518, it used to be the hospital belonging to the **Antonite Friary** (now in ruins).

There is the **Old Town Hall** between Castle Square and St Justin's Church with its characteristic stepped gable from the 16th century; the **Dahlberger House** at the western entrance to the town is the home of the Porcelain Manufactory; the **Greiffenclau House** with its decorated Renaissance gable, and the 16th-century **Kronberger House** with its late-Renaissance street facade.

Monumental palace: Immediately to the east of the old town is the **Neustadt**, the new town, conceived in 1768. Its focal point is the **Bolongaropalast**, a magnificent Baroque palace completed in 1780 and now occupied by the district administration. The palace was built by two businessmen, the Bolongaro brothers from Italy, who had made a fortune manufacturing snuff.

The ambitious Neustadt building scheme began and ended with the Bolongaro Palace and it wasn't until the 19th century that streets and new buildings started to be laid out around the old town. It was at this time that a small villa district came into being to the west of the old town. The centre of the district is marked by the elegant brick **Town Church** from 1882. Not far away is the neo-Romanesque Catholic **Church of St Joseph** whose interior contains some impressive *art nouveau* decoration.

Masterpiece of Expressionism: Modern architecture in Höchst is represented by the administrative offices of **Hoechst AG**, designed by the pioneering German architect Peter Behrens and built between 1920 and 1924. The building stands on Brüningstrasse; guided tours are available on request. The manufacturing areas of the company cover an enormous area to the west of the town.

Höchst also has a place in the contemporary cultural life of Frankfurt. Built in 1963 for the Hoechst AG's centenary, the **Jahrhunderthalle** has a fine reputation for concerts and cultural events.

Höchst's Castle Keep.

IG FARBEN

There is a product for which the postwar generation must surely be grateful to Hoechst AG: *Trevira*, the material from which creaseproof, non-iron dreams were made of. This man-made fibre of the economic miracle was one of the most popular creations of a chemical concern that has been making industrial history for more than 100 years.

It all began back in 1863 with the colour red. The chemist Eugen Lucius, who recognised a wonderful business opportunity in the production of synthetic dyes from the waste products of coal, founded the *Theerfarbenfabrik* (tar dye factory) *Meister, Lucius & Co.* in the little town of Höchst. *Fuschine*, a dye that turns anything and everything irrevocably red, was obtained from aniline oil and arsenic acid and, as a result, the firm was dubbed by the local populace "the red factory". The colour range was increased over the years, although colour alone was not enough to satisfy the experimental and commercial zeal of the owner. As early as 1883 the company started to produce drugs; the painkiller *Antipyrin* and the anti-syphilis drug *Salvarsan* were among the best-known.

However, the quest for scientific breakthroughs also resulted in the development of lethal products. From the waste materials of dye production the researchers at Höchst succeeded in sythesising chemicals of mass destruction. In World War I countless numbers of soldiers either died or were maimed by the poison gas the company produced.

Despite increasing successes in chemical research and exports, during the 1920s, the works at Höchst also hit on hard times. In 1925 the company joined forces with other firms such as BASF, Bayer and Agfa to established the *IG Farbenindustrie AG*.

The rise of the Third Reich turned out to be highly lucrative for I.G. Farben, which became heavily involved in supplying Hitler's war machine. The inglorious role that IG Farben played during that time also included the production of Zyklon B, the gas used by the Nazis at concentration camps such as Auschwitz. This and the 50,000 East European deportees who were working as forced labourers in its factories made IG Farben a partner in crime of the Nazi terror regime.

In 1945, the Allies attempted to liquidate the company by splitting it into Bayer, BASF and Hoechst. But before this had been fully accomplished, the Farbwerke Hoechst AG was founded anew in 1951. The tower with bridge, a stylised representation of the company's office block designed by Expressionist architect Peter Behrens in 1924, became the world-famous company logo.

The age of petrochemicals has opened up new possibilities for the company, with the manufacture of plastics. Shares in other chemical concerns allowed expansion into further fields of chemical research and production. The name "Farbwerke" soon no longer reflected the huge diversity of operations it controlled, and since 1974 it has been known simply as Hoechst AG. The company has always been open to new markets and today one of its points of emphasis is to be found in the fields of molecular biology and gene technology. The company is also playing its part in the search for a cure for AIDS. ■

One of IG Farben's riverside installations.

One of the things that will most surprise visitors to the congested metropolis of Frankfurt is the abundance of open countryside right on the doorstep. It's only a matter of stepping into a local train or the car and very soon you're in a totally different world; a world of medieval towns such as the nearby Offenbach and Hanau, with quaint half-timbered houses, of elegant spa resorts where the nobility used to come and take the waters, and of miles and miles of paths and trails linking castle to castle and village to village.

The nearest rural playground for the city is provided by the Taunus Mountains. At their feet, the town of Kronberg with its defiant castle dating from the 13th century can be reached in scarcely 30 minutes by S-bahn from the city centre. Visitors wanting to go a bit further afield can step aboard one of the steamers at the Main embankment and travel from the Main to the Rhine to visit such beautiful cities as Mainz and Wiesbaden and take in the vineyards, towns, monasteries and castles of the Rheingau, sampling some of the local vineyard produce along the way.

Further destinations beyond the city include the Vogelsberg, an extinct volcano rising to the north of the city which provides a wealth of recreational activities, and the Rhön, a much wilder expanse of upland away to the east where the city of Fulda provides the focal attraction and where non-motorised aviators take to the air in gliders and circle over the adjacent Thuringian Forest. To the south of the Rhön is the Spessart, one of the least spoilt of all German highland areas, whose idyllic valleys and quaint villages provide just the tonic for the stress of city life. The Spessart used to be the domain of robbers and highwaymen; nowadays travellers can relax as they drive past its woods and glades to such idyllic sights as the castle at Mespelbrunn, or as they follow the course of the River Main from one historic town to the next.

To the south, they can follow the old Bergstrasse, taking in a whole chain of castles and tasting the local wine before arriving in the Odenwald, the land of Hansel and Gretel. And rather than following the motorway, the visitor can continue along the same route down to the Neckar Valley at the southern edge of the forest, where the epitome of German Romanticism, the city of Heidelberg, lies waiting.

Preceding pages: the marketplace in Grünberg; Heidelberg Castle and the river Neckar; the facade of the Ysenburg Castle in Offenbach. **Left**, timber-framed house typical of the region around Frankfurt.

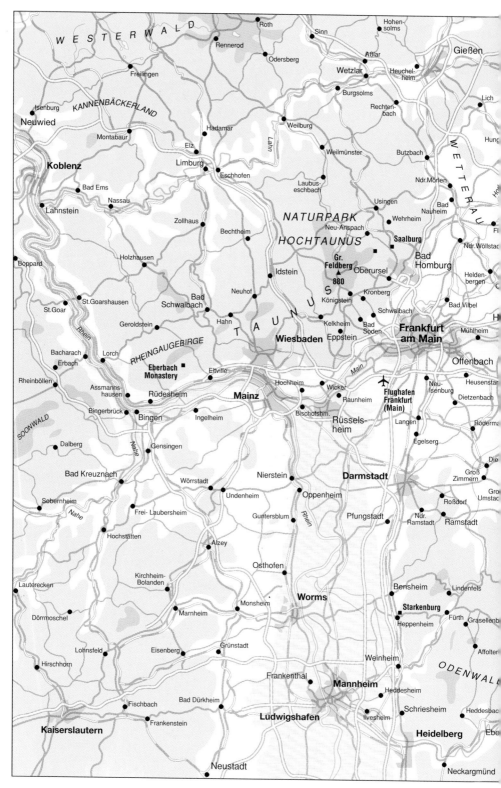

WESTERWALD

Roth

Sinn

Hohen-
solms

Gießen

Rennerod

Odersberg

Aßlar

Heuchel-
heim

Wetzlar

Freilingen

Burgsolms

Rechten-
bach

Lich

KANNENBÄCKERLAND

Isenburg

Weilburg

Hung

Neuwied

Hadamar

Montabaur

Elz

Weilmünster

Butzbach

W

Limburg

NDr.Mörlen

E

Koblenz

Eschhofen

T

Bad Ems

Laubus-
eschbach

Usingen

Bad
Nauheim

T

Nassau

Wehrheim

E

Lahnstein

Zollhaus

NATURPARK

Neu-Anspach

Ndr.Wöllstad

R

Bechtheim

HOCHTAUNUS

Saalburg

A

Holzhausen

Gr.
Feldberg

Bad
Homburg

Helden-
bergen

U

Boppard

Idstein

Oberursel

St.Goarshausen

Bad
Schwalbach

Neuhof

880

Kronberg

Bad Vilbel

St.Goar

Königstein

Schwalbach

Geroldstein

Hahn

TAUNUS

Kelkheim

Bad
Soden

Frankfurt
am Main

Mühlheim

H

Bacharach

Lorch

RHEINGAUGEBIRGE

Wiesbaden

Eppstein

Offenbach

Erbach

Eberbach
Monastery

Eltville

Hochheim

Wicker

Neu-
Isenburg

Heusenstar

Rheinböllen

Assmanns-
hausen

Rüdesheim

Mainz

Raunheim

Flughafen
Frankfurt
(Main)

Dietzenbach

Bingerbrück

Bingen

Ingelheim

Bischofshm.

Langen

Röderma

SOONWALD

Dalberg

Gensingen

Rüssels-
heim

Egelserg

Die

Bad Kreuznach

Wörrstadt

Nierstein

Darmstadt

Groß
Zimmern

Sobernheim

Undenheim

Oppenheim

Gro
Umstac

Nahe

Frei- Laubersheim

Guntersblum

Pfungstadt

Ndr.
Ramstadt

Ramstadt

Hochstätten

Alzey

Kirchheim-
Bolanden

Osthofen

Bensheim

Lindenfels

Lauterecken

Monsheim

Worms

Starkenburg

Fürth

Grasellenb

Dörrmoschel

Marnheim

Heppenheim

Lohnsfeld

Eisenberg

Grünstadt

Weinheim

Affolter

Hirschhorn

ODENWALD

Frankenthal

Mannheim

Fischbach

Bad Dürkheim

Heddesheim

Heddesbac

Kaiserslautern

Frankenstein

Ludwigshafen

Ilvesheim

Schriesheim

Heidelberg

Ebe

Neustadt

Neckargmünd

176

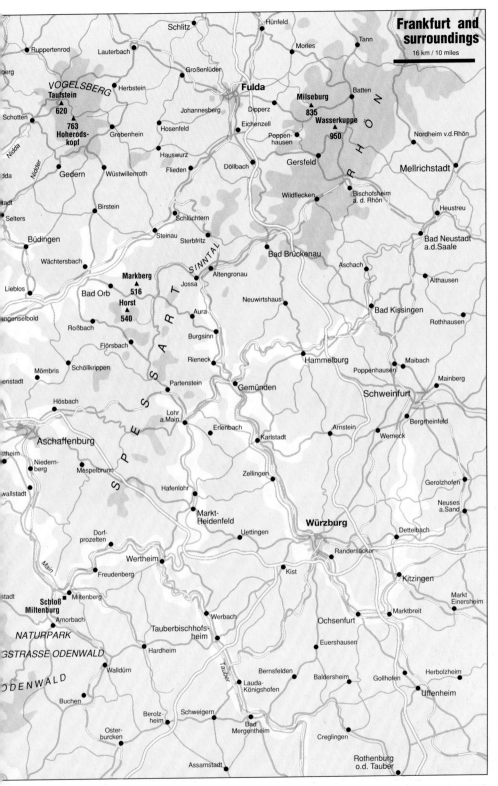

Ruppertenrod

Schlitz

Hünfeld

Morles

Tann

Lauterbach

Großenlüder

berg

VOGELSBERG   Herbstein

Fulda

Milseburg

Batten

Taufstein

▲
620

Johannesberg

Dipperz

835

Wasserkuppe

N

Schotten

▲
763
Hoherods-
kopf

Grebenhein

Hosenfeld

Eichenzell

Poppen-
hausen

▲
950

Nordheim v.d.Rhön

Ö

Nidda

Nidder

Hauswurz

Gedern

Wüstwillenroth

Flieden

Döllbach

Gersfeld

Mellrichstadt

R

dda

Wildflecken

Bischofsheim
a. d. Rhön

H

tadt

Birstein

Schlüchtern

Heustreu

Ö
N

Selters

Büdingen

Wächtersbach

Steinau

Sterbfritz

Bad Brückenau

Aschach

**Bad Neustadt
a.d.Saale**

SINNTAL

Altengronau

Markberg

▲
516

Jossa

Lieblos

Bad Orb

Neuwirtshaus

Bad Kissingen

Horst

Aura

Rothhausen

ngenselbold

▲
540

Roßbach

Burgsinn

Flörsbach

Rieneck

Hammelburg

Maibach

Mömbris

Schöllkrippen

Poppenhausen

Mainberg

enstadt

Partenstein

Gemünden

Schweinfurt

Hösbach

Lohr
a.Main

Aschaffenburg

Erlenbach

Karlstadt

Arnstein

Bergrheinfeld

Werneck

stheim

Niedern-
berg

Mespelbrunn

Zellingen

Gerolzhofen

wallstadt

Hafenlohr

Markt-
Heidenfeld

Uettingen

Würzburg

Dettelbach

Neuses
a.Sand

Dorf-
prozelten

Wertheim

Kist

Randersacker

Main

Freudenberg

Kitzingen

stadt

**Schloß
Miltenburg**

Miltenberg

Markt
Einersheim

Amorbach

Werbach

Ochsenfurt

Marktbreit

NATURPARK

Tauberbischhofs-
heim

Euershausen

GSTRASSE ODENWALD

Hardheim

Herbolzheim

ODENWALD

Walldürn

Tauber

Bernsfelden

Baldersheim

Gollhofen

Uffenheim

Buchen

Berolz-
heim

Schweigern

Lauda-
Königshofen

Oster-
burcken

Bad
Mergentheim

Creglingen

Assamstadt

Rothenburg
o.d. Tauber

OFFENBACH AND HANAU

"Oh, Offenbach", old-time Frankfurt residents say; "forget about it". They themselves would probably rather forget that this "open brook" (*offen Bach*) has been competing with its sister city of *Franconouvurd*, at least in name, since 977, the date of the first documented mention of Offenbach.

Rivalry between the two cities – which used to be so bitter that Frankfurt forbade Offenbach to build its own city wall – has remained in the popular consciousness up to the present day. Contemporary Frankfurt residents express their antipathy in dubious claims: the Offenbachers, for example, are said to be lousy drivers. For their part, Offenbachers describe Frankfurters as arrogant and concerned only with money.

Offenbach "flair": The people of Offenbach are quite different. They pride themselves on their town's neighbourly ambience and "flair" – a term to which they invariably resort when trying to come up with a description of their town's character. This "flair" may have resulted from the town's historical sense of hospitality. Offenbach has always provided shelter for those seeking asylum: in the 14th century, the Waldensians fled there from the French Inquisition; the Huguenots came in the 16th century, after the Saint Bartholomew's Day Massacre.

The Gallic influence is evident on market days, when Offenbach's town centre is reminiscent of a French provincial town: people stroll along contentedly, taking in their surroundings or stopping on the pavement to chat. All of this creates an ambience the flavour of which is only partially conveyed by the word "cosy".

Leather city: Perhaps all this explains why Offenbach holds a special attraction for citizens from abroad. The town's percentage of foreign residents (13 percent) is the second-largest in the Hesse region – after Frankfurt, of course. Offenbach, with over 100,000 inhabitants, has grown into Hesse's fifth largest town; an industrial town, moreover, with chemical and leatherworking plants. And because the chemical industry has associations with air pollution and foul smells, Offenbachers prefer to dub their town "the leather city", even though the leather industry here is not the most advanced.

Competition with Frankfurt: No matter which aspect of his town you choose to discuss with an Offenbacher, comparisons with Frankfurt are sure to creep into the conversation, although people do their best to maintain boundaries between the two. The Frankfurt Transport Authority's (FVV) uniform-fare public transportation system ends at the so-called "city border", the tram stop in Oberrad. Passengers have to get out and cancel tickets from the Offenbach transit system before getting back onto the same tram to travel the two remaining stops to Offenbach's town centre. Many

eft, the avilion in ffenbach ilipark. ight, ffenbach own Hall.

residents save themselves the cost of this short ride by completing the last kilometre on foot.

Tellingly, there's also no public-transportation link between Offenbach and East Frankfurt over Kaiserlei Bridge, which would be the shortest and easiest route between the two cities.

Markets galore: In the recent past there was still a little flea-market in Offenbach, on the Main Embankment behind Carl-Ulrich Bridge. There, in contrast to the flea-market in Sachsenhausen, everything was thoroughly unbureaucratic, and the policeman responsible for registration came by in person every Saturday to make sure that no professionals were trying to get a piece of the action. Soon enough, the little **Offenbach Flea-Market** had grown into a big one, which it remains today. It is an altogether more relaxed affair than the official Frankfurt flea-market in Sachsenhausen, and is well worth a visit.

Another insider tip is to visit the **Farmer's Market** in Offenbach. It was first held long before Frankfurt could bring itself to permit small farmers' markets in the town's various neighbourhoods in addition to the market hall in the town centre. The Offenbach farmer's market on **Wilhelm Square** is an old tradition. So extensive is the selection of vegetables, fruits, farm-fresh eggs, breads, and other edibles that the masses of people who flock to this market on the three days a week it operates are sure to get their money's worth.

Things are most hectic on Saturday morning; it can be extremely difficult to find a seat in one of the town's many cafés and, in some places, even standing room is scarce. But the tone remains calm and relaxed. For Frankfurt residents, familiar only with the hectic pace of weekend shopping, such composure is simply incomprehensible.

A cultural town: Offenbach's flair doesn't derive only from its almost small-town way of life. Culturally speaking, the town has quite a bit to offer. The **Büsing Palace**, for one, newly

Philippsruhe Castle in Hanau.

renovated and restored to its former ornate glory; the building houses a small stage, where rock concerts are sometimes held. All over Rodgau – the name of the region around Offenbach – word is out that the most interesting music groups appear in **Offenbach Hall** (perhaps because the public is more receptive here than in Frankfurt). Rodgau's particular brand of ironic humour has become known throughout Germany through the texts of the rock group "Rodgau Monotones", who made their first appearance in Offenbach. Summer concerts in **Leonard Eisner Park** further demonstrate that Offenbach is home to a specific brand of Offenbach rock.

If it's history you're after, visit the garden pavilion in **Lili Park** (named after Goethe's fiancée Lili Schönemann), or the Baroque castle in **Rumpenheim**. There are also institutions such as the **Offenbach Municipal Museum**; the **Klingspor Museum** (named for the typographer Karl Klingspor), where you can see displays about

modern publishing and printing; or Offenbach's best-known museum, the **German Leather Museum**. Situated in a converted warehouse in Ludwig Strasse, it provides an insight into the artistic and fashion use of leather from prehistoric times to the present day.

The **Shoe Museum** next door displays the caprices of human taste in footwear through the centuries.

Speculation: Offenbach has many interesting corners. Only a few steps away from the town centre's ugly 1960s-style concrete architecture are blackened *art nouveau* facades which survived the heavy bombardments of World War II – and which, one hopes, will soon regain their true colours through sandblasting and renovation. This is all to be financed by speculators, who stand to gain from an improvement in appearance of the town centre.

For Offenbach's future is already in the works; on Kaiserlei Field, at Offenbach's border with Frankfurt, construction is underway on a new office com-

Offenbach Farmer's Market.

plex, which will create some 30,000 new workplaces. High-tech workplaces, in fact, which are likely to attract settlers from throughout the land; these newcomers will then compete with the Offenbachers for living space. Frankfurt speculators have already begun buying up land in preparation.

But the Offenbachers would fight rather than let Frankfurt incorporate their town as a part of the larger metropolis. In such a civil war, all kinds of terrible things could happen: Offenbachers could blow up the two bridges across the Main and erect, at long last, a city wall; or, even worse, Offenbach's football team could return to the first division of the German Football League, forcing Frankfurt's team to the second rank – a nightmare scenario for Frankfurt fans.

Hanau: If a Frankfurt dweller makes his way to Hanau, it's usually because someone has given him a tip to go to "the Spaniard". The Spaniard is the **Centro Espagnol Democratico Obrero** on the corner of Eugen Kaiser Strasse, a real Spanish tavern with *tapas* and *vino tinto* and flamenco music. As most people who've come here stay until night has fallen over the town before trekking back into Frankfurt, few Frankfurt residents get to see Hanau's other attractions: the **Hanau Museum** in the Baroque castle of **Phillipsruhe**, for example, or the square before the Town Hall where stand the tarnished bronze statues of the **Brothers Grimm**. Collectors of folklore and fairytale, Jakob (1785–1863) and Wilhelm (1786–1856) Grimm were Hanau sons; their stories have been translated into more than 140 languages. But one can also visit Hanau simply to stroll along the Main, or take in sights such as the **Hessian Doll Museum** in the Comoedienhaus or the 16th-century **Goldsmithing Museum** in the Old Town Hall.

Hanau is a gem of a town, with half-timbered houses, parks and promenades. **Wilhelmsbad**, today a part of Hanau, was laid out in 1779 as a resort for Wilhelm IX of Hessen-Kassel; in those

The most famous local craft is in gold.

days Hanau was a summer residence of the Hessian counts. Originally, Hanau consisted of a little fortress on the river Kinzig; gradually, a town began to grow up around it. The settlement only began to take off economically with the advent of the Huguenots, who, persecuted in Flanders and Wallonia, were settled in Hanau by Count Ludwig II. These émigrés were wonderful diamond-cutters, expert gold and silversmiths. Hanau's prosperity was assured from this time on.

A less splendid, but no less lucrative, source of income was the trade of Prince Wilhelm IX of Hessen-Kassel, who conscripted soldiers from throughout the land, including Hanau, to rent out to his cousin George II in England. These Hessian troops were sent to put down the rebellion in the English colonies of North America, which, as it later turned out, wasn't enough to prevent the founding of the United States. The profits from this human trade were used to lay out the resort of **Wilhelmsbad** in the

very latest English style. Built around the mineral springs discovered by Hessian herb-sellers in 1709, the spa was fitted out to satisfy the demands of the world-weary upper classes. An amusement park was also built; here, guests could try to hack off wooden Turks' heads or impale St George's dragon on a lance from their mounts on a beautiful carousel. After visiting the park, one could adjourn to the casino and gamble away one's money – all to the good of the ducal treasuries.

You can find traces of this bygone world even today. The **Pump Room** and **Comoedienhaus** are still extant, and have been restored. And, if you sit very still on a park bench on a warm summer night, you may think you hear echoes of the titters of the ladies, and the murmured compliments of their enamoured escorts, borne to you on the wind. Of course, you may only be hearing the caterwauling of tomcats, who have also taken advantage of the cover of night to woo their sweethearts.

The Goldsmith's guild house in Hanau.

THE TAUNUS

The Taunus hills with their forests and gentle ridges lie just beyond Frankfurt's front door and provide an instant contrast to the hustle and bustle of city life. In the old days the region was simply known as "Höhe", meaning an area of high ground. Enclosed by the Rhine and the Main rivers in the south and the Lahn in the north, the highest elevation in the Taunus is the Grosser Feldberg, at a respectable 880 metres (2,887 ft) above sea level.

The Taunus not only provides a wonderful recreation area for the people of Frankfurt, but is also sought-after as a residential area by captains of finance and industry. Anyone who can boast a **Bad Homburg** or **Königstein** address commands some respect among the people of Frankfurt, and the limousines that roll into the city from here every morning are correspondingly smart. Only those not afraid of losing their image use the more environmentally friendly public transport system. But good quality of life doesn't have to be expensive. Society here likes to have its produce straight from the farm. A brochure from the Bad Homburg tourist office tells you where you can get your eggs, vegetables and flour as well as homemade sausages, Christmas goose, lamb and freshly-baked farmers' bread.

But this area is not just for tennis players, golfers and riders. Health resorts and spas such as Bad Homburg, Bad Soden and Königstein, with their half-timbered pensions and secluded hotels, provide an ideal getaway for discerning city dwellers. Those who enjoy hiking can leave their car and explore the region's castles or castle ruins on foot. Children will grumble until they have been to one of the leisure parks in the region. One of the best of these is the **Hessenpark**, which gives a fascinating insight into the history of the area since around 1700. Some of the oldest and most beautiful half-timbered buildings, churches and public buildings from all over the land have been assembled here. **Saalburg** takes you much further back in time – in fact, to the 1st century AD. It was one of the border posts built to protect the Roman empire from the unwelcome attentions of marauding Germanii.

Only 18 km (11 miles) from Frankfurt, the little town of **Oberursel**, the gateway to the Taunus, lies in almost rural tranquillity. It is best reached from the city centre with the U-bahn line 3 or the motorway 661. Getting off the train, the visitor will be struck by the cleanliness of the station area, with its well-tended parks and gardens. A number of large firms have their offices in the vicinity. The **Strachgasse**, with its rows of houses from the 17th century, leads directly to the main objective of this particular excursion, namely the former village centre of today's town, which celebrated its 1,200 years of existence in 1991.

The **Vortaunus Museum**, on the corner of Strachgasse and Rahmtor, provides a detailed insight into the history of the place, which gets its name from the *Urselbach* (Ursel stream) whose energy was responsible for drawing a variety of trades in the Middle Ages. The community, which was granted its charter in 1444, rapidly gained in economic importance through the armourers and later the cloth mills that set up on the banks of the stream.

When the town had to be rebuilt after a disastrous fire during the Thirty Years' War, flour and oil mills, as well as tanneries, became the basis of its prosperity. At one time there are said to have been no fewer than 47 mills strung out on the banks of the Ursel. The oldest is the **Herrenmühle**, which still exists today.

Walking around in the vicinity of the **Church of St Ursula**, it is easy to see why the locals are so proud of their town, with its many half-timbered houses, squares and narrow alleyways.

In the 1970s the historic old part was restored, partly on private initiative and partly with the help of local government grants. The dedication involved in this transformation can be seen from the display cases affixed to some of the houses, such as the one on house number 19 in the St Ursula Gasse, whose photographic display of "before and after" can only engender admiration. After this tour, satisfy your hunger with a hearty meal at the **Gasthof Zum Schwanen** ("The Swan"), and then continue to Hohe Mark at the end of the U-bahn line. This is where hiking trails through the Taunus start.

Alternatively, you can leave Oberursel by following the federal highway 455 towards **Kronberg**. After turning off at "Kronberg Nord", an inconspicuous sign marked "Schlosshotel" at the entrance to the town points the visitor to **Kronberg Castle**, a rambling Tudor manor with fine oriel windows, parapets and gables set in extensive grounds. During the week it is possible to tour the stately rooms and the fine library. At the weekend, however, this privilege is reserved for guests staying at the hotel who pay between 365 marks for a double room and 1,550 marks for the "Royal Suite". The 18-hole golf course and the grounds are open to all.

The lords of Kronberg were once the arch-enemies of Frankfurt, robbing the merchants and stealing the cattle. In May 1389, Frankfurt mustered a force of 2,000 men and laid siege to the old Kronberg castle. But then the cavalry arrived from the Palatinate and Hanau and the Frankfurt force was forced to beat a hasty retreat. Thus ended the largest military campaign ever mounted by the city of Frankfurt.

It is hard to imagine that bitter poverty reigned in Kronberg until well into the 19th century. Indeed it wasn't until 1894 that things started to improve. It was then that Victoria, Princess of Prussia and Princess Royal of England chose to move here in widowhood, her husband the emperor Frederick III having died of

The Taunus is a protected nature park.

throat cancer in 1888. Between 1945 and 1951 the castle building was impounded by the Americans, and was later used by General Dwight Eisenhower as overnight accommodation.

Schloss Strasse in the centre of the town does not in fact lead to the manor-cum-hotel, but to the much older Kronberg Castle. Built in the 13th century, this is where the old town originated. The pretty half-timbered houses, beer gardens and boutiques selling arts and crafts make for a pleasant stroll.

From Kronberg the B455 leads towards Königstein. On the way, **Falkenstein Castle** stands perched on a hill. From these ruins there is a path that leads westward through the forest to Königstein. Particularly on weekends, the 2-km (1-mile) path is probably a better bet than the main road, as the traffic tends to get rather congested on the B455. Alternatively, a popular local track leads east to the top of the Alter König mountain, with the overgrown remains of a Celtic ring-castle. The walk is rewarded with a scenic view of the Main Valley and Frankfurt.

Another attraction en route to Königstein is the **Opelzoo**, founded in 1956 by Georg von Opel. The cages and enclosures for hippopotami, African elephants, sheep, goats, ponies and many other species have blended in well with the landscape of the Rentbach Valley. Children can also take rides on camels and ponies, as well as investigate the adventure playground and the natural history museum.

The popularity of the health resort of **Königstein** tends to make the place pretty busy at weekends. The **Kurzentrum** (health cure centre), which is situated in the midst of the expansive forests, offers the full treatment to people with heart, circulatory and nervous disorders, as well as exhaustion and migraine. Nicotine addicts can even undergo hypnosis to cure them of their habit. The superbly renovated old town is clustered around the **Kurpark** in the centre. Restaurants and cafés, most of

them rather smart, provide meeting places for young and old.

By walking up the Burgweg from the old town, the visitor will arrive at the ruins of **Königstein Castle**. It was built at the beginning of the 13th century to protect the Imperial Road between Frankfurt and Cologne. It was only when roads to Limburg and Cologne as well as the long-distance connection to the Netherlands were laid through here that the community acquired enough importance to receive its own coveted city charter. Every summer a festival is held in the ruins in honour of the castle and the role it has played in the history of Königstein. The locals dress up as knights and maidens and the parade goes all the way through the town.

Having passed through the Burg Hain and past the Freiheitsfelsen, this tour can be broken temporarily at an open-air swimming pool surrounded by woods and fields. Those who still have the energy can continue from here along the European long-distance footpath E1 to arrive at the summit of the **Kleiner Feldberg** (825 metres/2,706 ft) after about one and a half hours.

There are a number of inviting inns in the vicinity of Königstein. They include the **Fröhliche Landmann** (happy farmer) with its stud farm and hotel and the **Zur Roten Mühle** (The red mill) in the Liederbach Valley. They are venerable old inns in the middle of the forest; both have large beer gardens and are about half an hour's walk from the Wiesenbadner Strasse side of town.

Fischbach, Eppstein and Idstein: On the way to Wiesbaden on the B455, you will come to the idyllic little town of **Fischbach**. The narrow road wends its way on through the Fischbach valley, in which numerous inns welcome travellers. Long-distance footpaths cross the valley, leading up to the Grosser Feldberg or to Idstein. Back in the Middle Ages, **Eppstein** in the quaint Schwarzbachtal, surrounded by woodland and cliffs, was home to one of the most prominent families in Hesse. Now, only

The Taunus mountains are popular in winter.

the ruins of the **Reichsburg Castle** remain to recall old glories. The **Eppstein Automobile Museum** contains a curious steam engine that was capable of travelling at 40 mph (64 kph), and a Rolls-Royce Phantom III built in 1936.

Following the Bremtal for another 25 km (15 miles) and crossing the *autobahn*, you will come to **Idstein**. The **Idstein Palace**, which now houses a grammar school, is only a stone's throw from the historic town centre. Dominating the old city walls rises the original **Castle Keep**, which after the witch-hunts, trials and burnings in the 17th century was renamed the **Hexenturm** – the witches' tower.

The old town lies on the other side of the archway. At its centre, **König Adolf Platz** is surrounded by beautifully restored half-timbered houses. Many of the buildings now contain cafés and restaurants where it is possible to sit outside. Locals tend to congregate at the fountain in the middle. The **Killingerhaus** has a particularly interesting his-

tory. It used to stand in Alsace, but then, at the beginning of the 17th century, the owner Killinger, a servant of Duke Johannes, was summoned to Idstein. He came, but not without dismantling his house and bringing it with him, re-erecting it on its present site. Today the building houses the **Tourist Office** and the **Municipal Museum**. Directly opposite is the **Town Hall**, which has served as such for over 300 years.

The oldest house in Idstein can be found in the Obergasse, number 2. Just like the **Unionskirche**, it dates from the 14th century, although the latter underwent numerous alterations over the following centuries. With its rich decorative elements including paintings, wall panels and ceiling frescoes, the interior of the church looks more like a museum of art than a house of God. Most of the wall and ceiling paintings were executed by the Rubens School in Antwerp. Equally decorative are many of the half-timbered houses in the vicinity; many of them are also painted with fine murals.

Open-space chess in the Homburg Kurpark.

Bad Homburg and Grosser Feldberg: The town of **Bad Homburg vor der Höhe** is like the living room of Frankfurt: clean, dignified and luxurious. And here money changes hands just as often as in the metropolis on the Main. Through its Casino, founded in 1841 by François Blanc, the spa town became a favourite playground of the European elite. It was closed for a spell in 1872 by the Prussians, who in their typical frugal style wanted to return the place to some semblance of order and uprightness. Visitors to Bad Homburg can take advantage of the S-bahn line 5 which offers a regular service. Alternatively, from 2pm every afternoon there is a special hourly bus service, the Casino Express Bus, which picks up tourists and professional gamblers alike from the south side of Frankfurt's main station, or from the Poseidon House at the Trade Fair Centre. Visitors with no car in Bad Homburg can hire bicycles locally.

A stroll from Bad Homburg's **Kurhaus** through the expansive 44-hectare (109-acre) **Kurpark** gives the visitor a good initial impression of some of the merits of the town. This is one of the largest and most attractive spa gardens in Europe and contains the first tennis courts on the Continent as well as Germany's oldest golf course. The **Siamese Temple** was donated by the King of Siam (now Thailand) in 1907 in appreciation of the recovery he made here.

Even today, the **Kaiser Wilhelm Spa Baths**, completed in 1890, help maintain Homburg's reputation as a health spa. One need only look at the building to appreciate that 100 years ago luxury knew no bounds. As far as the local waters are concerned, there are 14 springs of which seven are used for mineral water cures. The cures are said to be beneficial in the treatment of stomach, bowel, gall bladder and liver disorders, as well as metabolic diseases.

The **Casino** is rather less conspicuous and is located right next door. In the summer, sessions of roulette and blackjack are held outside on the terrace. The

Pharmacy with a long tradition in Homburg.

visitor can indulge in lobster, game or fish – none of which are terribly expensive – in the **Casino Restaurant**. Should one have had the same run of bad luck as the Russian novelist Dostoyevsky, then one can always still sample the waters at the fountains of the Ludwig and Kaiser spring or the Louise and Landgrave spring free of charge.

The place where the Frankfurters themselves go to recover from the toils of city life is the noble **Taunus Thermen** baths at the eastern edge of the Kurpark. Here, businessmen sit next to clerks, all packed like sardines into one of the nine Finnish saunas in the steam bath; or they sprawl out naked in an artificial rocky landscape.

After this thorough fitness programme, return to explore the other side of Bad Homburg: the historical part of the town. The Dorotheenstrasse, in the 18th-century home for employees of the court and wealthier burghers, leads directly to the **Palace**. Built by landgrave Friedrich II in the 17th century, it stands on the site of the old castle, of which the **White Tower**, the symbol of Bad Homburg, is the only part still standing. The restaurant and café **Landgrafen** now occupies part of the palace courtyard and its attempts to provide service fit for a king are matched by princely prices.

Through the archway on the left and past the royal chapel, the visitor will arrive at the palace gardens, linked to the old town by the **Ritter von Marx Bridge**. It was to the left of this bridge that a craftsmen's settlement was established back in the early 14th century. It acquired civic rights in 1330 and provided the core of present-day Homburg. The old town which grew up around it has been painstakingly restored, although the houses of the various trades are now occupied by cafés and boutiques. After following the Schulberg and crossing the Marketplace (weekly market), stroll along the modern pedestrian precinct of Louisenstrasse before winding up back at the Kurhaus. In the **Hat Museum** are examples of the fa-

he lisabethen-runnen, a untain with edicinal ualities, in e Homburg urpark.

mous "Homburg" hat which many a statesman has worn with pride.

Roman journey: Only 7 km (4 miles) from Homburg is the **Saalburg**, an old Roman fort, which was built in the 1st century AD as a border post and camp for Roman troops. It was part of the *limes*, the fortified border that the Romans built between occupied Upper Germania and the region of free German tribes to the north. It was the German equivalent of Hadrian's Wall.

The Saalburg was carefully reconstructed between 1898 and 1907 and can now once again be entered through the main gate flanked by two watchtowers. Immediately to the right, in the reconstructed *horreum* (store, magazine) is the **Museum**. It is best to go here first, because then one gains an immediate impression of what conditions were like for soldiers stationed here on the outer limits of the empire. Among the exhibits is a model of the bath house. Even here, it seems that hygiene was very important. The soldiers also had the

luxury of underfloor heating and there is a detailed description of how the system worked. The many artefacts recovered from the site, including all the craft tools, indicate that the garrison was not only interested in battle but also produced its own everyday utensils. The soldiers themselves cooked and baked. Instructions for bathing indicate that the Romans recognised and used the medicinal properties of the region's mineral springs.

The main building, the *principia*, was erected in the middle of the fort compound. In Roman times it was here that the soldiers assembled for duty. The building was also the headquarters of the military administration. From the fort a 15-km (9-mile) path leads east along the *limes*, passing the small Heidenstock fort and countless excavated Roman remains, to **Sandplacken**.

Down the hill from Saalburg is the **Lochmühle Recreation Park**, accessible either by road or the E3 long-distance path. Centred around the old farm-

Producing charcoal in the Hessenpark.

house, the 4-hectare (10-acre) park contains just about everything a child's heart could desire. It includes an enclosure where they can stroke pigs, dwarf goats and donkeys. There are threshing machines and tractors that have been converted into climbing frames; pony trots and carriage rides; trampolines and distorting mirrors; a big wheel and water slides. Families can also take advantage of the barbecue facilities located in the park. The historical **Lochmühle**, an old mill, is next to the park. It houses a splendid hotel and restaurant.

Hessenpark Open-Air Museum: The idea of creating a monument to Hessian culture and architecture was first proposed in the 1950s. It was then that experts realised the extent of the irreplaceable loss of numerous historical buildings, not just by war but by the subsequent reconstruction boom. If the state of Hesse could not be protected, then at least there must be a way of preserving certain typical local buildings in one place. Work began on this museum in Neu-

Anspach in 1974 with the construction of the timber frame of the church in Niedermörlen. In the meantime a total of six villages have been established on the generous 60-hectare (150-acre) site northwest of Homburg and millions of marks have been spent in the reconstruction of historical buildings threatened by decay and demolition.

The villages in the museum are separated by meadows, fields, pastures, woods and lakes. Many of the houses can be explored, providing the visitor with a clear impression of what rural life was once like. You can see the farmer's daughter slaving over a hot stove, or the blacksmith at work. The museum also demonstrates the homesickness of the country girls who had left to find work in the city, and the efforts of the Hessian soldiers involved in the American War of Independence. Relevant again today are the problems of Hessian settlers in Eastern Europe and deepest Russia.

The village store with its original furnishings sells postcards and souvenirs. Traditional craft workshops such as weaving mills and potteries are also to be found in the Hessenpark. They actually operate for a few hours a week and their products are for sale. As well as a baker's shop and a town hall, there is also an almshouse. You can get a good idea of how the locals used to do the washing and bleaching.

It is the attention to detail that has made the Hessenpark so successful. With a bit of imagination, the visit can really turn into a journey back in time. Having completed the tour, visitors can then have a meal at the **Zum Adler** (the eagle) guesthouse.

Nearby is the **Grosser Feldberg**. With a height of 880 metres (2,887 ft), it is just about impossible to miss, and is best scaled from the village of Oberreifenberg, although the route to the summit is marked everywhere, whether from Oberursel, Bad Homburg, Königstein or on foot from the Hessenpark. On the mountain, eagles and vultures can be seen in Hesse's oldest falconry.

asket-
eaver at
ork.

FROM THE MAIN TO THE RHINE

First impressions of **Wiesbaden** do not deceive: this spa town on the Rhine, which in the 19th century had more visitors than inhabitants, really is an extremely elegant place. The poshest part of town at the foot of the Neroberg, Wiesbaden's local mountain at the edge of the Taunus, gives the impression of being one vast open-air museum. If you forget about the cars, then you can well imagine how the Wiesbaden upper crust together with their equally rich guests once whiled away their days in the lap of absolute luxury, particularly in the town's golden age from 1870 to 1914.

Just as in the days of the emperors Friedrich and Wilhelm, the **old funicular**, built in 1888, still trundles up the **Neroberg**. The car coming down is filled with water to give it the weight required to pull the other one all the way up to the so-called **Greek Chapel**, which is in fact a Russian Orthodox church. Duke Aldolph of Nassau had the edifice built in 1850 as a fitting tomb for his wife the Grand Duchess Elizabeth Mikhailovna from St Petersburg, a niece of Tsar Nicholas I. He had married her in 1844 when she was 17 years old, but she died barely a year later together with the daughter she had just born him.

By viewing the city from the forecourt of the chapel, the visitor will be able to take in all the other fashionable residential districts of this the capital of the State of Hesse; a fine place indeed, with all its stucco, marble and brick, spires and exquisitely designed gables, oriels, balconies and columns. The first view of Wiesbaden – a love at first sight, so they say. Or is it? An English administrator, Sir Francis Head, enjoying the same view in 1834, was more critical in his observations: "The town of Wiesbaden is evidently one which does not appreciate the luxury of 'home sweet home!' for it is built not for itself, but for strangers; and though most people ad-mire the size of the buildings, yet, to my mind, there is something very melancholy in seeing houses so much too fine for the style of inhabitants to whom they belong… "

You can get to the Neroberg railway terminus by taking the bus from the main station, passing the spa gardens and the old spa house with the casino and the state theatre and along the city's elegant boulevard, **Wilhelmstrasse**. From above, from the Neroberg, the powerful buildings from the *Gründerzeit* don't look much larger than the set of a model railway. Above the sea of houses rises the triple-naved **Marktkirche**, a neoclassical evangelical edifice built in 1862. Organ concerts take place here every Saturday at 11.30pm and entrance is free. In front of the church and within view of the state parliament building, the people of Wiesbaden erected a bronze statue in memory of Prince William I. Also known as William the Silent, as the eldest son of William, Count of Nassau-Dillenburg, he was

also the prince of Wiesbaden. He became one of the wealthiest noblemen in Europe. Born a Catholic, he was a man of liberal views and supported the Reformation. Having converted to Protestantism, he succeeded in liberating the Spanish Netherlands from the Duke of Alva's oppressive regime.

New rulers: The new rulers of Hesse in Wiesbaden are called minister-presidents. They have been here since the foundation of the state of Hesse and the elevation of Wiesbaden to its capital in 1946, and they reside all year in an elegant *Gründerzeit* villa in Bierstädter Strasse. The parliament itself is housed in the neoclassical palace of the counts of Nassau built in 1842. In the 1920s it was used as a museum and continues to house sculptures and wall and ceiling frescoes of varying styles. The hall under the dome contains figures from Greek mythology. A guided tour takes place at 11am on the first Saturday of each month.

Black Jack and the "Apaches": The old spa district lies between the spa gardens, the marketplace and the Kochbrunnen Fountain. In Wiesbaden, your money need not just be spent on smart clothes, jewellery or dinner for two. You also have the choice of gambling it away. The **Casino** in the former Kurhaus is open from 3pm, and you only need a stake of 5 marks to join in the roulette or blackjack. Wiesbaden was the "roulette capital" in Dostoyevsky's novel *The Gambler*. And, just as the gambler did, it is still possible to pour money away to your heart's content on the green baize. "Excited by the game, I took out all I had left, placed the same bet as before and lost yet again, whereupon I withdrew totally mesmerised from the table. After that, I spent the whole time staggering around the park".

You have to wear a tie in the casino, but you can go to the concerts, operas and performances in the state theatre next door in jeans. And free of charge are the countless summer concerts held in the relaxed atmosphere of the spa

The Gutenberg Museum in Mainz.

gardens outside. If you still have enough to splash out after your visit to the casino, then try the Italian restaurant **Laterna** in Westendstrasse, on the noble Sedanplatz.

Wiesbaden is not a place for the average earner. The costs of rents here are the second highest in the country. "Wiesbaden is tops," say the locals – in almost every respect. The folk festivals, such as the Wilhelmstrassenfest or the Rheingau Wine Week, are veritable orgies of eating and drinking. The people of Wiesbaden have their old Kaiser Wilhelm II to thank for that; the city was his summer residence right up until the outbreak of World War I. Wiesbaden became the capital of the Second Empire for months on end when, together with his entourage, he would visit the theatre and the spa's thermal springs.

The modern face of Wiesbaden is displayed at the "Theatrium" festival performances held at the end of May or beginning of June, when the streets are decorated with flags. Around 200,000 visitors converge on the city to enjoy the performances of numerous ensembles. Here, it is the more unconventional performers who tend to go down best with the inhabitants. People enjoy experiment in a city that otherwise looks as if time has stood still. And it is this that makes Wiesbaden such an unusual place, a noble idyll with discriminating people, who out of their fondness for things nostalgic and their very own brand of cosmopolitanism have created a philosophy of life in which there is no room for trivia.

Printing city: Situated on the other side of the river is the city of **Mainz** (pop. 190,000), the capital of the Rhineland Palatinate. The city was founded by the Romans as *Mongotiacum* in 38 BC. Mainz has prospered ever since AD 747 when St Boniface, the "German Apostle" arrived here and made it an archbishopric. The city developed into the centre of Germanic Christendom. The archbishops of Mainz were not only spiritual shepherds, but in simultane-

Barge on the river Rhine.

ously performing the role of chancellor to the Reich and elector of the emperor, they became one of the strongest secular powers in the Holy Roman Empire of German Nations. Back in the Middle Ages, Mainz was one of those cities that was able to wrest certain freedoms from the bondage of feudalism. A leading member of the Rhenish League of Cities from 1254, Mainz succeeded in releasing the Rhine from the grip of the robber knights, who during the great Interregnum (1250–73) had gained a hold on most of Germany.

The mighty Romanesque **Cathedral** (begun 975) remains the dominant feature of a city that practically had to be rebuilt after the devastation of World War II. Opposite the cathedral in the marketplace is the **Gutenberg Museum**. It was in Mainz, in 1445, that Johannes Gutenberg is credited with making one of the most important of all inventions: printing with moveable letters. The building contains a replica of the master's workshop and the original

printing apparatus. The most valuable "publication" on display is one of the 47 extant 42-line Bibles, a lasting testimony to the amazing revolution that Gutenberg began. The restored late-Renaissance **Electoral Palace** today houses the **Roman Germanic Central Museum**, where artefacts and remains from the Roman period are on view. The banqueting hall is used for performances during the *Mainzer Fassnacht*, the annual Lenten carnival that with its masked balls and fools' processions attracts hordes of visitors.

But it isn't only during carnival time that one can savour the atmosphere of the old city. In one of the many wine bars you can enjoy the light white wines of Rhine Hesse with *Handkäs mit Mussig* – curd cheese garnished with vinegar, oil and diced onions. Mainz's role as the centre of the Rhineland-Palatinate wine trade is clearly demonstrated by the cellars of the giant *sekt* producer **Kupferberg**. Hundreds of thousands of bottles of sparkling white wine are stored

Mainz, with the cathedral in the background.

in these vaulted premises, which themselves bear traces of Roman and medieval occupation.

The Rheingau: The inhabitants of Wiesbaden maintain that their city is the "gateway to the Rheingau". But for years now this title has been hotly contested by the people of **Wicker**. The small community of Wicker in the Main-Taunus district is, as it were, the bridgehead of the Rheingau-Riesling route from Frankfurt, which wends its way along the Rhine between the river and the vineyards for 62 km (38 miles) before arriving in the little redwine town of Assmannshausen. The road is officially known as the B42.

If you wish to go wine-tasting along the Riesling route, then it's probably best to leave the car behind. Back in the 18th century Goethe explored the delights of the Rheingau by carriage, and nowadays, sensible wine-bibbers tend to take the bus. The central booking office for tours in the Rheingau is the tourist information office at the main station in Wiesbaden. Those who want to see the area in style by floating gently down the Rhine can, if they wish, embark at the Eiserner Steg in Frankfurt. The disadvantage with these cruises is that they call in only at certain destinations such as Rüdesheim or Eltville; the real Rheingau which lies hidden behind the vineyards is not part of the tour.

Hock: In the Lower Main region between Frankfurt and the Rhine, Wicker is the first place one comes across with wine-tasting stalls and the typical inns of the area, the "Straussewirtschaften" where a garland hanging outside indicates that wine is being poured. The locals drink their wine from *Schoppen* (glass goblets), often in accompaniment with home-made sausage or cheese sticks. Things are a little more refined in neighbouring **Hochheim**, with its top-quality wines. This little town on the other side of the Main has supplied the English royal household with its wines for more than 150 years. Because the name Hochheim was too difficult to

pronounce for English lips, Queen Victoria simply called the wine "Hock", and the name stuck: "Good Hock keeps off the Doc" was the motto. The Hochheim wine market in the summer and the Hochheim Fair in the late autumn draw thousands of visitors every year, with livestock sales and market stalls. A fun park adds to the gaiety of the event.

The Riesling route continues via Kostheim and Wiesbaden and into the Rheingau proper. The small town of **Niederwalluf** is the oldest wine-producing community in the region, vines having been cultivated here ever since AD 779. A "Vintner steak" in the local winegrowers' hall is best washed down with a glass of *Fitusberg* or *Walkenberg*, drunk from the classic "Roman" glass with its green bottom. This type of glass is typical of the Rheingau and you will doubtless drink from it again upon arrival in the town of **Eltville**. This old Roman settlement of *Alta Villa* received its first official mention in 937, and then went on to acquire civic rights in 1332.

Once the summer residence of the archbishops of Mainz, it is a neat little town with fine half-timbered houses. The formidable castle of the prince-bishops provides a stark contrast to the **Crass Castle** at the entrance to the town which was rebuilt in the style of German Romanticism. The little castle, just about choked in creepers, was one of the primary destinations of illustrious visitors to the area at the beginning of the 19th century, the poets who came to explore and write about the "Romantic" Rhine.

Gregorian chants: A few kilometres away from old father Rhine is the Gothic wine village of **Kiedrich**. In medieval times, Kiedrich was an important place of pilgrimage, after the nearby monastery at Eberbach donated a relic of St Valentine to the community in the 14th century. Under episcopal patronage, the people proceeded to build their Gothic **St Valentine's Church**, with its St Michael's chapel and charnel-house on the foundations of the old Romanesque Church of Dionysos. A late-Renaissance gallery and choir were added later.

But the church, with its unicum Rheingau Madonna with wine leaves on the sceptre and crown, has also long been a destination for pilgrims of a different kind. The main attraction here is the unique boy's choir. As long ago as the 14th century the men of the community sang their Gregorian chants with the village school master and the Kiedrich boys. The choir has remained true to chanting following the Gothic "hob nail" notation; here one can appreciate pure Gothic art both optically and acoustically.

The Name of the Rose: "The abbot sat in the middle of his raised table, festively dressed in an embroidered purple robe, holding his fork high like a sceptre. Next to him drank Jorge from a large wine goblet and at the lectern was the scorpioid figure of Remigius who devoutly read out the lives of the saints." This scene, described by Umberto Eco in his novel *The Name of the Rose*, is actually set in an imaginary abbey in

The Rheingau is renowned for its wine.

northern Italy. The film of the same name, however, was made by Jean-Jacques Arnaud in a real live monastery, namely **Eberbach Monastery** in the Rheingau, hidden in a valley above Kiedrich. Sean Connery came here to play his part some 900 years after the monastery's founding in 1136. And, just as in Eco's film, this monastery was indeed a scene of conflict between the strictly religious Cistercians and the Benedictines who were not averse to enjoying worldly pleasures. The rule for monks of *ora et labora* was interpreted by the Eberbach Cistercians as meaning that the monks were to worship and the lay brothers were to work. This definition of roles repeatedly led to bloody revolts on the part of the exploited non-monk monastery community. And so it happened that in 1261 lay brothers did away with the abbot.

However, by this time the Cistercians of Eberbach had long since ceased to follow the same strict principles that had led to conflict with the Benedic-

tines. They had become rich through the wine trade; wine now flowed in the monks' veins and every day was open day at Eberbach Monastery. The general chapter responsible for the establishment soon felt it necessary to issue a decree that, at least at Christmas time, the gates of the monastery remain closed, except for the entrance to the church.

The year 1500 was a bumper one for wine and it is said that the merry monks of the late Middle Ages stored it in a vat with a volume of 70,000 litres that had taken them three years to build. During the Peasants' Revolt, this wine vat was the first military objective of the local Rheingau population, and only after it had been captured and emptied was the uprising over. Monastical life was finally ended by Napoleon's troops in 1803 with the dissolution of the monastery. It subsequently became a lunatic asylum and then, after the 1848 revolution, a military prison.

Nowadays the complex is used by the administration of the Hessian State Wine

Preparing the casks.

Estates. The very best of the Rheingau wines (200,000 bottles) mature in the vaulted cellars, and in nursery vineyards around the monastery experiments are carried out on new varieties of grapes. Because the monastery was continually developed by the abbots who resided here, the building presents an interesting mix of architectural styles, even if the whole is dominated by the purely medieval building complexes. The dormitory for the lay brothers, which was built in the mid-13th century, remains the largest non-sacred interior space of any building in Germany (83 metres/ 272 ft long). Particularly at weekends, high-quality classical concerts are held in the monastery church. And just as in the golden days, when the powerful abbot general would come to the Rheingau, so today do the cream of society gather here for wine tasting at the invitation of the state premier.

From Eberbach Monastery, a road leads past **Johannisberg Castle**, whose vineyards are exclusively for the cultivation of Riesling, back to the Rheingau-Riesling route and the village of **Winkel**. This is famous as the location of the Brentanohaus, the house of the German poet Clemens Brentano.

The Drosselgasse: The town of **Rüdesheim**, with its famous **Drosselgasse** (thrush alley), has somehow managed to market itself to millions of visitors as your typical, quaint wine "village". There is actually very little to distinguish Rüdesheim from other settlements along this stretch of the river. All have the typical half-timbered houses and narrow back alleys and *weinstuben* (wine bars). The Drosselgasse itself can be very busy.

With its *Asbach* (a kind of brandy) distillery and its *sekt* (German sparkling wine) cellars, Rüdesheim also has a number of sights that are well worth seeing. There is the **Brömserburg** (9th century), a moated castle which today houses the fascinating **Rheingau Museum of Wine History**, as well as the impressive ruins of the Boosenburg. In the Brömserhof, near the castle of the same name, is a unique collection of music boxes from around the world, from street organs to tiny musical snuffboxes. It is from the Brömserhof that the Rüdesheim "Winzerexpress" departs. This little train takes visitors on a round tour of the vineyards.

From Rüdesheim, a cable car climbs to the 37-metre high **Niederwald Monument** (unveiled in 1883), whose scale and position high above the Rhine are breathtaking indeed. Created as an expression of Wilhelmenian aspirations of power after the Franco-German war (1870–71), the statue they call *Germania,* symbolically depicted as a sword-brandishing Valkyrie, gazes defiantly across the river. The top dignitaries of the Reich, who had gathered together for the inaugural celebrations, would all have gone up in smoke had the two anarchists Reinsdorf and Küchler been prepared to pay more for waterproof fuses: because of torrential rain the night before, the charge of dynamite failed to detonate, the nobility was spared and the two would-be assassins ended up paying with their lives. Germany's national monument survived.

The final destination of this trip through the Rheingau is **Assmannshausen**, a village which produces the only red wine on the right bank of the Rhine. It can be tasted in such venerable establishments as the **Krone**. Ferdinand Freiligrath (1810–76), one of the leaders of the 1848 revolution, was a regular in the Krone, as was Hoffmann von Fallersleben (1798–1874), the composer of *Deutschland, Deutschland über Alles*, which became the German national anthem in 1922.

From either Assmannshausen or Rüdesheim, one can cross the Rhine by ferry, past the legendary **Mouse Tower**, to the town of **Bingen** at the confluence of the River Nahe. On a weekend in July the spectacular "Rhine in Flames" firework display takes place on this stretch of the river, and is best witnessed from the rails of one of the steamers.

Grape picking on the slopes of the Rheingau.

THE VOGELSBERG

The most beautiful route to the Vogelsberg is marked on the map by a thin blue line. This is the River Nidda, which after the River Main is the second-longest river in the Frankfurt area. It flows through the city for some 20 km (12 miles) and when the sun shines its banks provide a popular escape for city dwellers. Walkers, cyclists and even anglers all take advantage of the Nidda. There are display boards located at regular intervals which explain the flora and fauna on and in the river.

Leaving the city area behind, one can continue to follow the river to the north to arrive at the **Vogelsberg**. This is where the Nidda has its source, at a height of 720 metres (2,362 ft) above sea level.

The High Vogelsberg is an oasis of green situated between the built-up areas of Frankfurt, Giessen and Fulda. Only 80 km (50 miles) from Frankfurt, it is easily reached by car along country roads or the *autobahnen* that run at a tangent to its western and southern flanks. However, a much more rewarding way is to follow the course of the Nidda; tracks and cycle paths follow the river just about the whole way.

Through the Wetterau: The start of the journey along the Nidda involves hopping from park to park. The site of the National Garden Show in 1989, the Frankfurt **Niddawiesen** (Nidda Meadows) have meanwhile been converted into an expansive area of parkland. In the little Hessian spa town of **Vilbel**, situated just to the north of the city limits, the river flows right past the spa gardens.

Going further out, the highly industrialised agriculture of the **Wetterau** is characterised by its large fields of cereal crops. It is a very fertile area whose high yields have led the locals to call it the "golden" Wetterau. In the rugged Vogelsberg, however, the farms are only small; there was never much of a living to be made from the soil here and cattle farming is the main industry.

The Wetterau has been the region's granary ever since the days of the Romans. The fortifications that the Romans constructed to defend the area were expanded into a veritable fortress by the Staufen rulers; the Wetterau "castle triangle" whose northern boundary ran between Friedberg, Büdingen and Gelnhausen. Even today, most places are dominated by their old castles. In **Florstadt-Staden**, a small town on the Nidda, the castle now houses a hotel.

The gateway to the Vogelsberg is considered to be the town of **Nidda**, 60 km (37 miles) from Frankfurt. It is a jewel of medieval, half-timbered architecture. Further on, the hill resort of **Schotten** calls itself the "heart of the Vogelsberg". It lies in the Vogelsberg National Park. From here the road climbs sharply upwards.

An extinct volcano: A sign on the Hoherodskopf reads "Attention! you are

Preceding pages: flying kites at Drachenstein in the Wetterau. **Left**, Alsfeld town hall. **Right**, a bunch of flowers brightens the day.

ng on a volcano". This might cause ty in some visitors. While this gen- ... ll may appear decidedly inconspicuous, it is in fact the largest single basalt massif in the whole of Europe and covers a total area of some 2,500 sq. km (965 sq. miles).

Millions of years ago impressive rivers of lava poured from the flanks of the Vogelsberg and flowed all the way to present-day Frankfurt. The volcanic ruin that remains reaches its highest point with the **Taufstein** at 773 metres (2,536 ft). The nearby **Hoherodskopf**, which is the more famous of the two peaks, tops out at 764 metres (2,506 ft).

The Vogelsberg is also an important natural reservoir. In this connection, the people of Frankfurt have developed a special bond with "their" mountain; it serves the city population not only as a recreation area and location for second homes in the country, but also provides them with much of their drinking water. One-third of all Frankfurt's water needs are pumped out of the Vogelsberg and it is not without good reason that scientists and ecologists fear that this natural water tank will gradually run dry. The fact that the water table has sunk has not only led to structural damage in buildings, but it has also had a detrimental effect on the local ecology.

From a height of about 600 metres (1,968 ft), the Vogelsberg plateau is covered in a mantle of pine and beech forest. Even in the 1920s, nature lovers from local environmental groups campaigned for the protection of the forest and the rare animal and plant species it contained. Success, however, only came in the 1950s after the area became a popular tourist destination. The **Vogelsberg National Park** was created; with an area of 400 sq. km (154 sq. miles) it is, after the Luneburg Heath, the second oldest national park in Germany.

Tourist infrastructure: Be that as it may, it is difficult for visitors to the Vogelsberg to feel that they are out in the wilds. As is the case with most of Germany's scenic areas, the authorities have made **Outdoor pursuits.**

things as easy as possible. Each of the countless car parks provides access to circular hiking trails, with grill stations and rest areas, huts and playgrounds for the children.

For those keen on winter sports, apart from the three ski lifts there are also about 50 km (30 miles) of cross-country tracks. For tobogganists a 750-metre long summer slide with a gradient of 18 percent has been installed on the flanks of the Hoherodskopf.

The plateau itself is disected by a dense network of footpaths. Because the forest is small enough to cross in a single day, the tracks tend to avoid any difficult obstacles. The most popular route skirts the bizarre rock formations on the Taufstein and Geiselstein, continues over the high moorland and wet meadows of the **Breungeshainer Heath** and takes in the source of the Nidda. On the Hoherodskopf, the focal point of excursions, there are a number of restaurants and places to spend the night.

Nature walks: In fact, what likes to be presented as a happy medium between environmental protection and tourism, does actually turn out to be a bitter conflict of interests. On weekends, the invasion of motorised visitors puts the national park under increased strain. Although the legendary motor-cross rally "around Schotten" came to an end in 1955, the Vogelsberg remains a place for driving pleasure. There is an information centre on the Hoherodskopf with information about the ecological aspects of the region. In order to ensure effective environmental protection, more and more areas are being designated as preservation areas and are being closed to the public.

The tourist business is concentrated on the southern and eastern side of the Vogelsberg, where the weather is best. On the northern side, locals would prefer to forget that their mountain has a traditionally bad reputation as being the "Siberia of Hesse". Extremely high levels of precipitation and an inordinately high number of foggy days combine

Women footballers.

with severe winters and the proverbial poverty in the region to produce anything other than an attractive tourist destination. This can, of course, be seen from a more positive aspect, namely that particularly in the northern and western parts the character of the landscape has not been changed beyond recognition by the superimposed infrastructure for tourists. Here, the most problematic changes will be brought about by the gradual decline of farming in the region.

A walk on the wild side: The best way to appreciate the delights of the northern side of the Vogelsberg is on foot. Starting at the source of the Nidda in the high moorland, a marked path leads for 25 km (15 miles) down to the town of **Lauterbach**. It crosses the remotest part of the high forest and its route is so planned that the attractions of the landscape can be fully appreciated without having to pass through villages or cross any roads. The countryside here is wild. Beyond the forest, the vegetation gives way to the hedges and green fields so typical of the area.

Despite the large-scale and ecologically disastrous reparcelling of arable land that took place in Germany in the 1950s and '60s, pasture farming was not greatly affected, and here the traditional role of farming in shaping the landscape has been preserved.

Shortly before Lauterbach stands **Eisenbach Castle**. The building is often referred to as the Wartburg (a castle in Thuringia) of Hesse. Work on the edifice still standing today was commenced in the 13th century. Visitors will be pleased to discover that there is a restaurant within its walls. From the picturesque old town, a track leads to the so-called **Haining**, which is an old Germanic sacred site, and folk festivals still take place under the 400-year-old oak tree.

In the climatically more favourable south and east, tourism is now something of a tradition. Despite the fact that the Vogelsberg does not contain a sin-

Swift-running river in the Vogelsberg.

gle natural lake, even in centuries past the necessity of regulating the water supply led to the creation of man-made lakes and ponds. The last dam to be built was on the Nidda near Schotten. The resulting **Nidda Lake** is now an attractive place for excursions, appreciated just as much by nature lovers as by swimmers and surfers. There are a number of campsites and the hotel industry in Schotten itself has expanded to cope with demand.

The **Gedener See** further to the east is almost entirely given over to leisure activity, and the same goes for the **Niedermoser See**. The **Obermoser See**, on the other hand, is protected and its waters and banks reserved for migratory birds. A number of health resorts here advertise their mild climate and clear air; the town of **Herbstein** has meanwhile had a thermal baths installed. In just about every town and village there are special deals offered for stays lasting several days. These packages are typical of the standard fare for other German central highland areas and include, for example, rides in covered wagons and carriages, bread baking, riding, nine-pin bowling, fishing, a holiday on the farm and "hiking without back-packs".

Traditional architecture: In **Schotten**, just as in Laubach, Grünberg, Herbstein and Lauterbach, there has also been extensive restoration work to the old half-timbered houses. In the open-air cafés and restaurants around the marketplace there is almost a Mediterranean atmosphere. While in the traditionally poor high-ground areas of the Vogelsberg there isn't much in terms of representative architecture, in Schotten the half-timbered ensemble of houses really is one of the finest examples to be found anywhere.

Asfeld, too, situated just to the north of the Vogelsberg, boasts many fine buildings. It has received the rare accolade of being named by the Council of Europe as "European model town for the preservation of monuments".

THE RHÖN

Another area of beautiful upland scenery easily accessible from Frankfurt is the Rhön. It lies about 50 km (30 miles) to the east of the city, between the towns of Fulda in Hesse, Meiningen in Thuringia and Bad Kissingen in the Lower Franconian part of Bavaria.

Steep and rugged cliffs, volcanic extrusions, rounded limestone hilltops, basalt and coloured sandstone are some of the geological features that contribute to the highly varied nature of the region's topography. The climate is harsher and the hills bleaker than in other highland areas of central Germany. Snow is pretty well guaranteed in the winter, making it a popular destination for winter sports enthusiasts.

Nothing much grows on these storm-battered hills. Visitors can get a good idea of how the Rhön farmers used to live by visiting the **Museum Village** in **Tann**. For the people of the Rhön, prosperity simply meant a modest, cosy existence; traditionally, the Rhön was always a poor area.

Fulda: At the beginning of the 8th century, the Anglo-Saxon missionary Boniface, whose common name was Wynfrith and who later came to be known as the "Apostle of the Germans", was commissioned by Pope Gregory II to Christianise the east-Hessian part of Thuringia. The eastern border of the young Frankish kingdom had to be defended against the marauding Saxons by both the sword and the Word. He met with startling success and founded countless monasteries including the one at **Fulda** in 744, which he had the Benedictine monk Sturmius build on the ruins of the old Merovingian castle. After Boniface had died his martyr's death in Friesland on 5 June 754, his mortal remains were brought here and laid to rest in the crypt.

In ensuing centuries, the bishops of Fulda, much like their counterparts in Mainz, attained ever greater secular power. They even took to the field against the lords of Würzburg in order to expand their domains. This alliance of spiritual and secular interests bequeathed Fulda with a host of splendid historical buildings. The **Palace** dates from the beginning of the 17th century when the prince-bishops had the former Renaissance palace remodelled and extended. Dedicated at the beginning of the 18th century, the baroque **Cathedral** was built on the foundations of the old basilica. This had been built at the beginning of the 9th century after the old sepulchral church of St Boniface could no longer accommodate the ever increasing stream of pilgrims.

Today, the **Tomb of St Boniface** lies in the cathedral crypt. A baroque alabaster relief framed with black marble depicts the martyrdom of the saint.

Jewish cemeteries: Following the edge of the Rhön, an old trading route connected southern Germany with Leipzig and eastern Europe, and it was this trad-

ing route that even in early times attracted Jewish communities to settle in the area. They were flour and wheat traders, craftsmen, farmers and school teachers. But there is little to remind one of their presence now, although photographs of some of the families once again hang in the tiny local museum at Hünfeld, which is housed in the former village school.

There is a large Jewish cemetery in **Rhina** and another one in **Burghaun** which can be reached by walking across the fields from Hünfeld. It lies hidden above a bend in the road at the exit to the village. The simple grey gravestones stand between the trees. The Hebrew inscriptions were carved by Catholic masons.

Art and computers: In the 1980s, a certain amount of prosperity came to the Rhön. The little town of **Hünfeld**, for example, was done up. Hünfeld is only a stone's throw from the line of the old border with the former GDR. When reunification came, the place was suddenly awoken and became a major traffic junction just about overnight, to the delight of the hotels and restaurants.

But even before this happened the people of Hünfeld were busy bringing the world to their door. They offered the professor of art Jürgen Blum space for his modern art collection in the painstakingly restored gas works, where a selection of over 2,000 of his lithographs and sculptures is now on display. The **Museum of Modern Art** is to be kept up to date through the acquisition of new collections. Hünfeld even houses works by such famous names as Joseph Beuys, Uecker, Christo and Warhol.

Hünfeld's most famous citizen is undoubtedly the computer pioneer Konrad Zuse, who is now over 80. Zuse constructed the first operational general-purpose programme-controlled calculator, known as the Z 1, a replica of which can be seen in the local museum. It functions with a mechanical memory and calculator, whose lead components Zuse originally cut with a fret-saw. The

Rural idyll with vine.

programmes were punched in strips of old cinema film. The exhibits in the museum date from the 1950s and were assembled in his factory in neighbouring Bad Hersfeld.

Gliding on the Wasserkuppe: The highest mountain of the Rhön is the 950-metre high (3,117-ft) Wasserkuppe. While a number of rare medicinal herbs still grow on its flanks, the summit has grown more and more barren in recent years. The forests of spruce have succumbed to the pollution fanned over the high Rhön from industrial areas in both east and west. But originally they weren't part of the scenery; the indigenous forest is deciduous, primarily beech.

It was on the Wasserkuppe that gliding in Germany was born. After World War I, the Treaty of Versailles stipulated that the Germans were never again to build up an air force. So the Germans took to the air in gliders and, although flying here began as early as 1910, it was this restriction that provided the major impetus for later development.

Today, when the wind is blowing in the right direction, pilots will take passengers up with them for a fee. For those who get the chance, the Rhön from above provides truly breathtaking vistas. Gliders can now cross the point where until 1990 they had to turn round to avoid East German airspace, and can continue to do their acrobatics over Thuringia, which, with its emerald green forests and valleys and bubbling streams, is even more inviting and unspoilt than the Hesse side of the mountains. In the meantime, model aircraft enthusiasts and hang-gliders have also arrived on the mountain.

Those who prefer to use their hands and feet to gain height can do so on the 42-metre (138-ft) high crags near **Poppenhausen**. Those more geologically inclined can take to the **Geological Path** on the western flanks of the Wasserkuppe.

A small monument in **Schönau** recalls a sport of a totally different kind. It was built to the memory of one Otto

Winter coat.

Flick, the inventor of the Rhön wheel. The contraption consisted of two large rings (up to 7 feet in diameter) of tubular steel to which gymnasts would clamp their hands and feet and then proceed to roll along either in a straight line or in twists, or even jump up or pirouette. Nowadays, Rhön wheels have more fans in the US and Japan than they do in their country of origin.

Moors, Celts and pilgrims: In Germany high moorland areas are something of a rarity. That the Rhön possesses two moors, the **Black Moor** and the **Red Moor**, is thanks to the campaigns of foresters and environmentalists which succeeded in bringing an end to peat farming. In an effort to promote "ecological" tourism, corduroy paths lead the visitor across the terrain so as to avoid any great disturbance to the animal and plant world. Sundew grows here, as does cotton grass and erica. When the mist descends over the moors in the autumn one becomes aware of how easy it would be to get lost in this wilderness, and is thankful for the path.

The much-travelled naturalist Alexander Humboldt called the **Milseberg** the most beautiful mountain that he knew. And one can understand why; it rises sharply out of rolling landscape, and its wooded cliffs can be seen from far and wide towering over the valleys. According to legend, the giant Mils is buried under this mountain. Along the **Prehistoric Path**, display boards provide information about the lives of the Celts who inhabited the area more than 2,000 years ago. High up on the mountain they built the keeps in which they took refuge from their enemies.

On the western side of the mountain forestry is not practised and so it still maintains an almost primeval character. Climbers can test their skill on the crags of the **Kleiner Milseberg** or the Kälberhutstein. The chapel on the summit of the mountain is dedicated to St Gandolf.

Another famous mountain is the **Kreuzberg** (930 metres/3,051 ft) which

The Orangerie at Schloss Fulda.

rises above Bischofsheim in the Bavarian part of the Rhön. On its broad, bleak summit stands a 26-metre (85-ft) high wooden cross which is said to have been erected by the Irish monk St Kilian, the "Apostle of Franconia" in 668. Just below the western side of the summit is a Franciscan monastery founded in 1644. The Kreuzberg has always been an important place of pilgrimage, and to satisfy the thirst of penitent pilgrims the monks here have always brewed their thick, dark beer. There is a magnificent view from the summit: Franconia to the south, the High Rhön to the north, Thuringia to the east and the Vogelsberg away to the west.

The Merkers Cavern: The most magical place of all in the Rhön has only been accessible since reunification. It lies, as befits this mythical region, deep under the ground in Thuringia. For 10 years the miners at the potash mines in **Merkers** kept quiet, and it was only in the summer of 1991 that they revealed their discovery: a massive, glittering crystal cavern. Now it is possible to go down the mine and view this wonder of nature. However, you should book first as there is capacity for only 150 people a day. You are taken by monorail through the mine, which is like a huge underground city.

Since the opening of the border, environmentalists have been fighting for the preservation of the eastern Rhön's natural habitats. While the river Werra is salty from potash mining, the water in its tributaries is still clear, and the banks have not been regulated; they remain a paradise for kingfishers. When it was discovered a few years ago that there was still some life to be found in the brine of the Werra, West German scientists were amazed. After finding tiny crabs that otherwise only live above river estuaries between sweet and salt water, they experimented by introducing a stock of young flounders into the river. These sea fish actually survived and to the amazement of anglers made it downstream as far as Kassel and beyond.

The Fasanerie, a palace south of Fulda.

THE SPESSART

If you climb up one of Frankfurt's towers (Henninger Tower or the TV tower), on a clear day you'll get a splendid view of the hills of the Taunus in the north, the Odenwald in the south and the Spessart away to the east. The latter is a rolling upland region, whose national park is the largest in Europe. The Spessart hills rise between the river Kinzig in the north, the Sinn in the east and the Main, which flows around them in a U-shape in the south. The region is famed for its very special scenery of forested hills, gentle valleys and cosy hamlets in which the romance of 19th-century Germany remains largely intact. In times gone by the dense forest provided ideal cover for bandits and highwaymen, and travellers always crossed the region as quickly as possible for fear of being held up and forced to hand over their loot, or worse.

No such worries for the traveller of today, however. The first port of call after leaving Frankfurt along the Kinzig Valley is **Gelnhausen**, some 40 km (25 miles) east of the Main metropolis. Here are the remains of the **Imperial Palace** commissioned by Emperor Frederick Barbarossa. This was an important junction of routes running through his empire, and in 1170 he united the three settlements in the area to create the "imperial city" of Gelnhausen. The first imperial Diet was held here in 1180 and the town maintained its strategic importance all through the Middle Ages.

The route continues to the east to **Wächtersbach**, which has retained the magic of a small royal town nestled between the national parks of the Vogelsberg and the Spessart. As in many other towns on the route, the road is lined by medieval half-timbered houses.

The health resort of **Bad Orb**, nestling in the hills of the Orb Valley to the south, is a tranquil place. Salt was mined here until the turn of the century, but today the economic mainstay of this town of 8,000 people is the visitors recovering from illness and the rigours of everyday life, who between treading water and gymnastics and other healthy activities stroll around the old town and, when the walking gets too much, then recover in one of the many cafés or restaurants.

Visitors not content to spend their afternoon indulging in coffee and cake might attempt an ascent of one of the surrounding hills like the Hühnerberg (340 metres/1,115 ft) or the Grosse Kuppe (410 metres/1,345 ft). Suitably exhausted, they will probably then head for one of the town's many wine bars; Bad Orb lies on the **Franconian Wine Road**, and Franconian wine in its distinctive *boxbeutel* bottles is well-worth tasting. Fitter mortals may try staggering up the Horst (510 metres/1,673 ft), the Mark Berg (516 metres/1,692 ft) or the even higher Schwarzer Berg (black mountain), but will probably be frustrated by groups of screaming children racing past them to the top.

The visitor touring the area by car will not be aware of the trials and tribulations of the town's recuperating guests. As he speeds up and out of town and then along the Spessart Hohenstrasse (high road) to enter the dark spruce forest and descend into the Jossgrund, he is much more likely to reflect on how much darker this forest must have been before a hurricane called "Wibke" flattened many of the trees when it passed through here a few years ago.

One can enter the Spessart hills either from Bad Orb or by first travelling along the motorway further towards the east, past the idyllic spa of Bad Soden and on to **Steinau**, a small romantic town at the heart of the picturesque "Bergwinkel" (mountain nook) on the northern flanks of the Spessart. This is where, in the old **Amtshaus**, the brothers Grimm, Jakob and Wilhelm, spent their childhood. Visitors to Steinau should make a point of seeing the **Teufelshöhle** (devil's cave) a short distance to the north. **Schlüchtern**, 8 km (5 miles) further on, is an old

monastery town nestled in the rolling hills. The **Bergwinkel Museum** recalls the life and works of the Grimm brothers as well as Ulrich von Hutten (1488–1523), the famous humanist who wrote satires and pitched himself against the Pope; he fought all his life for a strong and united German empire free from foreign and church domination.

The North Hessian National Park: From Schlüchtern you can head south to join the Spessart Hohenstrasse coming from Bad Orb, descending to the east into the picturesque **Jossgrund Valley** through which the Jossa flows on its way to meet the River Sinn, the eastern boundary of the northern Spessart. The Sinn flows through the **Sinngrund Valley**, past the villages of Oberzell, Sterbfritz, Mottgers, Zeitlofs, Altengronau, Jossa, Obersinn, Mittelsinn, Burgsinn and on to Aura im Sinngrund. Every bit as delightful as the names is the landscape through which the river passes. And when you see a freight train rolling across the viaduct on its way from **Summer in Spessart.**

Gemünden to Schlüchtern, you may get the feeling of not being in the real world, but instead in the perfectly idyllic landscape of some model railway with all that that might include; neat half-timbered houses, village greens, church spires and watermills.

There is nothing better than to while away the afternoon on the banks of the Sinn between Altengronau and Zeitlofs, rod in hand waiting for the trout to bite. And even if one doesn't, because the summer heat also makes the fish feel lazy, then you can simply wander through the woods and see if all those bilberry gatherers have missed any. Or, if it is autumn, then you can go searching for mushrooms; horn of plenty under the beech, golden boletus under the larch, chanterelle in the mixed woodland. The Spessart is a paradise for nature lovers.

And for those who have worked up enough appetite, there are also a great many country pubs where you can get wild boar stew or leg of venison, real

specialities when served with homemade potato dumplings, red cabbage and cranberries. If you are looking for the loneliness of the forest, then you can still find it in the Spessart. The little hamlets and villages tucked away in the valleys are separated by expansive areas of forest: hiking trails lead you to little inns solitarily perched on the rounded summits.

Here and there you'll find some old forts and castles such as **Reinau Castle**, **Ramholz Castle** and **Brandenstein Castle** near Schlüchtern, the ruins of **Steckelsburg Castle** near Sterbfritz, the moated castle, the new castle or the **Fronhofschlösschen** in Obersinn, or **Rieneck Castle** in Rieneck. And between them is forest and more forest.

Travelling down the River Sinn, you cross from the Hessian part of the Spessart into the Franconian part. The Sinn meets the river Saale immediately to the north of **Gemünden**. Between the two rivers there is an attractive campsite with a swimming pool and facilities to

hire boats. If you're thinking of visiting the area on a weekend, then book a place for your tent or caravan in advance.

From here, the river then flows under the bridges of the town into the River Main, and this short stretch of water provides the opportunity for shooting the rapids by kayak or Canadian canoe. If you have the energy you can trek up to the castle keep of **Scherenburg** or further on to the ruin of the **Slorburg**; or else you can simply take in the atmosphere of the pedestrian precinct by sitting in one of the many cafés and waiting for the brass band to start playing in the marquee down on the riverbank, calling locals and visitors alike to fried sausage and beer.

The Main Spessart: The Spessart is enclosed to the west, the south and also partly to the east by the River Main. If you've seen the Main further downstream, where it transports all of Frankfurt's industrial waste and that between Höchst and Mainz into the Rhine, then you'll hardly recognise the river as it flows its serpentine course around the Spessart. Its waters are still relatively clean and tranquil here, although it has been regulated for transport, and every half hour or so a barge slides past, its wash lapping against the banks of the river. Barges aside, it is the ducks and swans and fish and mosquitos that share this peaceful idyll with the campers, anglers and canoeists.

To the south of Gemünden is the town of **Lohr**. The electoral castle contains the **Spessart Museum** where the visitor can find out more about the arts and crafts of the region, including the furniture typical to the Spessart. Further to the south, **Rothenfels Castle** towers 224 metres (735 ft) above the river. The earthworks, the dungeon and the lower storey of the castle date from the 12th and 13th centuries. Beyond lies the town of **Marktheidenfeld**, which has an attractive market square surrounded by pretty half-timbered houses.

Continue southwards along the meandering course of the Main to **Wert-**

Travelling craftsman offers his services.

heim, the old Franconian town at the confluence of the Tauber and Main rivers. The Main-Franconian character of the town is determined by its narrow alleys and the pointed gables of the buildings around the marketplace, particularly the **Haus zu den Vier Gekrönten** ("house of the four crowned heads"). From the top of the castle keep is a wonderful view of the Main valley.

Other attractive settlements on this stretch of the river include Faulbach and Hasloch. **Henneburg Castle** in **Stadtprotzelten** is a fascinating old ruin dating back almost 1,000 years. It's your typical knight's castle; a great place to explore and climb up the towers and peer into the underground passages.

Those not so keen on these kinds of activities, and who prefer wine to water, are strongly advised to head for **Miltenberg**, one of the best-preserved medieval towns to be found anywhere, with quaint alleyways and picturesque half-timbered houses. The perfect architectural ensemble is completed by a fountain in the middle, the former **wine cellars** dating from 1541, which now houses an interesting local museum, the famous tavern **Zur Gülden Cron** dating from 1623 and the **Weinhaus am Altenmarkt**. Another famous tavern is the **Gastof Zum Riesen,** reputed to be the oldest preserved inn in the whole of Germany, having been established as far back as 1590. The town itself is dominated by its old **Castle** built in 1210, and other sights of interest include Löwenstein Castle and Engelberg Monastery.

At Miltenberg you leave the Main and cross the Spessart, following the road to Grossheubach and then via Eschau and Hobbach to the little town of **Mespelbrunn**. Before the town gates, in a clearing in the forest, stands the handsome moated **Mespelbrunn Castle**. Completed in 1564 in Renaissance style, it remains the property of the family of the counts of Ingelheim. The interior of the castle is preserved in its original state.

Ideal mountain bike country.

ODENWALD, HEIDELBERG AND THE BERGSTRASSE

If you want to go in search of the authentic romantic Germany, then head south of Frankfurt towards Heidelberg. To the east, the motorway is accompanied by a low range of hills, just high enough to be called mountains. The range is partially forested and crowned by castles and fortresses, and well worth closer inspection.

The Bergstrasse: Even the Romans realised that travelling was easy along the foot of this range of hills. It is they who gave the *Via Strata Montana*, the Bergstrasse (mountain road), its name. A fertile loess soil and a mild climate (the spring starts earlier here than anywhere else in Germany) together allow fruit to flourish along the Bergstrasse. Apricots, peaches, nuts and almonds are harvested in vast quantities. But the main attraction of the Bergstrasse is not the early blossoming of the fruit; nor is it the numerous castle ruins on the hilltops; no, it is the wine that draws people here. On this western slope, the soil warms up quickly enough to give the Riesling, Müller Thurgau and Ruländer grapes just the right Oechsle degree. Experts maintain that the wines are mild, balanced and full-bodied.

Such wine can be found, for example, in the wine pubs of **Bensheim**, a distinctly medieval town of 33,000 inhabitants. If, in addition to admiring the two churches from the 15th and 17th century, you wish to see a real castle, you only have to go up the **Schönberg hill** with its castle of the same name, or to the district of **Auerbach**. Practically every hilltop in this part of the world is crowned by a castle or at least a ruin. The one near Heppenheim is called the **Starkenburg**.

Farther to the south, **Weinheim** (pop. 42,000) lies at the foot of the 347-metre (1,138-ft) high **Saukopf** (Pig's Head). This is a good place for wine and has the added attraction of well-preserved half-timbered houses huddled around its 16th-century town hall. Some sections of the old town wall have also been preserved. Opposite the Saukopf, **Wachenburg Castle** still stands sentinel over the town.

Further destinations for those who want to walk a bit between wine tasting include **Strahlenburg Castle** near Schriesheim, **Alsbach Castle** and **Heiligenberg Castle** near Jugenheim and the ruins of **Frankenstein Castle** near Pfungstadt. The latter used to be the venue for hallowe'en parties – until the practice became too spooky for the locals. The quality of the wine pubs below the castle hill goes without saying; just follow the German hikers' code: "mountains from below, churches from the outside and pubs from the inside."

The Odenwald: The lovely area of highlands between the Rhine, Main and Neckar rivers is both romantic and easy to reach from Frankfurt. Travelling through the Odenwald by way of the Nibelungenstrasse or the Siegfriedstrasse, contrary to what these names

Preceding pages: Otzberg Castle in the Odenwald. **Left**, the old town of Heidelberg. **Right**, the entrance to Heidelberg Castle.

might infer, you will not be confronted by any bombastic Wagnerian overtures. There are no dark forests here, but green woods and blooming meadows where cows contentedly graze in the sun. This is the Germany of Hansel and Gretel; the Germany straight out of *Grimms' Fairytales.*

According to legend, the Nibelungs came here to hunt. The Odenwald lay right in front of their door. It was in Worms on the left bank of the Rhine that the kings of Burgundy resided until the invasion of the Huns in 437. And when their indulgent feasting left nothing more on the table, all they had to do was cross the river and go hunting deer or stag, wild boar and other game. To follow the trail of the Nibelungs, take the *autobahn* past Darmstadt to **Lorsch** and from there follow either the **Nibelungenstrasse** via Bensheim or the **Siegfriedstrasse** via Heppenheim into the Odenwald. The region can also be reached more quickly by driving in a southeasterly direction from Frankfurt along the B45 through Dietzenbach, Dieburg and Gross-Umstadt.

The first castle is in Breuberg, just before the spa town of **Bad König**. The visitor should have a break at **Michelstadt**, and stroll around the narrow cobblestone alleys and the completely intact **Marketplace** with its half-timbered town hall dating from 1484; the fountain in the market place dates from 1541, and the **Church of St Michael and St Kilian** was built between 1461 and 1507. Also worth visiting is the **Odenwald Museum** with artefacts from Celtic and Roman times.

The quickest way from Michelstadt to the Neckar Valley and Heidelberg is to continue due south down the B45 to Eberbach.

If you have more time, turn east along the Nibelungenstrasse to **Amorbach**, a town famous for its 8th-century **monastery**. The monastery church, originally built in the Romanesque style and then rebuilt in Baroque between 1742 and 1747, is a unique example of German

Wahlen in the Odenwald.

236

rococo. The church still contains the wrought-iron trellis that separated the monks from the laymen; and the organ – which, with no less than 3,000 pipes, is the second largest Baroque organ in Germany.

One can also head further east to **Walldürn** with its pilgrimage Church of the Sacred Blood and an interesting Ivory Museum. Just to the east are the remains of a **Roman fort**, which formed part of the *limes*, the string of fortifications that the Romans built to protect their empire from the marauding Germanii.

Elves and forests, castles and palaces, caves and churches, streams and meadows: in short, the Odenwald Romanticism was what inspired Wolfram von Eschenbach to write his *Parzival* in the **Wildenburg Castle** to the south of Walldürn, of which only ruins now remain. *Parzival* provided the basis for Wagner's libretto *Parsifal*.

Another attractive route from Amorbach is the Siegfriedstrasse which leads

back towards the west. From **Kailbach** there is an attractive detour southwards to **Gaimühle** and **Antonslust** and the 626-metre (2,053-ft) high **Katzenbuckel** hill. From there one can follow the idyllic **Sensbach Valley** and rejoin the Siegfriedstrasse at Hesseneck. From the **Marbach Dam**, the Siegfriedstrasse leads westwards to Fürth back to the real Odenwald myth, the *Nibelungenlied*; it is said that this was the place where Hagen finally did away with Siegfried.

Even if you head straight down the B45, you should at least stop in **Erbach** for a quick look at the Renaissance and Baroque palace with its lordly weapons' collection, as well as the **German Ivory Museum** which recalls the fact that, until elephants were put on the list of endangered species, local Odenwald craftsmen busily chiselled away at ivory sculptures.

The beautiful Neckar Valley is reached at the town of **Eberbach** with the ruins of Eberbach Castle, which was

Fine grapes grow on the Bergstrasse.

built between the 11th and 13th centuries and used to be the largest fortress of the Hohenstaufen emperors.

The road which follows the Neckar is known as the Burgenstrasse (castle road), and passes through one of the most beautiful of all German river landscapes. To the east, it leads past such impressive bastions as the 13th-century **Zwingenberg Castle** and **Hornberg Castle** near Mosbach; the latter was the property of Götz von Berlichingen (1480–1582), who is immortalised in Goethe's drama of the same name. A museum in the tower is dedicated to the heroic deeds of this intrepid knight.

Heidelberg: Nestling against the southern slopes of the Odenwald forest which drops down to the River Neckar and dominated by its famous castle, the city of Heidelberg retains the same beauty it has always had.

The first people who came here did so about half a million years ago; at least that is the age of the jaw bone of *homo heidelbergiensis* – the oldest human bone ever discovered in Europe – which was dug up in the vicinity. Much later came the Celts; they were followed by the Romans who constructed a fort. The city was first officially documented as "Heidelberch" in 1196; from 1214 it was ruled for almost 500 years by the powerful counts of the Palatinate who controlled the Electoral College responsible for electing the German kings. And despite the vicissitudes of history, notably the Thirty Years' War and the Palatine War of Succession in the 17th century, Heidelberg bears the counts' unmistakable mark to this very day: the city's major landmarks are the Castle, the world-famous University and the Church of the Holy Ghost.

The first sight on the agenda of any visitor is likely to be the **Castle**. It can be reached either by walking up from the Kornmarkt at the eastern end of the old town, or by taking the funicular. It demonstrates a 400-year evolution of building styles, all the way from Gothic to **Flower market in Heidelberg.**

Baroque. The oldest part of the complex is the **Gothic House**, the residence of the Elector Ruprecht I. The northern part of the courtyard is occupied by the **Friedrichs Building** (built between 1601 and 1607), whose impressive Renaissance facade is decorated with the statues of German kings.

The facade of the **Ottheinrichs Building** (which now houses the German Apothecary Museum) on the eastern side is one of the best examples of German Renaissance architecture; with its composition of statues and ornamentation, it presents a picture of utter harmony. Any tour of the castle will also include the famous **Heidelberg Vat**, said to be the largest wine vat in the world. It was guarded by Perkeo, the court jester, who was known for his legendary thirst. It is said that he died after being persuaded to drink a cup of water rather than the wine to which he was accustomed.

Although much of its architecture is dominated by elegant Renaissance and Baroque buildings, the **Old City** is of Gothic origin and the medieval atmosphere is retained in the narrow lanes lined by slim houses. You should start exploring at the **University**. Founded in 1386 by Ruprecht I, it is the oldest in Germany. It lost much of its importance during the wars of the 17th century and only revived after its reinauguration by Karl Friedrich of Baden in 1805. Student life today does not quite compare to the riotous student days of yore. Until 1914 the former **Studentenkarzer** (student lock-up) in Augustinerstrasse served as a jail for students guilty of particularly indecorous behaviour in public. The walls of the cells are covered with humorous graffiti.

In the oldest part of the city around the **Marketplace** and the Kornmarkt, you can visit such traditional student pubs as **Zum Sepp'l** (Sepp's Place) and **Roter Ochsen** (The Red Cow). But there are also a large number of modern pubs, restaurants and cafés packed into the old quarter of town.

The late-Gothic **Church of the Holy Ghost**, the largest church in the Palatinate, stands to the north of the Kornmarkt. Its founder, Ruprecht III, lies buried within, and his tomb and the former Palatinate Library, pillaged by General Tilly during the Thirty Years' War, are worth closer inspection. The **Hotel Ritter** opposite had more luck and retains one of the most beautiful Renaissance facades in Germany. The adjacent former **Court Apothecary**, a Baroque building, is also well worth seeing.

The Old Bridge which crosses the Neckar at this point, is another of the city's symbols; Goethe considered it to be one of the wonders of the world, largely on account of the beautiful view it affords upstream of the **Benedictine Monastery of Neuburg**, and downstream of the valley gradually widening out into the Rhine Plain. As one looks back, the city is perfectly framed by the archway of the bridge gate. This is Germany at its most romantic.

Cobbled street in Heidelberg.

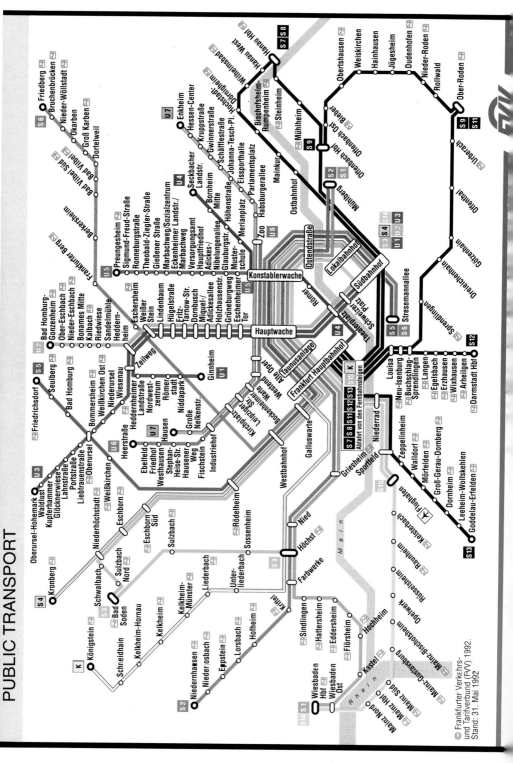

© Frankfurter Verkehrs-
und Tarifverbund (FVV) 1992.
Stand: 31. Mai 1992

TRAVEL TIPS

GETTING THERE

BY AIR

Frankfurt is continental Europe's key centre of trade and the money markets. Its central position in both Germany and Europe make it a major traffic junction; the airport is Europe's second-busiest after London Heathrow, catering for no fewer than 28 million passengers and 320,000 departures and arrivals each year.

Arriving at Rhein-Main Airport in Frankfurt is a fairly easy procedure. Regular scheduled airline connections exist between Frankfurt and a total of 216 other cities. The airport itself consists of 3 large terminals designated Terminals A, B and C and there is a subterranean railway station located in Terminal A. If you are in possession of a valid plane ticket it is possible to travel to or from the airport without additional charge on board one of the Lufthansa express trains. These expresses run to and from Düsseldorf, Cologne and Stuttgart (arrival A, Level C). New arrivals will also find train connections to the main railway station or into the city centre and Sachsenhausen via the S-Bahn (fast train) on Level C. The fast trains (Line S 15) depart every 20 minutes between 4.33am and 11.53pm; the last train leaves at 12.33am (subject to slight variation in accordance with the summer or winter timetables). The trip into the city centre takes about 10 minutes.

Although they also stop at the main railway station, Intercity Trains (passengers pay a 6 DM additional charge prior to boarding or 7 DM once on board) mainly serve transit connections leaving directly from the airport to all large cities in Germany, as well as, for instance, to and from Vienna, Zurich, Basle, Amsterdam, Paris, Luxembourg, Brussels, Copenhagen and Prague.

All car-rental agencies maintain counters on Level B, just below the main airport entrance (Arrival A) next to the German Federal Railways Ticket Office.

Avis, tel: 6902777
Airport Car, tel: 6902790
Eurorent, tel: 6905250
Hertz, tel: 6905011
Inter Rent, tel: 6905464
Sixt Budget, tel: 6905237

There is a taxi stop located at ground level by the airport's main entrance (Arrival A). The journey by taxi into the city centre takes about 15 minutes and costs between DM 30 and 35, depending on traffic conditions.

Local commuter bus connections operating within the Rhine-Main area from the area are as follows: Number 62 to and from Schwanheim and Kelsterbach, Number 68 to and from Zeppelinheim and Neu-Isenburg, Number 70 to the airport freight centre, Number 900 to and from Dietzenbach via Neu-Isenburg, Number 915 via the *autobahn* to and from Bad Homburg and Number 964 to and from Sprendlingen.

There are approximately 30 different shops housed in the airport which stock both practical necessities as well as luxury items. Most of these shops are open between 7am and 9pm (including Saturdays). Exchange offices stay open until 9pm. There's also a well-known disco called Dorian Gray which is open 10pm–4am during the week and until all hours of the morning on the weekends. The airport is also known for its sex shop and cinema.

RESERVATIONS

The main information services at the airport are:
Passenger Information, tel: 6903051
Parking Information, tel: 6906889
Reservations, tel: 230621

Flight tickets can be purchased directly at the following airline offices:
Air Canada, tel: 250131
Air France, tel: 6902625
Austrian Airlines, tel: 6905440
British Airways, tel: 250121
Delta Air Lines, tel: 668041
Lufthansa, tel: 6902111
Luxair, tel: 6902854
Malaysian Airlines, tel: 6905477
Middle East Airlines, tel: 6903321
South African Airways, tel: 6903925
Swissair, tel: 6903303

It is also possible to book a flight through the Iata-Service in any of the numerous travel agencies located throughout the city centre.

BY ROAD

Travelling to Frankfurt by motorway isn't exactly a pleasurable experience. The orbital motorway surrounding the city is not quite finished and its eventual completion is still a matter of controversy because the missing eastern segment would have to pass through a nature reserve.

The city can be looked upon as the eye of the needle with regards to western German north-south traffic. Accordingly, the Frankfurt North-West Intersection (Frankfurter Nordwest-Kreuz) and the Frankfurt Intersection (Frankfurter Kreuz) in the southwest are infamous for their frequent traffic jams. If at all possible, try to avoid driving in during the morning rush-hour and in the late afternoon on

THE COLOUR OF LIFE.

A holiday may last just a week or so, but the memories of those happy, colourful days will last forever, because together you and Kodak Ektachrome films will capture, as large as life, the wondrous sights, the breathtaking scenery and the magical moments. For you to relive over and over again.

The Kodak Ektachrome range of slide films offers a choice of light source, speed and colour rendition and features extremely fine grain, very high sharpness and high resolving power.

Take home the real colour of life with Kodak Ektachrome films.

LIKE THIS?

OR LIKE THIS?

A KODAK FUN PANORAMIC CAMERA BROADENS YOUR VIEW

The holiday you and your camera have been looking forward to all year; and a stunning panoramic view appears. "Fabulous", you think to yourself, "must take that one".

Unfortunately, your lens is just not wide enough. And three-in-a-row is a poor substitute.

That's when you take out your pocket-size, 'single use' Kodak Fun Panoramic Camera. A film and a camera, all in one, and it works miracles. You won't need to focus, you don't need special lenses. Just aim, click

and... it's all yours. The total pict▪

You take twelve panoran▪ pictures with one Kodak Fun Pa▪ ramic Camera. Then put the cam▪ in for developing and printing.

Each print is 25 by 9 centimet▪ Excellent depth of field. True Kodak Gold colours.

The Kodak Fun Panoramic Camera itself goes b▪ to the factory, to be recycled. So that others too can capture one of those spectacular phooooooooooootoooooooooooooos.

Sundays. If you're planning to leave the city on a Friday, it's wise to have left by 1pm; on the remaining days of the week it's a good idea to be out of the city by 3pm, before the afternoon/evening rush-hour commences. Unfortunately, you can be sure of additional delays and obstructions if it's raining or snowing. Along certain stretches of the motorway where 4 lanes are in operation there are traffic jam alert signals which recommend a specific speed for each separate lane. These speed recommendations really do aid in keeping traffic moving and should be heeded.

There are signs posted for Park and Ride car-parks with fast train and underground connections departing at regular intervals located at all *autobahn* exits (except at the "Messe" exit). During the times when trade fairs are held, the Rebstockgelände (it has its own exit; just follow the "Messe" signs) is available to trade fair visitors for parking.

Parking in the city itself can be a problem, particularly in the city centre, the Nordend and Westend, as well as in Sachsenhausen. This is not surprising when one considers that there is practically one car for every two inhabitants, added to which comes all the commuter, business and tourism traffic. For car drivers Frankfurt truly constitutes a realm of the unknown with its hundreds of one-way streets. Although parking spots are rare and intentionally so, there are sufficient multistorey parking garages situated throughout the city centre. Petrol stations are located along all arterials heading in the direction of the motorway. The following automobile associations will come to your aid in the case of a serious breakdown either on the motorway or in the city centre:

ACE: Wilhelm-Leuschner-Strasse 69-77. Tel: 235158 (Helpline: 232929)
ADAC: Schumannstrasse 4-6. Tel: 7430-0 (Helpline: 19211)
AvD: Lyoner Strasse 16. Tel: 6606300 (Helpline: 6606600)

BY RAIL

Frankfurt main station is a terminal, and therefore not all trains on the German north-south routes stop here; some go round the city. Be that as it may, Frankfurt remains the busiest passenger station in Europe, handling a total of 255,000 passengers and 1,640 departures every day. But it may be necessary if you arrive late at night to transfer at Mainz in the west, at Mannheim in the south and in Würzburg in the east when entering the city. A subterranean railway route for Intercity trains – similar to the one currently in operation at the airport – which would help to remedy the log-jam produced by an old-fashioned terminus, is being considered for some point in the future. Direct connections aboard Intercity trains (passengers pay a 6 DM additional charge prior to boarding or a 7 DM additional charge once on the train) and on Intercity Express trains (no additional charge), exist to all big cities in Germany as well as to and from Paris, Prague, Warsaw and Vienna.

The shops in the main railway station remain open until 10pm. There's also a food centre here called "MiB" ("Markt im Bahnhof") which contains a butcher's shop, bakery and a variety of good snackbars. The post office located on the first floor at the main entrance is open around the clock; on the ground floor there is a money machine which will accept the most common currencies.

Other rail connections (local fast train commuter traffic) within the Rhine-Main Region are found on the underground Level B, to and from Wiesbaden (S 1), Niedernhausen (S 2), Bad Soden (S 3), Kronberg (S 4), Friedrichsdorf (S 5), Friedberg (S 6) and Mainz via the airport (S 14). The fast trains operating along the regular lines travel to and from Darmstadt (S 12), Goddelau-Erfelden (S 13) and Königstein (Line K), as well as to and from Hanau (S 7 and S 8) and Rödermark (S 9) (the latter two via Offenbach).

Buses leave regularly for Prague, Athens, Istanbul, Barcelona, Paris and London from the bus station located at the southern exit of the main railway station.

RESERVATIONS

Tickets for the German Federal Railway System can be purchased in the city at any of the following DER (Deutsche Reisebüro) travel agencies (Eschersheimer Landstr. 25, tel: 15660; the main railway station, tel: 230911 and 236139; Hauptwache/Passage, tel: 291704; the airport, tel: 693071), as well as at the ticket counter in the main railway station. On journeys of 50 km (about 30 miles) or more it is possible to buy a ticket on board an Intercity or Intercity Express train for a small additional fee. For journeys of less than 50 km this surcharge is disproportionately expensive. When travelling within the Rhine-Main transport network you must in any case purchase your ticket before boarding the train. Otherwise, the "surcharge" may cost you 60 DM.

TRAVEL ESSENTIALS

VISAS & PASSPORTS

Members of other European Community countries are not required to have a visa for an intended stay of up to 3 months; different regulations apply to citizens of non-EC countries visiting Germany. To make sure you have accurate, up-to-date information concerning entry regulations, enquire at your local German embassy.

CUSTOMS

There are no restrictions on the import of currencies. You can also bring in any personal belongings as well as food for your own consumption. EC citizens can import (duty free) 300 cigarettes or 150 cigars or 400 gm tabacco; 1½ litres of wine; 750 gm of coffee beans; 75 gm of perfume and ³/₈ litres of toilet water.

TIME ZONE

Local time in Frankfurt during the winter months corresponds to Standard Central European Time. From April until September city clocks tick in accordance with Central European Daylight Savings Time. When it's 12 noon in Frankfurt (as well as in Paris, Rotterdam and Rome), then it's:
11am in London
8am in Buenos Aires
6am in New York and Montreal
4am in Denver
1am in Honolulu and Anchorage
12 midnight on the Midway Islands
1pm in Athens
2pm in Moscow
4pm in Karachi
9pm in Sydney

CLIMATE

Frankfurt enjoys a relatively temperate climate without excessively cold winters or unbearably hot summers. However snow in the winter and humid days during the summer are the rule rather than the exception. On average the temperature in Frankfurt is always 2°C warmer than it is in the surrounding countryside. Thus far there has been no danger of a smog-alert.

Average monthly temperatures (given in Celsius) are as follows: January: 0.9°; February: 2.3°; March: 5.3°; April: 9.4°; May: 13.9°; June: 17.3°; July: 18.8°; August: 18.1°; September: 14.6°; October: 9.7°; November: 5.0°; December: 1.6°.

Average monthly precipitation (given in millimetres): January: 16.8; February: 13.1; March: 14.4; April: 14.6; May: 15.0; June: 14.0; July: 12.7; August: 13.1; September: 10.7; October: 12.2; November: 16.7; December: 15.3

Average amount of sunshine (given in hours per month): January: 31.2; February: 64.3; March: 107.5; April: 178.6; May: 220.3; June: 205.5; July: 203.4; August: 205.7; September: 144.9; October: 76.6; November: 36.9; December: 27.2
Source: The German Weather Bureau

WHAT TO WEAR

During the winter bring warm clothing; the thermometer can drop to –10°C. In the summer when temperatures reach 30°C, minimal, lightweight clothing is suitable citywear. Although the city is not markedly fashion-conscious, the general atmosphere is decidedly one of liberality when it comes to accepting more unusual clothing styles.

BUSINESS HOURS

With the exception of a few shops located at the main railway station and airport, all others are generally open Monday–Friday 9am–6.30pm. On Thursdays many stores remain open in the city centre until 8.30pm. Business hours on Saturday are 9am–2pm. The first Saturday of each month is designated "Long Saturday". On this particular day shops are open until 4pm, and during the month prior to Christmas they open until 6pm every Saturday.

Many banks as well as the main post offices located in the railway station and airport maintain extended business hours. It is also possible to exchange money – for a slightly higher commission, of course – in hotels. The following are a list of places where you can exchange money or cash travellers or Eurocheques after regular business hours, on Sundays and holidays:
Bank für Gemeinwirtschaft, airport, Departure B, tel: 694025-27, Fax: 694648. Open daily 7am–9.30pm.
Commerzbank, airport, Arrival B, tel: 6979030. Open daily 7.15am–9pm.
Deutsche Bank, airport, Departure B, tel: 6903208/10. Open daily 7am–9.30pm.
Deutsche Verkehrs-Kredit-Bank, airport, Arrival B, tel: 6903506. Open daily 6am–11pm; main railway station (south side), tel: 2648201. Open daily 6.30am–10pm.
Dresdner Bank, airport, Departure A, tel: 6979044. Open daily 7am–9.30pm; airport Transit B, tel: 6979043. Open daily 7am–9.30pm.

GETTING ACQUAINTED

GEOGRAPHY

Precisely stated, Frankfurt is situated at a longitude of 50° 06' 42.5" north and at a latitude of 8° 41.94" east. Expressed less exactly, the city lies in the middle of Germany in the German state of Hessen. It is located at about the same degree of latitude as Paris and Prague. The highest point in Frankfurt at 212 metres (about 710 ft) above sea level is the Berger Warte in Seckbach; the lowest point is the Mainwiesen (Main Meadow) between Frankfurt-Sindlingen and Okriftel at 88 metres (295 ft) above sea level. The city encompasses a total surface area of about 249 sq. km (96 sq. miles) with the distance from east to west measuring 23.4 km and that from north to south 23.3 km (about 14.5 miles). Nevertheless, the city limits are mostly an administrative technicality. The fact of the matter is that Frankfurt is the centre of the larger Rhine-Main Region which extends east-west from Wiesbaden to Hanau and north-south from the Taunus to Darmstadt.

THE MODERN CITY

In 1861 the city had a total of 72,000 inhabitants; in 1914 this number rose to nearly 450,000. Through the incorporation of outlying towns, Frankfurt expanded to the east in 1877, to the west in 1895, to the south in 1900 and to the north in 1914. In 1914 the university was established and in 1936 the Rhein-Main Airport was opened. By the year 1933 the population of Frankfurt had reached 550,000. The tyranny of the National Socialist Party lead to the persecution of political opponents, the extermination of the Jewish community and the destruction of the old part of the city. However, soon after 1945 Frankfurt was again on its way to becoming a significant and vital city of international trade. In the 1949 election carried out to decide which city would become the capital of Germany, Bonn just barely won over Frankfurt. The first segment of the city's underground system was completed in 1968 and the Old Opera House (Alte Oper) was reopened in 1981. As the centre of German high-finance, the city of Frankfurt presents a constantly and rapidly changing physical profile. Today the population stands at 635,000, with 1.5 million in the greater Frankfurt region.

RELIGION

There are a total of 137 churches in Frankfurt including a countless number of independent religious congregations. There's even a Koran school located in the red-light district by the railway station. Due to the high percentage of foreigners living in this traditionally liberal city, nearly all world religions are represented. The Protestant Church with 76 congregations and 203,000 members is about as well-represented as the Catholic Church with its 56 congregations and 210,000 members. The Jewish tradition, in a congregation of 4,894 members, and the Islamic religion are also quite visibly present.

Frankfurt Cathedral (Catholic) once served as the site for imperial coronations beginning in the year 1152 and Frankfurt was never a diocesan town; moreover, as early as 1848 St Paul's Church (Protestant) relinquished its purely religious role to take on more worldly tasks (it became the seat of the first German Parliament); all these pointers highlight Frankfurt's traditionally rather liberal attitude. St Katherine's Church (located at the Hauptwache) has long served as the stage of the Frank Moritz Theatre Ensemble. (The further use of the church in such secular ways is currently being debated in church circles.)

Religious services (recorded message) and other announcements. Tel: 1157
Spiritual Welfare (24-hours a day), Protestant, tel: 11101; Catholic, tel: 11102
Anglican Church, Sebastian-Ritz-Strasse 22. Tel: 550184
Greek Orthodox Church, Solmsstrasse 1. Tel: 777421
Russian Orthodox Church, Am Industriehof 18. Tel: 7894140
Mennonite Congregation, Eysseneckstrasse 54. Tel: 590228
Jewish Congregation, Westendstrasse 43. Tel: 740721
Christian-Islamic Documentation Centre, Guiolett-strasse 35. Tel: 726491

COMMUNICATIONS

POSTAL SERVICES

Main Post Office, on the Zeil near the Hauptwache (telefax and telex services). Open Monday–Friday 8am–6pm, Saturday 8am–noon. After-hours service, tel: 211-0. Open 6am–8pm Monday–Friday noon–6pm, Saturday and Sunday noon–4pm.

Post Office in the **main railway station** (located on the first floor), tel: 2615113/22. Open 24 hours per day. Services offered after 6pm: regular letter service, giro transfer order via telegram, Eurocheque and Post Office Savings Bank services; no parcel service offered at this time.

Airport Post Office, Departure B. Tel: 6056275. Open daily 6am–10pm (giro transfer order via telegram and telex services offered). Transit office: Monday–Saturday 7am–9pm, Sundays and holidays 8am–4.30pm.

NEWSPAPERS & MAGAZINES

Frankfurt's daily newspapers make a point of presenting articles of national interest. Accordingly, the subtitle of the largest German daily – second in popularity only to the widely-distributed tabloid paper *Bildzeitung* – is "Zeitung für Deutschland" ("Newspaper for Germany"), the *Frankfurter Allgemeine Zeitung* (FAZ), (Hellerhofstrasse 2-8), which has the reputation of being simultaneously staunchly liberal and nobly conservative. Despite the fact that the commentaries on the front page tend to be rather basic and straightforward, the feature section is one of the very best in the entire country. The sports section is generally held in high esteem and the financial pages are pretty much mandatory reading for both supporters and opponents of the market economy. Supplements like "Nature and Science", "Travel", and "Technology and Motors" are qualitatively good, which is to say that is they are written to appeal to a wide variety of readers rather than to an exclusive group of experts.

On Fridays the FAZ Magazine appears along with the regular newspaper. The section dealing with local matters is rather neutral in its overall tone, presents a clear overview of the events of the day and is only distributed within the Rhine-Main Region. On Sundays – also only in the Rhine-Main Region – the FAZ Sunday edition is published in 4-colour splendour. This issue includes articles concerning

current politics, a TV guide, culture and sports sections, all of which are neither particularly exciting nor inspiring; but – recently on the market – already an institution.

Although it isn't quite as clear in its presentation as the FAZ, the *Frankfurter Rundschau* (FR) is also an institution and focuses primarily on left-wing-liberal issues and events throughout the country. The political section emphasises issues of social and international importance. The paper is popular due to its up-to-date reporting (the *Frankfurter Rundschau am Abend* appears at noon with the very latest news printed on its front page followed by reports from the previous day).

The *Frankfurter Neue Press* is the smallest of the daily papers. It is not available nationwide, nor is its editorial emphasis that of a cosmopolitan city newspaper's. However, a definite advantage of the *Frankfurter Neue Press* is that it seems to reduce the city to much more manageable and less overwhelming proportions.

The *Bild-Frankfurt* – like all tabloid papers everywhere – is very popular. The newspaper regularly presents special, critical consumer reports, for example concerning the overall quality of hospitals located in Frankfurt or the conditions of public swimming pools in the city.

The city magazine *PflasterStrand*, published by ex-revolutionary Daniel Cohn-Bendit, was legendary as a nationally approved source of the opinions of the left-wing scene. In 1990 it was transformed under the editorship of Matthias Horx into a slick magazine and in the wake of increased competition merged with the illustrated *Auftritt* to become *Journal Frankfurt*. In its present form the magazine is issued every 14 days and contains the most up-to-date calendar of events happening within the city. Every year in June the *Journal Frankfurt* publishes the gastronomic guide *Frankfurt Geht Aus!* ("Frankfurt Goes Out!"), and in October the shopping guide *Frankfurt Kauft Ein!* ("Frankfurt Goes Shopping!"); both also available in English.

The *andere Zeitung* (az) is primarily popular in the districts and environs of Frankfurt, appears every four weeks and is oriented decidedly towards the left-wing scene.

The city magazine *Prinz Frankfurt* corresponds to the *Bild-Zeitung*. Cover stories that appear in the different monthly editions of *Prinz* are identical throughout the country and are intended for a fairly youthful audience. The more positive aspects of the publication are found in the city tests, for instance which discos, which parks, or which saunas are the best. In addition to these, there are also 2 other magazines published monthly which can be picked up for free at various pubs and cafés: the *Skyline* is a purely commercial publication financed by advertising and the *Strandgut* is a must for all avid cinema-goers. In this latter magazine you'll find the programmes of all the city cinemas.

THE KODAK GOLD GUIDE TO BETTER PICTURES.

Good photography is not difficult. Use these practical hints and Kodak Gold II Film: then notice the improvement.

Move in close. Get close enough to capture only the important elements.

Frame your Pictures. Look out for natural frames such as archways or tree branches to add an interesting foreground. Frames help create a sensation of depth and direct attention into the picture.

One centre of interest. Ensure you have one focus of interest and avoid distracting features that can confuse the viewer.

Use leading lines. Leading lines direct attention to your subject i.e. – a stream, a fence, a pathway; or the less obvious such as light beams or shadows.

Maintain activity. Pictures are more appealing if the subject is involved in some natural action.

Keep within the flash range. Ensure subject is within flash range for your camera (generally 4 metres). With groups make sure everyone is the same distance from the camera to receive the same amount of light.

Check the light direction. People tend to squint in bright direct light. Light from the side creates highlights and shadows that reveal texture and help to show the shapes of the subject. If shooting into direct sunlight fill-in flash can be effective to light the subject from the front.

CHOOSING YOUR KODAK GOLD II FILM.

Choosing the correct speed of colour print film for the type of photographs you will be taking is essential to achieve the best colourful results.

Basically the more intricate your needs in terms of capturing speed or low-light situations the higher speed film you require.

Kodak Gold II 100. Use in bright outdoor light or indoors with electronic flash. Fine grain, ideal for enlargements and close-ups. Ideal for beaches, snow scenes and posed shots.

Kodak Gold II 200. A multipurpose film for general lighting conditions and slow to moderate action. Recommended for automatic 35mm cameras. Ideal for walks, bike rides and parties.

Kodak Gold II 400. Provides the best colour accuracy as well as the richest, most saturated colours of any 400 speed film. Outstanding flash-taking capabilities for low-light and fast-action situations; excellent exposure latitude. Ideal for outdoor or well-lit indoor sports, stage shows or sunsets.

A P A
INSIGHT
GUIDES

ARE Going Places:

INSIGHT
pocket
GUIDES

Ci VEDREMO·
PRESTO!

See You Soon! In Italy

Daily News (recorded message), tel: 1165
News for the Blind (recorded message), tel: 1155
There are over 13 public libraries and numerous archives located in Frankfurt. Amongst them are the City Archive, the Federal Archive, the Albert Schweizer Archive, the Hindemith Archive, the Historical Archive of the German Book Trade, the Schopenhauer Archive, the Chaplin Archive and the Manskopfsche Collection.

EMERGENCIES

Important telephone numbers:

Emergency Legal Services in Criminal Matters, tel: 283083
Medical, Dental and Veterinary Emergency Services and chemists on emergency duty, tel: 11500 (for a recorded message)
Transportation for Physically Disabled Persons, tel: 439665
Medical and Meteorological Information – Pollen Prediction, tel: 11601
Fire Brigade, Ambulance, First Aid, tel: 112
Lost and Found, tel: 7500-2403
Johannite Accident Aid, tel: 543002
Hospital (the University Clinic), tel: 6301-1
Maltese Emergency Services, tel: 676790, 410454, 452200
Police Emergency, tel: 110
Helicopter Rescue Service, tel: 441033
Red Cross, tel: 7191910, 233364
Credit Card Loss or Theft, tel: 740987
Locksmith Service (around the clock), tel: 626262, 545454, 565652
Emergency Dental Aid, tel: 6607271

GETTING AROUND

INFORMATION CENTRES

The Frankfurt Tourist Information Office offers a variety of diverse services tailored to fit the needs of specific tourist groups, whether they be shopping enthusiasts from Japan (Tourist Board Information Office, tel: 21233677), American businessmen with only enough time for a brief sightseeing tour (City-Tours, tel: 253253), visitors who intend to stay in the city for a longer period of time (Tourist Information Office/Room Reservations, Kaiserstrasse 52, tel: 21238800, Fax: 21237880), trade fair and congress participants (Congress Service, tel: 21234137), business employees taking part in their company's incentive programme (Incentives, tel: 21238551), or those who have just recently moved to the city (Römertelefon, tel: 21234000/4100).

The tourist information office located in the main railway station directly across from Platform 23 may be of service to visitors who have just arrived in Frankfurt. Open Monday–Saturday 8am–10pm (1 November–31 March 8am–9pm), Sundays and holidays 9.30am–8pm, tel: 21238849/51. There is also a tourist information office located in the airport, Arrival A. Open daily 7am–10pm, tel: 693153. Yet another tourist information office is situated at a place where all visitors to the city manage to wander by sooner or later, the Römer; Am Römerberg 27. Open Monday–Friday 9am–7pm, Saturday and Sunday 9.30am–6pm, tel: 21238708/9. Information useful to travellers either departing from Frankfurt or for those continuing further is available at the headquarters of the German Tourist Board, Beethovenstrasse 69. Tel: 75720, Fax: 751903.

PUBLIC TRANSPORT

Frankfurt and its environs are served by a public transport system (FVV) with a total of 124 lines and 1,262 stops. The system includes the S-bahn (fast suburban trains), the U-bahn (underground), trams and buses. If you arrive at the airport, then take the S-bahn line 14 or 15 to the city centre. The most important stops here are the main station, the Hauptwache (at the beginning of the Zeil shopping street) and the Konstablerwache at the end of the Zeil. Lokalbahnhof is the stop for the apple wine district of Alt-Sachsenhausen on the south bank of the river, or you can take the number 36 bus. The

Römer can be reached from the main station or the Konstablerwache via the U 4. Six further U-bahn lines connect the city with the districts in the south (Sachsenhausen) and the north, via lines U 1, 2 and 3 (Ginnheim, Gonzenheim, Bad Homburg and Hohemark). In an west-east direction, lines U 6 and U 7 link Hausen with Bergen-Enkheim, calling at Bockenheim, Alte Oper, Konstablerwache and Zoo. Line U 5 runs from the Konstablerwache via the Nordend to Preungesheim.

Tickets for the FVV can be obtained from blue ticket machines, and presently cost DM 1.90 for adults (in the peak periods 7–8.30am and late afternoons 4–6.30pm DM 2.60). Tourists are well advised to take advantage of the "Tageskarte" (cheap day ticket); for DM 5 you can travel as often as you like. The whole of the city area falls within the "yellow zone", but it is necessary to pay more if you want to travel beyond the city limits (to Hanau in the east, Darmstadt in the south, Friedberg in the north and Mainz/Wiesbaden in the west. Businessmen should note that the Tourist Board now offers a special Congress Ticket for congresses and meetings. Organisers and hotels can order FVV tickets for their visitors at considerable savings. These tickets are convenient and time-saving as they are supplied in advance along with other meeting documents. Handling and billing are done directly between the tourist board and the organiser.

Night buses are in service on Fridays and Saturdays, and run every hour after 2am from Konstablerwache: N1 from Nordweststadt to Sachsenhausen, N2 from Preungesheim to Rödelsheim, N3 from Fechenheim to Schwanheim, N4 from Enkheim to Höchst. Further information as well as timetables can be obtained from the FVV main office in the B level of the Hauptwache, tel: 2694-0.

TAXIS

Short wave radio equipped taxis operate 24 hours a day. Tel: 250001, 230033 or 545011. There is no pick up charge, just a flat rate DM 3.60 which applies day or night. Every kilometre costs DM 2.05 and waiting time DM 36 per hour. The price on the meter is the valid price, regardless of how many passengers or how many pieces of baggage are being transported. All major credit cards are accepted. Further information can be obtained from the Taxivereinigung Frankfurt e.V., Schönstrasse 22. Tel: 232568 or 253534.

Visitors should bear in mind that getting a taxi may prove to be quite difficult during a trade fair. After a fair closes for the day the competition for cabs is intense. In general, plan on having to wait at least 20 minutes. There are taxi stands at all prominent places in the city centre.

ORIENTATION

Frankfurt is surrounded by beautiful hilly and forested scenery: the Rheingau, Taunus, Vogelsberg, Spessart and Odenwald. The best view of the city and its environs can be seen from the Television Tower in Ginnheim; at 331 metres (1,086 ft) it is the tallest building in Western Europe. The high-speed lift takes you to the viewing lounge at 222 metres (728 ft), where there are panorama windows with monitors to help you with orientation. The multi-media "Frankfurt Experience" starts every half hour and relates the development of the city with the aid of lasers, wind machines and the like. The panorama lounge is open daily 10am–6pm and costs DM 7. The Sky Fantasy discotheque takes place here on Wednesdays, Fridays and Saturdays. The exclusive restaurant Windows is to be found one floor below, at a height of 218 metres (715 ft). It is an ideal place for business dinners and is open Tuesday–Saturday 7pm. Booking a table in advance is advisable; tel: 533077.

Further landmarks offering a good view of Frankfurt are the tower of the Cathedral, the Goethe Tower which dominates the city forest above Sachsenhausen, and the tower of the Henninger Brewery in Sachsenhausen itself. At a height of 120 metres (394 ft) there is a Museum of Brewing as well as a restaurant serving Frankfurt specialities.

An easy 2-hour stroll will give you a good first impression of the city. Begin at the Alte Oper, which before its reopening as a concert and congress centre in 1981, was referred to as "Germany's most beautiful ruin". From there the route follows the Fressgass, Frankfurt's gourmet mile. Turn into Börsenstrasse, and you'll come to the largest and most important stock exchange in Germany, which has been operating since 1585, and located at this site since 1879. The visitor's gallery is open Monday–Friday 11.30am–1.30pm.

If you then follow Schillerstrasse, you'll come to the Hauptwache, the "heart of the city". The building is a reconstruction of the original guard house and a café is now housed within. Opposite is the Church of St Katherine (1678–1681) in which the city's most famous son, Goethe, was baptised. To the right of the church are signs to the Goethe House and Goethe Museum (Grosser Hirschgraben 23) in which the poet spent his childhood and youth until 1775. Cross the nearby Berlinerstrasse to arrive at the famous Paulskirche (1789–1833), which in 1848–49 was the seat of the German National Assembly, the first German parliament.

Diagonally across to the right is the town hall, the Römer, which was acquired by the city in 1405 and subsequently expanded. The Tourist Information Office is on the corner. The Fountain of Justice in front of the Römer was erected in 1611. On the facade of the Römer are the statues of the four emperors to be crowned in Frankfurt. The houses of the Römer–Zeile opposite were all destroyed in World War II, but were subsequently reconstructed.

In the Schwarzer Stern house on the left of the Römer there is a café of the same name. Further to the left is the City Historical Museum and the Apple Wine Museum, and the Kunsthalle Schirn art gallery behind, with changing international exhibitions. In front of the Schirn are the Historical Gardens, with remains of some of the city's Roman walls as well as the foundations of a Royal Hall dating from the Carolingian period (9th century AD). Behind the Schirn is a new row of impressive "post-modern" buildings. To the east is the Cathedral, in which no less than 36 coronations took place. Back to the left on the Berliner Strasse is the new Museum of Modern Art designed by Hans Hollein, which because of its shape is known locally as "the piece of tart".

TOURS

It is also possible to board a bus for tours around the city. In the summer (1 March–31 October) the Panoramabus leaves the Tourist Information Office at the Römer every day at 10am and, May–September, again at 2pm. Both these services can be joined 15 minutes later at the main railway station. The tour lasts 2½ hours, is available in English and German and costs DM 28.

For visitors who wish to tour the city on their own, the Tourist Information Office provides Walkmans for a deposit of DM 50 together with cassettes in English, German or Japanese costing DM 12.

Three special tours costing DM 70 per hour are entitled "Architek-Tour" (banks, museums, skyscapers, housing estates and their designers); "Judaic History" and "Kult-Tour" (on Goethe's trail). For further information contact the Tourist Board, Kaiserstrasse 52. Tel: 253253.

A rather unusual excursion in the city centre is to hop aboard the historic steam-powered Harbour Railway with its buffet car, which runs along the right (north) bank of the Main one weekend in the month, Saturday and Sunday. Precise departure times can be obtained by calling 436093. Adults pay DM 9 and children DM 2.50. A ride in the driver's cabin costs DM 15.

A very special Frankfurt speciality, its apple wine, can be sampled while taking a trip on a tram designed specially for the job, the "Ebbelwoi Express"; this enables you to get a good first impression of the city and sample some of its culinary delights at the same time. The "Ebbelwoi Express" departs every 35 minutes between 1.32 and 6.28pm from Bornheim central and runs past the Zoo, Römer/Paulskirche, main station, Sachsenhausen, and back. In addition, it can be hired for excursions along the city tramway network. For information call the municipal authorities on 2132-2425.

The Apfelkelterei Possmann (Possmann apple press) Eschborner Landstrasse 156–162, tel: 789904-22) produces famous apple wine. You can learn about how it is made Monday–Thursday 1.30–4.30pm.

Frankfurt Airport offers a bus sightseeing tour lasting 50 minutes. It begins at the observation deck, the most-visited place in Germany after Neuschwanstein Castle in Bavaria, and in summer departs daily at 11am and 2pm (Saturdays and Sundays also 1pm and 3pm). Tickets cost DM 9 (children DM 6).

IG Farben in Höchst is such a huge chemical concern that tours are arranged only for specific areas of production. It is necessary to book 6–8 weeks in advance.

INCOMING PARTNERS

All of the following agencies offer individual programmes and group travel arrangements:

American Express International Inc., Kaiserstrasse 8, 6000 Frankfurt 1. Tel: 210548, Fax: 283398; special agent for visitors from overseas, especially the US.

Becker's Travel Frankfurt GmbH, Gutzkowstrasse 75, 6000 Frankfurt 70. Tel: 622018, Fax: 626055; groups and individual travel from around the world, also for trade fairs.

CC Int'l Tours and Travel GmbH, Pfingstweidstrasse 10, 6000 Frankfurt 1. Tel: 430181, Fax: 430185; tailor-made programmes for incentives and special interest groups.

CTI Compass Tours Incoming, Wiesenhüttenplatz 39, 6000 Frankfurt 1. Tel: 231091, Fax: 231044; hotel reservations, transfers, congresses, meetings, bus rentals, special events.

DER Deutsche Reisebüro GmbH, Emil-von-Behring-Strasse 6, 6000 Frankfurt 50. Tel: 9588-3650, Fax: 9588-1010; special and group travel, individual reservations, incentives.

Deutsche Touring GmbH, Am Römerhof 17, 6000 Frankfurt 90. Tel: 7903-219, Fax: 706079; international travel agency, bus transportation throughout Europe, bus charter and incoming.

Hapag-Lloyd Reisebüro GmbH, Kaiserstrasse 14, 6000 Frankfurt 1. Tel: 2162-268/28065. Fax: 2162288; specialising in trade fairs, meetings, tours, particular groups, individual travel.

Melia Travel, Grosse Bockenheimer Strasse 54, 6000 Frankfurt 1. Tel: 9200380, Fax: 295786; transfers, guide and interpreting services, package tours, car rentals and chauffeur driven cars, hotel reservations.

Primus Travel Organisation, Am Hauptbahnhof 10, 6000 Frankfurt 1. Tel: 230017, Fax: 233102; own buses and private car services for individual travel throughout Germany and Europe.

Team Travel Service GmbH, Westendstrasse 52, 6000 Frankfurt 1. Tel: 7240407, Fax: 728991; specialist for complete incoming services for Germany for both groups and individuals, including tours, fairs and special programmes.

TOURS BY BOAT

A relaxing way of getting to the Rheingau and the Loreley, to Seligenstadt in the Odenwald and Michelstadt or Aschaffenburg, is by taking a river boat. Several companies offer round trips as well as cruises to all places of interest on the Main and Rhine rivers. Departure and booking office for all trips is at the Eiserner Steg (iron footbridge across the Main in Frankfurt).

The **Primus Line** leaves there for Rüdesheim at 8.30am (DM 32); for the Loreley at 8.30am (DM 45); for Seligenstadt at 9am (DM 21) and for Aschaffenburg at 8.30am (DM 29). Further information regarding days of departure can be obtained by calling 282884.

Main-Rhein-Tours leave for Miltenberg in the Odenwald at 8am (DM 37); for Phillipsruhe Palace in Hanau at 10am (DM 21); for Seligenstadt at 8.30am (DM 29) and for Rüdesheim at 9am (DM 32). For further information call 293960 or 282886.

The **Köln-Düsseldorf Line** operates a service to all points on the Rhine right up to Cologne and Düsseldorf, running daily 11 April–12 October, leaving from the quayside in Mainz at 8.45am and 10.15am and from Wiesbaden-Biebrich at 9.05am and 10.15am. From Frankfurt the Köln-Düsseldorf Line also offers trips lasting several days to Trier on the Moselle (DM 780), to Cologne via Trier (DM 1,170) and a 7-day round tour Frankfurt–Trier–Cologne–Frankfurt (DM 1,456). Between 26 April and 18 October the boats depart on Sunday, and additionally on Friday 3 July–9 October. For reservations, tel: 285728.

PARKS & GARDENS

The Municipal Forest (Stadtwald): Frankfurt is proud of the fact that it is home to the largest area of municipal forest in Germany. Covering the entire southern fringes of the city, it is criss-crossed by a multitude of paths. From the Goetheturm above Sachsenhausen it is possible to see as far as the Taunus in good weather. The park also contains a number of play parks for children (Monte Scherbelino, Scherwald and Louisa). Tram 14 towards Neu-Isenburg stops at the Oberschweinstiege, one of the nicest departure points for a long walk along the Jacobi pond. There is a game park at the Louisa S-bahn station (S 11, S 12 towards Darmstadt).

Grüneburgpark: This is a popular place for Frankfurters, particularly in the summer. Take the U-bahn (U 1, 2 or 3) and get out at Holzhausenstrasse. A small café in August Sibert Strasse is a meeting place for sun-worshippers who come here in their hundreds on hot sunny days.

The **Palm Garden** (Palmengarten) lies to the south of the Grüneburgpark and is best reached from the U-bahn station Bockenheimer Warte (U 6 and 7). With its tropical hothouses, cactus houses, rockeries, palm tree houses and orchid gardens, it is one of the finest botanical gardens in Europe. In the new tropical hothouse, the only one of its kind in the world, it has been possible to simulate conditions in a tropical rain forest. Waterworks, rowing boats and a garden railway are further attractions of the garden. Opening hours: November–February 9am–4pm, March 9am–5pm, April–September 9am–6pm, October 9am–5pm. Admission: adults DM 5, children DM 2.

The **Zoological Gardens** is one of the oldest zoos in Germany, founded in 1858 as a result of a campaign by a local action group. Alongside its 6,500 animals and 650 species, the Zoo's biggest attraction is the *Nachttierhaus* (Exotarium), which is open till 9pm. Penguins in arctic climate, alligators in tropical conditions and insects in damp conditions are generally more active at night. Opening hours: 16 March–30 September 8am–7pm; 1–15 October 8am–6pm; 16 October–15 February 8am–5pm; 16 February–15 March 8am–6pm. Admission DM 9.50 (children DM 4.50), with FVV ticket U-bahn station Zoo, (U 6 and 7) DM 7.50 (children DM 3.50).

The **"Nizza"** is the name given to the broad green promenade running along the north bank of the Main. But it is also possible find lawns to relax on the other side of the river as well.

The **Rampart Park** (Wallanlagen) is a 5-km (3-mile) long green belt around old city on the site of the former fortifications. Office workers like to come here during their lunchbreak, but parts of the parks are seedy and frequented by drug users.

OUTLYING DISTRICTS

Especially romantic and well-preserved are:

Höchst: First documented in AD 790, Höchst now stands on a medieval foundation. Its principal attractions include Höchst Castle (1366), St Justin's Church (Frankfurt's oldest church, built AD 850) and the Bolongaro Palace, built in 1755 by Italian snuff manufacturers, and today the venue for summer jazz concerts. The old porcelain manufactory (Brüningstrasse 50) still sells its original Höchst porcelain in Bolongarostrasse 186. The Höchst Castle Festival takes place on the first weekend in July, Friday–Monday. Höchst can be reached in 10 minutes from the city centre by taking the S 1 or the S 2 from Konstablerwache or the main station.

Bergen-Enkheim: Situated in the northeast of the city, Bergen-Enkheim has an attractive medieval core with traditional apple wine pubs. The place comes alive particularly on the first Tuesday in September; the "Berger Markt" takes place on this and the four preceding days and includes a unique cattle market. Bergen-Enkheim can be reached on the U 7 from Konstablerwache.

Seckbach: Some of Frankfurt's most traditional apple wine pubs can be found in Seckbach, also in the northeast of the city. On the Lohrberg, an adjacent hill is Frankfurt's one and only vineyard.

There are nice views of the Main river and pleasant strolls to be had through the orchards. Seckbach can be reached on the U 4 from the main station, Theaterplatz or the Römer; then take the 38 or 43 bus from the end station Seckbacher Landstrasse.

THE ENVIRONS

To the north lie the Taunus hills and the spa town Bad Homburg; to the west is the wine region of the Rheingau and the spa town of Wiesbaden, in the east along the River Main is Aschaffenburg and the Spessart hills, and to the south lies the Odenwald with its picturesque little valleys and the smallest area of wine cultivation in Germany.

The Taunus can be reached by taking line K to Kronberg (change in Höchst) or the U 2 to Gonzenheim (= Bad Homburg). One of the attractions here are the Taunus Thermal Baths, one of the best adventure pools in Germany (Seedammweg, tel: 06172 4738; admission for 4 hours DM 28). After that you can try your luck in the Homburg Casino (the "mother of Monte Carlo"), and be transported back into the elegance of the Wilhemenian era. It is open daily from 3pm and the price includes bus transfer back to the main station; tel: 06172 170170. Further attractions include the Opel Zoo near Kronberg, which is great for the kids because there is an enclosure where they can stroke the animals, open daily 8.30am–6pm, admission DM 6 (children DM 4); the Lochmühle Recreation Park in Wehrheim (8am–6pm), the Hessenpark open-air museum in Neu-Anspach which is open 1 March–31 October except Mondays, 9am–6pm (in winter only Sundays and national holidays 10am–5pm) and can be reached from the *autobahn* Bad Homburg exit on the B 3041, admission DM 4, and finally the Saalburg, a Roman fort on the *limes* (open daily 8am–5pm), reached by taking the Oberursel exit in the direction of Feldberg and Sandplacken from the Bad Homburg *autobahn*. From here you can take a delightful walk along the line of what was once the northern border of the Roman Empire.

To get to Wiesbaden (the state capital of Hesse), take the S 15 via the airport and Mainz which leaves every 20 minutes. From the station, the elegant Wilhelmstrasse passes the Spa Gardens on its way to the Museum of Wiesbaden (admission free, open Tuesdays 10am–9pm, Wednesday, Thursday, Saturday and Sunday 10am–4pm) and on to the Casino and the adjacent Hesse State Theatre with its beautiful colonnades to the Nassauer Hof Hotel containing the legendary Die Ente von Lehel restaurant. Behind the hotel the road leads left past the Kochbrunnen spring to the water-powered funicular that leads up the Neroberg to the Greek Chapel. Also of interest is the Women's Museum in Wörthstrasse 5 (admission DM 3).

The Rheingau lies to the west of Wiesbaden and extends along the Rhine as far as the town of Lorch. Rüdesheim, the "capital" of the Rheingau is famous for its wine pubs strung out along the Drosselgasse. Especially recommended is the climb up to the tower and a trip through the vineyards aboard the "Vintner Express" (DM 5, children DM 2.50). Groups of 20 persons or more can go wine tasting in the old cellars of the Brömserburg. In the summer months a visit to Siegfried's mechanical music box with over 400 automatic musical instruments is well worth a visit (Oberstrasse 19, admission with guide DM 6).

For further excursions from Frankfurt, for example to Heidelberg, to the Rheingau or the Odenwald, you can hire a guide for DM 60 per hour who will show you all the main attractions and cater to any special wishes. For further information, contact the Tourist Board at Kaiserstrasse 52, tel: 253253.

WHERE TO STAY

Each year around 9 million visitors to Frankfurt stay in approximately 19,000 hotel beds. Accordingly, during trade fairs the larger hotels are usually overbooked and rooms in those near to the Messe are frequently reserved as much as a year in advance. The Frankfurter Touristen-Information/Zimmervermittlung (Frankfurt Tourist Board/Accommodation Office), Kaiserstrasse 52, tel: 212-36869, Fax: 212-37880 is happy to accept written requests for reservations. You can also inquire here about private lodgings. This latter service is becoming increasingly popular as, on the one hand, guests are glad to rely on recommendations made by natives of the city, and, on the other, those offering private rooms welcome the additional income in view of the horrendous Frankfurt rentals they themselves have to pay. Thus accommodation in private homes can be very comfortable. The Frankfurter Mitwohnerzentralen (Frankfurt Accommodation Centre) may also be of help in your search for lodgings. Below is a selection of hotels.

LUXURY HOTELS

The following list of venues can be used for conferences and meetings and have office facilities, fax and a secretarial service. The first group is of hotels located in the proximity of the airport and will therefore be of use to travellers and business people who are just passing through. The second group is of hotels in the city centre and near the trade fair centre, in the Westend.

NEAR THE AIRPORT

Arabella Congress Hotel, Lyoner Strasse 44-48. Tel: 416760, DM 180/365. 400 rooms, indoor swimming pool, sauna, sunbed, steam bath. Banqueting capacity for 260 people, exhibition space, video sytems, overhead/flip chart, 9 conference rooms and a board room.

Dorint, Hahnstrasse 9. Tel: 66306-0, DM 190/400. 183 rooms, indoor swimming pool, sauna and sunbed. Banqueting capacity for 200 people, exhibition space, 8 seminar rooms, modern technical equipment upon request, 4 conference rooms.

Steigenberger Frankfurt Airport, Unterschweinstiege 16. Tel: 6975-0, DM 245/430. 380 rooms, 38 suites, rooftop pool, sauna and massage. Banqueting capacity for 600 people, exhibition space, discussion microphones, tape recorder, slide projector, movie projector, overhead/flip chart, 12 conference rooms.

Holiday Inn Conference Centre, Mailänder Strasse 1, 6802-0, DM 265/445. 400 rooms, 3 suites. Fitness centre and much more. Banqueting capacity for 180 people, exhibition space, 2 seminar rooms, discussion microphones, large scale visual projection, overhead/flip chart, simultaneous translation equipment, movie projector, slide projector, conference centre with 10 rooms and a board room.

Queens, Isenburger Schneise 40. Tel: 67840, DM 248/336. 263 rooms, 3 suites. Banqueting capacity for 300 people, exhibition space, loudspeakers, microphone, overhead/flip chart, VHS video system, projection screen, 14 conference rooms.

Sheraton, airport, Terminal Mitte. Tel: 69770, DM 295/530. 2,100 beds; single/double 1,020, suites 30, indoor swimming pool, sauna, sunbed, gift shop, barber shop. Banqueting capacity for 1,000 people, exhibition space, tape recorder, movie projector, slide projector, overhead/flip chart, video system, 6 interpreter cabins in the Congress Center, all technical equipment available on request.

NEAR THE TRADE FAIR CENTRE

Arabella Grand, Konrad-Adenauer-Strasse 7. Tel: 2981-0, DM 350/470. Single rooms 121, double rooms 217, suites 39, indoor swimming pool, sauna, sunbed, massage, fitness centre. Banqueting capacity for 240 people, exhibition space, 12 conference rooms with modern conference facilities.

Steigenberger Frankfurter Hof, Am Kaiserplatz. Tel: 21502, DM 295/500. Single rooms 200, double rooms 200. Banqueting capacity for 400 people, exhibition space, discussion microphones, overhead/flip chart, tape recorder, movie and slide projector, conference centre with 15 rooms, business services.

Frankfurt Marriott, Hamburger Allee 2-10. Tel: 2605-0, DM 300/495. Single rooms 368, double rooms 193, suites 24, executive levels 4. Banqueting capacity for 1,000 people, exhibition space, inhouse engineering department and ultramodern technical equipment upon request. 10 conference rooms.

Hessischer Hof, Friedrich-Ebert-Anlage 40. Tel: 75400, DM 295/575. Single rooms 54, double rooms 50, suites 11. Banqueting capacity for 300 people, video system, overhead/flip chart, movie projector, slide projector, 8 conference rooms.

Intercontinental, Wilhelm-Leuschner-Strasse 43. Tel: 26050, DM 320/495. Single/double rooms 736, suites 64, indoor swimming pool, sauna, sunbed, fitness centre. Banqueting capacity for 800 people, exhibition space, discussion microphones, overhead/flip chart, tape recorder, slide projector, video system, 10 conference rooms.

Parkhotel, Wiesenhüttenplatz 8-38. Tel: 26970, DM 259/440. Single rooms 203, double rooms 79, suites 17. Banqueting capacity for 250 people, exhibition space, discussion microphones, overhead/flip chart, tape recorder, slide projector, movie projector, video system, 10 conference rooms.

Pullmann Hotel Savigny, Savignystrasse 14. Tel: 75330, DM 190/340. Single rooms 71, double rooms 54. Banqueting capacity for 80 people, exhibition space, discussion microphones, overhead/flip chart, slide projector, video system, 5 conference rooms.

Ramada Hotel, Oeserstrasse 180. Tel: 39050, DM 225/395. Single rooms 79, double rooms 157, indoor swimming pool, sauna and sunbed. Banqueting capacity for 350 people, 10 conference rooms.

Scandic Crown, Wiesenhüttenstrasse 42. Tel: 273960, DM 215/360. Single rooms 104, double rooms 44, indoor swimming pool, sauna, sunbed, massage. Banqueting capacity for 180 people, exhibition space, discussion microphones, overhead/flip chart, slide projector, video recorder, 6 conference rooms.

MODERATE HOTELS

Below is a selection of hotels which all offer friendly and attentive service and are well situated for transport connections. Prices per night up to DM 300.

Altea, Voltastrasse 29. Tel: 79260, DM 170/308, 852 rooms, sauna, conference rooms.

Am Dom, Kannengiessergasse 3. Tel: 414955, DM 100/200, 300 rooms.

Am Holzhausenpark, Holzhausenstrasse 62. Tel: 1520090, DM 55/180.

Am Zoo, Alfred-Brehm-Platz 6. Tel: 490771, DM 70/155, 140 rooms.

Astoria, Rheinstrasse 25. Tel: 745046, DM 120/195, 100 rooms, sauna, conference rooms.

Carley Apparthotel, Nibelungenallee 31-35. Tel: 550190, DM 100/330, 50 rooms, conference rooms.

Gerbermühle, Deutschherrnufer 105. Tel: 655091, DM 135/210, 18 rooms.

Lian-Yi, Niddastrasse 39-41. Tel: 235915, DM 80/300, 120 rooms, conference rooms.

Meyn, Grüneburgweg 4. Tel: 590170, DM 91/235, 35 rooms.

Novotel Frankfurt Messe, Voltastrasse 1b. Tel: 793030, DM 190/260, 470 rooms, sauna, conference rooms.

Schwille, Grosse Bockenheimer Strasse 50. Tel: 92010-0, DM 145/260, 80 rooms, conference rooms.
Spener-Haus, Dominikanergasse 5. Tel: 2165-410, DM 90/200 41 rooms, conference rooms.
West, Gräfstrasse 81. Tel: 778011, DM 73/156, 35 rooms.
Westend, Westendstrasse 15. Tel: 746702, DM 90/250, 40 rooms, conference rooms.

CHEAPER HOTELS & PENSIONS

The following hotels are at the lower end of the range, but are nevertheless well-maintained. They are for people who simply want to sleep rather than indulge in any kind of luxury. Prices per night up to DM 150.

Am Anlagenring, Eschersheimer Anlage 23. Tel: 590769, DM 60/140, 60 rooms.
Atlas, Zimmerweg 1. Tel: 723946, DM 48/95, 14 rooms.
Backer, Mendelssohnstrasse 92. Tel: 747990, DM 25/60, 30 rooms.
Brukner, Stuttgarter Strasse 9. Tel: 253545, DM 45/78, 13 rooms.
Diana, Westendstrasse 83. Tel: 747007, DM 51/130, 34 rooms.
Genève, Kurhessenstrasse 67. Tel: 524050, DM 45/118, 8 rooms.
Hotelschiff "Peter Schlott", Mainberg. Tel: 315480, DM 60/130, 20 rooms, conference rooms.
Motel Frankfurt, Eschersheimer Landstrasse 204. Tel: 568011, DM 82/132, 121 rooms, conference rooms.
Pauli, Rebstöckerstrasse 93. Tel: 731850, DM 50/120, 24 rooms, conference rooms.
Römerhof, Oranienstrasse 1. Tel: 573318, DM 55/136, 15 rooms.
Weisses Haus, Jahnstrasse 18. Tel: 554605, DM 59/102, 53 rooms.
Zur Rose, Berger Strasse 283. Tel: 451762, DM 48/120, 23 rooms.

ACCOMMODATION CENTRES (MITWOHNZENTRALEN)

Accommodation Centre, Klingerstrasse 9, tel. for those looking: 284340/47; for those who have something available: 296111
Frankfurt Accommodation Centre, Sandweg 106, tel. for those looking: 441020; for those who have something available: 452030.

YOUTH HOSTEL

Haus der Jugend, Deutschherrnufer 12. Tel: 619058. 500 beds: 8-bed room up to the age of 20, DM 16; from the age of 20, DM 20, breakfast included; 4-bed room DM 25; single room DM 38; double room DM 29.

FOOD DIGEST

WHERE TO EAT

There are over 1,300 restaurants and bars in Frankfurt (see Eating Out chapter on page 89). Here is a small selection:

TOP-CLASS RESTAURANTS

Willi Tetz's Humperdinck is a minor sensation, not only as far as cooking is concerned, but also for its novel ideas. Here you can get a "One-star Whopper", the gourmet's answer to fast food. Grüneburgweg 95, tel: 722122. Open Monday–Friday noon–2pm and 7–10.30pm and Saturday evening.

Katherina Hessler is the secret star of Frankfurt's gourmet cuisine; despite the fact that her restaurant is not in the city itself, she cooks with amazing creativity and produces health food dishes of the highest quality. Located in Maintal-Dörnigheim, Am Bootshafen 4, tel: 06181 492951. Open Tueday–Saturday noon–2pm and 7pm–1am.

Klaus Trebes' Gargantua has emerged from being an "in" restaurant of the "alternative scene" to become one of the top addresses in town. Friesengasse 3, tel: 776442. Open Monday–Saturday 7pm–1am.

Erno's Bistro (Guy Bastian) provides the finest cuisine. Liebigstrasse 15, tel: 721997. Open Monday–Friday noon–2pm and 7–10pm.

Bistro 77 run by the Mosbach brothers is a veritable jewel of French provenance, a treat for the eyes and the palate. Ziegelhüttenweg 1–3, tel: 6140140. Open Monday–Friday noon–3pm and 7pm–1am, Saturday 7pm–1am.

INTERNATIONAL CUISINE

Erzherzog Johann is every bit as Austrian as the Austrians themselves – as charming as it is jovial, with a good choice of new wine and original specialities from the Wachau. Schloßstrasse 92, tel: 573800. Open Monday–Saturday 7pm–1am.

The Tse Yang is considered to be the best Chinese restaurant in Frankfurt. Authentic cuisine, with big portions and the freshest ingredients. Kaiserstrasse 67, tel: 232541. Open daily noon–11pm.

The Sushimoto is not only popular amongst the Japanese; it is a meeting place for the international community at large. Konrad Adenauer Strasse 7, in the Arabella, tel: 280045. Open 6pm–10pm.

L'Emir is a Lebanese restaurant which has such a fantastic selection of tempting starters that the visitor could easily forget the good line-up of main dishes. Baseler Platz 2, tel: 230123. Open noon–4am.

The **Tamnak Thai** is that business restaurant with a difference, with light and tasty dishes created with a lot of imagination. Berliner Strasse 64, tel: 287833. Open noon–3pm and 6pm–2am.

The **Suvadee** is the alternative Thai restaurant; it is somewhat smarter and its creations are spicier. Baumweg 19, tel: 4940764. Open Sunday–Thursday 6pm–1am, Friday 6pm–2am, Saturday 7pm–2am.

ITALIAN

La Galleria is the business meeting place in the BfG building. The quality is first class, the service superb and the prices definitely for the expense account. Theaterplatz 2, tel: 235680. Open Monday–Saturday noon–2.15pm and 6.30pm–midnight.

The **Incontro** has no competition as the sauce king of the Italian restaurants. The terrace is especially attractive. Kettenhofweg 64, tel: 725881. Open Monday–Friday noon–3pm and 6–11pm, Saturday and Sunday 6–11pm.

Da Enzo's speciality is fish, which is served up in variety of exciting ways. Feldbergerstrasse 10, tel: 723220. Open Monday–Friday noon–3pm and 6pm–midnight, Saturday 6pm–midnight.

The **Isoletta** always has a fresh choice, and good-sized portions of everything. Feldbergstrasse 31, tel: 725881. Open 11.30am–2.30pm and 5.30–11.30pm, Sunday from 5pm.

The **Casa Nova** offers generous portions at reasonable prices and has friendly service. Stresemannallee 59, tel: 632473. Open Sunday–Friday noon–3pm and 6pm–midnight.

FRANKFURT SPECIALITIES

Fine and wholesome at the same time: *Grüne Sosse* (green sauce), *Rippchen (*chops from cured loin of pork), *Handkäs mit Mussig* (and curd cheese with onions on bread) are the three traditional accompaniments to Frankfurt's very own beverage, its apple wine (*ebbelwoi*). All can be enjoyed in the apple wine pubs dotted around Sachsenhausen, Bornheim and Heddernheim. Here is our recommended selection:

Germania (Sachsenhausen): Textorstrasse 16. Tel: 613336. Hours: Tuesday–Thursday 4pm–midnight, Friday–Sunday 11am–midnight .

Fichterkränzi: Wallstrasse 5. Tel: 612778. Open Monday–Saturday 5–11pm.

Momberger: Alt-Heddernheim 3. Tel: 576666. Open Monday–Friday 4.15pm–midnight, Sunday 10.15am–1pm and 3pm–midnight.

Stalburg: Galuburgstrasse 80. Tel: 557934. Open Monday–Saturday 1–11pm, Sundays and public holidays 5–11pm, closed Thursdays.

Solzer (Bornheim): Bergerstrasse 260. Tel: 452171. Open Sunday–Sunday 4– 11pm.

In addition to apple wine, normal wine also plays a significant role in local drinking habits. Original Frankfurt wine is available directly atop the Lohrberg where it is grown, and can be enjoyed right along with the wonderful view out over the city: **Lohrberg-Schänke** (Seckbach), Auf dem Lohr 9, tel: 479944. Open Tuesday–Sunday: 10am–8pm.

The **Wielandstubb** which offers good plain wholesome fare, is a typical down-to-earth Frankfurt restaurant. Wielandstrasse 1, tel: 558551. Open Monday–Friday 11–1am.

Mutter Ernst is a traditional establishment catering for bankers and brokers right in the heart of the city. Alte Rothofstrasse 12, tel: 283822. Open Monday–Friday 9am–9pm, Saturday 9am–6pm.

Zum Rad in Seckbach is another of the above-mentioned apple wine pubs. It sells rare specialities such as *Karlinche-Spiess* (kebab) and Seckbach curd cheese on bread. Leonhardsgasse 2, tel: 479128. Open Monday–Friday, 4pm–midnight, Saturday and Sunday 3pm–midnight, closed Tuesday.

The **Wäldches Wirtshausbrauerei** is a small Frankfurt brewery with own bar and good Frankfurt cuisine. Woogstrasse 52, tel: 520522. Open Monday–Saturday 11.30–1am, Sunday 11–midnight.

When the weather is good, the **Gerbermühle** is the most popular garden pub. Situated on the Sachsenhausen bank of the Main. Deutschherrnufer 105, tel: 655091. Open Monday–Saturday 5pm–midnight, Sunday 11am–midnight.

DAY-TIME VENUES

Designers seem to be tireless in their preoccupation with transforming Frankfurt's cafés, bistros and "in" spots into cool, post-modern salons. The most important of these include:

Sacco & Vancetti is located in the Museum of Modern Art. Just like the whole building this café resembles a piece of tart. Braubachstrasse 25, tel: 289007. Open 9am–10pm.

Hildebrandt's is the latest arrival amongst Frankfurt's elegant bistros. Right next to the theatre, it is a popular meeting-place before and after performances. It was designed by Dudler. Untermainanlage 8, tel: 238515. Open 7.30–1am.

Lux is situated right in the heart of the city centre. It is a good place to go while shopping. Kornmarkt 11, tel: 281529. Open Monday–Thursday 11.30–1am, Friday and Saturday 11.30am–10pm, Sunday 6pm–1am.

The **Orfeo** is not only one of the best cinemas but also a top-class restaurant close to the trade fair centre. Hamburger Allee 45, tel: 709118. Open Monday–Friday noon–3pm and 7pm–1am, Saturday and Sunday 6pm–1am.

The **Plus** is one of Sachsenhausen's elegant establishments. It serves first-class cuisine during the afternoon when the kitchens of other restaurants are closed. Oppenheimer Landstrasse 31, tel: 615999. Open Monday–Sunday 10–1am.

CULTURE PLUS

Detailed information regarding daily events can be found in all the daily newspapers as well as in the city magazines *Prinz* and *az* (monthly), and in the *Journal Frankfurt* (published every 14 days). Monthly programmes put out by all the most important entertainment promoters in the Rhine-Main Region are available at ticket outlets throughout the city. These same promoters advertise in the monthly magazine *Strandgut*, which can be picked up for free in many cafés and bars.

MUSEUMS & COLLECTIONS

Since 1977, Frankfurt's most important museums have been strung out like beads along both banks of the Main. Together, they constitute the most varied collection of museums in Germany, and include such famous institutions as the Städelsche Kunstinstitut (Städel Institute of Art) and the much admired new building of the Museum für Kunsthandwerk (Museum of Applied Arts). All museums are closed on Mondays, but compensate for this by being open on the weekends. As a rule museums are open 10am–5pm and on Wednesdays until 8pm.

The easiest way to reach the Museum Bank (Museumsufer) is by going from the main railway station across Wiesenhüttenplatz and then crossing the Holbeinsteg bridge to arrive on the south bank of the Main. The museums below are listed by the order at which you arrive at them:

The **Städel Art Institute and Municipal Gallery** (Schaumainkai 63) contains one of the world's major art collections, with paintings from the 14th to 20th centuries, sculptures from the 19th and 20th centuries, plus a graphics collection.

The **German Postal Museum** (Schaumainkai 53, admission free) displays the history of communications in Germany and the international development of telecommunications.

The **German Museum of Architecture** (Schaumainkai 43, admission DM 4) is Germany's only museum on the subject of architecture. It provides a critical summary of the development of modern architecture in Germany and contains drawings, models and photos as well as the famous "house in a house" by Ungers.

The **German Film Museum** (Schaumainkai 41, admission free, cinema DM 6) contains a permanent exhibition relating to the origins and history of film making. The adjoining Kommunales Kino (cinema) shows films in their original versions which may well be of interest to foreign visitors. There are daily showings at 5.30pm and 8pm.

The **Ethnological Museum** (Schaumainkai 29, admission free) has changing ethnological exhibitions with critical emphasis on Third World Countries.

The **Museum of Applied Arts** (Schaumainkai 17, admission free) contains no fewer than 30,000 examples of European and Asian handicraft from medieval times to the present day. It also looks at contemporary trends in design, graphics and goldsmithing.

The **Museum of Iconography** (Brückenstrasse 3–7, admission free) contains a representative collection of mainly Russian icons.

The **Museum of Modern Art** (Domstrasse 10, admission DM 6) is Frankfurt's newest museum and is visited not only for its 150 works of art and sculptures from the 1950s to the present, but also for its unusual form, which resembles a "piece of tart" and was designed by Hans Hollein.

The **Cathedral Museum** (Domplatz 1) displays relics and sacristy objects from throughout the cathedral's history. Open Tuesday–Friday 10am–5pm, Saturday and Sunday 11am–5pm.

The **Schirn Kunsthalle** (Am Römerberg, admission varies) is an art gallery with changing exhibitions of international modern art, retrospectives of Russian Constructivism and the avant-gardists of the 20th century, and exhibitions dealing with individual artists such as Edvard Munch and Il Guercino.

The **Historical Museum** (Saalgasse 19, admission free) documents the history of Frankfurt from the Middle Ages to the present day. Also of interest is the Coins Collection, the Graphics Collection, the Library and the Children's Museum. Directly adjacent is a small museum devoted to apple wine.

The **Museum of Pre- and Early History** (Karmelitergasse 1, admission free) exhibits archaeological finds from the Frankfurt area. The museum regularly organises special exhibitions, and there are exhibits that cater for the blind and visually handicapped.

The **Judaic Museum** (Untermainkai 14/15, admission free) provides a sensitive portrayal of the history of Jewish life in the city.

The **Goethe Museum** (Grosser Hirschgraben 23–15, admission DM 3) is housed in Goethe's parents house. There is a collection of personal memorabilia as well as a picture gallery documenting the great man's life. This is where he wrote *Götz von Berchlingen* and *The Sorrows of the Young Werther*.

The **Museum for Ancient Sculpture** in the Liebieghaus (Schaumainkai 71, admission free) was opened in 1909 and exhibits sculptures from Ancient Greece, the Middle Ages, Renaissance, Baroque and from the age of Classicism.

The **Senckenberg Museum of Natural History** (Senckenberganlage 25, admission DM 5) ranks among the top five such museums in the world. It has an impressive collection of fossil remains and is actively engaged in the preservation of the famous Messel Fossil Beds near Darmstadt.

The **Stoltze Museum** (Töngesgasse 34–36) contains photo documentation, manuscripts and a selection of furniture from the estate of the poets Friedrich and Adam Stoltze.

The **Struwwelpeter Museum** (Hochstrasse 45–47) pays homage to the famous children's book author and physician Dr Heinrich Hoffmann, the father of "Struwwelpeter", a puppet. The museum contains original drawings from his estate as well as rare editions of "Struwwelpeter" and parodies from the 19th and 20th centuries.

OTHER MUSEUMS & ARCHIVES

Albert Schweitzer Archive, Neue Schlesinger Gasse 22. Tel: 284951.

Charlie Chaplin Archive, Klarastrasse 5. Tel: 524890.

Heinrich Hoffmann Museum, Schubertstrasse 20. Tel: 747969.

Carmelite Monastery. Tel: 212-34761.

Kommunale Galerie. Tel: 212-388847.

Museum für Höchster Geschichte (History Museum of Höchst), Höchster Schlossplatz 16. Tel: 303249.

Palmengarten (Tropical Garden), Palmengartenstrasse. Tel: 212-33382.

Schopenhauer Archive, University Library, Bockenheimer Warte. Tel: 7907-249.

City Archives, Karmlitergasse 5. Tel: 212-33374.

Steinhausen Stiftung (Steinhausen Foundation), Wolfgangstrasse 152. Tel: 5972326.

Stiftung Buchkunst (Art of Books Foundation), Sophienstrasse 8. Tel: 70808.

Uhren- und Schmuckmuseum (Museum of Clocks and Jewellery). Tel: 303030.

Verkehrsmuseum (Museum of Transport). Tel: 212-36893.

Zeppelin Museum, airport. Tel: 694390.

Zoological Gardens, Alfred-Brehm-Platz. Tel: 212-33715.

FRANKFURT FESTIVALS

Frankfurt's urban lifestyle is enlivened by almost 100 annual festivals and special outdoor markets. The city administration organises about 50 of these events, many of which are renowned well beyond Frankfurt itself. Here is a selection:

End of February: Carnival, **Shrove Tuesday** festivities on the Römerberg and in Heddernheim (Klaa' Paris).

From the middle of April until the beginning of May: **Springtime Dippemess** along Ratsweg. The two Frankfurt Dippemess (see also autumn Dippemess) have a tradition going back to medieval times. The Dippemess originated from a pottery (Dippe = pot) market held every year during the Middle Ages. Today the Dippemess features modern carnival attractions and many kinds of handicrafts. It rates as one of Germany's top folk festivals.

The Tuesday following Pentecost: **Wäldchestag** at the Oberforsthaus in the Municipal Forest. Wäldchestag follows an old tradition dating back to medieval times. In those days, on the Tuesday following Pentecost, the guilds trekked out to the countryside for a picnic. Now the day is known as Frankfurt's national holiday.

Middle of June: **Apple Wine Street Festival** on the Römerberg.

Around the 4th of July: **German-American Folk Festival** along the Ratsweg. One of the few occasions where Americans and Germans come together.

Middle of July: The **Höchst Castle Festival**.

Middle of August: **Main Festival** on the Römerberg and along the Main. The Main Festival dates back to 1393 to a fishermen's festival where contests of skill and fun were held along with medieval Passion Plays. Today, the Römerberg and the Main river banks become a huge outdoor beer garden.

The **Bornheim Fair**.

End of August/Beginning of September: **Rheingauer Wine Week** along the Fressgass'.

Last Weekend in August: **Museum Bank Festival** and the City Administration Open House.

Middle of September: **Autumn Dippemess** along the Ratsweg.

December: The **Christmas Market**. The Christmas Market in Frankfurt is one of the largest in Germany with about 3 million visitors. The historic setting at the Römerberg where Frankfurt's Christmas tree, a 30-metre high Norwegian spruce, stands, guarantees a unique atmosphere. At the Christmas Market are the traditional characters *Bethmännchen*, made out of marzipan, and the comical *Quetschmännchen* (made from prunes).

THE THEATRE SCENE

Frankfurt offers more theatre per head of the population than almost any city in the world. Alongside the four independent theatre houses are the municipal stages, no fewer than 50 independent companies and some 25 private theatres. For information regarding theatre and opera performances (recorded message) dial: 11518.

The **Theater am Turm** (Eschenheimer Landstrasse 2, tel: 1545-110) can look back on a long and distinguished history; this is where Rainer-Werner Fassbinder and Claus Peymann first made names for themselves, and it has now become one of the most significant centres for avant-garde performances in the European dramatic scene.

Theaterplatz is the location of what is now one of the world's most modern theatres, the **Oper Frankfurt** (Untermainanlage 11, tel: 236061). This is the home of the Frankfurt Ballet under the artistic direction of William Forsythe, a leading figure of European contemporary dance theatre who has extended the classical ballet vocabulary into a language all his own. The **Schauspielhaus** (Playhouse) is also housed here, as is the intimate theatre through the rear entrance. The **Bockenheimer Depot**, a beautiful barrel-shaped theatre in a former tram depot is also used for occasional performances.

The main house of national and international independent theatre is the **Mousonturm** in Bornheim. The building was converted in 1925 from a former soap and perfume factory. In 1988 the Mousonturm was transformed into a site for cultural events such as theatre, music, literature and painting and was placed at the disposal of artists in the city and the surrounding region. The OFF-TAT Theatre is located in the Mousonturm. Many prize-winning theatre presentations are performed here. The annual Summertime Festival is also organised by the OFF-TAT. The theatre has been known to put on operas in such unusual places as train repair yards and underwater concerts in one of the city's indoor pools.

Just as important are two independent theatre houses: **Das Freie Theaterhaus** in Schützenstrasse 10, which also puts on performances for children and young people (tel: 2998610) and the oldest independent Frankfurt theatre, the **Gallus Theatre** in Krifteler Strasse 55 (take the tram out towards Höchst) with a programme that caters to individual groups (children, gays, etc.). Tel: 7380037.

Of particular interest to the visitor whose command of German may not be the strongest is the **English Theatre** in Kaiserstrasse 52, near the station. It was founded in 1979 to satisfy the need for a professional English-speaking theatre, and presents traditional and modern American and English plays in the original language, including such classics as *The Mousetrap*. After performances actors chat with visitors in the theatre's own café, which is also well-suited for private or business occasions. The theatre has now also become a cultural and educational institute, with theatre courses offered to the public via adult education classes (Volkshochschule).

The **Tigerpalast-Varieté** in Heiligkreuzgasse 16–20 (near the Konstablerwache) has made a name for itself beyond the borders of Frankfurt. International acrobats and magicians and a humorous Master of Ceremonies attempt to revive the "good old days" of the city's variety theatre of the 1920s.

There are also countless private theatres which have a classical repertoire, such as the **Fritz-Remond Theater** (at the Zoo), the **Komödie** (next to the Schauspielhaus) and the **Goethetheater** (underground station Leipziger Strasse). Frankfurt is also home to two permanent cabaret theatres: **Die Schmiere** (in the Carmelite Monastery not far from Theaterplatz), and **Die Maininger** (located on Neue Rothofstrasse, parallel to Fressgass).

· THE MUSIC SCENE

For information about concert performances (recorded message) dial: 11516 (classical) and 11518 (entertainment and dancing).

The centre for both classical and contemporary musical performances is the **Alte Oper** (Old Opera House) at Opernplatz (tel: 1340-400). There's bound to be something to please every taste here, from musicals to jazz to premiere performances of brand new compositions – all presented in an opulent setting. Every year the emphasis of the so-called "Frankfurt Festivals" is on modern music, although there are also some classical music performances.

Concerts take place several times a month in the **Jahrhunderthalle** in Höchst (Silostrasse/Pfaffenwiese, tel: 3601-240), in the **Palm Garden** (Palmengartenstrasse, tel: 212-33939) and in the studios of the **Hessische Rundfunk** (Bertramstrasse 8, Tel 155-1). A good tip for chamber music fans is the **Finkenhof** (underground station Grüneburgweg, near the College of Music). Performances of the Frankfurt "Ensemble Modern" have a worldwide reputation.

Jazz in Frankfurt has a long and venerable tradion. Alongside the countless appearances by well known jazz musicians in the Summertime Programme, especially in the gardens of the **Bolongaro Palast** in Höchst, jazz is also staged in the venerable **Jazzkeller** (Kleine Bockenheimer Strasse 18a, tel: 288537) which having been on the go for 40 years is now one of the oldest jazz clubs in Germany. While the original performers included such greats as Louis Armstrong, today it is often new talent on stage here. Occasionally visitors from the international jazz scene will still turn up, and may even start a spontaneous session.

In addition, there are a large number of small piano bars and stages which provide for original and lively jazz. The most important are the **Jazzkneipe**, a free-standing pavilion on Berliner Strasse 70 (tel: 287173), the **Jazz Life Podium** with Dixieland and Swing in the Kleine Rittergasse 22/26 (tel: 626346), the **Schlachthof** (the abattoir) at Deutschherrnufer 36 (tel: 623201), which holds matinées of Dixie and Swing on Sunday mornings. Last but not least is **Down by the Riverside** at Mainkai 7 (tel: 292150).

Rock and Pop bands on their world tours generally play in the **Waldstadion** in the Riederwald. Big rock and pop concerts otherwise take place in the **Festhalle** located on the trade fair grounds. Further live music can be heard in the legendary **Batschkapp** in Eschersheim (Maybachstrasse 24, tel: 531037): this was always the cradle for rock and pop developments in the city, and even today hopeful bands from all over the world come to play here.

Every bit as venerable an institution is the **Sinkkasten** near the Zeil (Brönnerstrasse 9, tel: 280385). The appeal of the place is its atmosphere; the audience sits in cinema chairs and the bar resembles a tropical hot-house.

For so-called multicultural musical performances, the **Brotfabrik** in Bachmannstrasse 2–4 in Hausen has proved itself an excellent venue. Larger scale concerts take place in the **Volksbildungsheim** at Eschersheimer Tor, and smaller sessions are staged every evening in the numerous pubs in Alt-Sachsenhausen.

Frankfurt's discotheques are famous for developing new musical trends by themselves, especially the **Omen** in Junghofstrasse and the **Techno Club** which takes place every Friday evening at the airport (see Nightlife/Discotheques).

Tickets for concerts can be bought in advance at the Sandrock ticket office in the B-level of the Hauptwache (tel: 20115), at Hertie on the Zeil (tel: 294848) and at Concert Poster on the Liebfrauenberg 52–54 (tel: 293131).

LITERARY FRANKFURT ·

The centre for literary events in Frankfurt is the **Literaturhaus** at Bockenheimer Landstrasse 102 (underground station Bockenheimer Warte, tel: 748470). In addition to readings by famous and contemporary authors, the resurrection of forgotten works and events concerning more or less remote byways of literature are held here regularly. The **Hessische Literaturbüro** (Hessian Literary Centre), located in the Mousonturm (Waldschmidtstr. 4, tel: 40589523) is an institution in which local authors are invited to present their often quite considerable talents: Eva Demski, Ulla Berkéwicz and also the city writers from Bergen-Enkheim have all introduced works in this forum. Every month, a variety of people associated with writing – from radio playwrights to book publishers – discuss their craft. And last but not least the former stonghold of the Frankfurt literary scene is the **Romanfabrik** at Uhlandstrasse 21 (tel: 4980811), where a cartoonists' meeting takes place once a month, as well as increasingly noteworthy readings and discussions.

Don't forget to check out the big bookstores like Huss'sche Universitätsbuchhandlung (Kiesstr. 41, tel: 776050), the Kohl'sche Buchhandlung (Rossmarkt 10, tel: 298904-0) and the former left-wing bookshops Ypsilon (Berger Str. 18, tel: 448738), the Autorenbuchladen (a bookstore operated by authors), (Reuterweg 57, tel: 722972), the Frauenbuchladen (Women's Bookstore), (Kiesstr. 27, tel: 705295), Karl Marx (Jordanstr. 11, tel: 778807) the Lesecafé (Diesterwegstr. 7, tel: 622523 and Land in Sicht (Rotteckstr. 13, tel: 448738). Generally speaking, all these bookstores have guest authors' readings at least once a month.

CINEMAS ·

For a recorded telephone message concerning city centre cinemas (A-F) dial 11513; for city centre cinemas (G-Z) the number is 11514. For cinemas located outside Frankfurt (drive-in and airport cinemas) call 11512 and for cinemas located in Frankfurt suburbs call 11511; in Offenbach dial 11515.

The biggest cinema by far is the Royal, situated not too far from the Konstablerwache in Schäfergasse 10 (tel: 287874). There are cinema centres on the Zeil 85-93 (tel: 285105), at Weissfrauenstrasse 12 at

the theatre (tel: 283128) and at Hauptwache (tel: 285205 and 285789). Good cinemas which run premier films include the Orfeo at Hamburger Allee 45 (near the trade fair grounds, tel: 702218), the Berger-Kino at Berger Strasse 177 (tel: 456405) and the Harmonie in Sachsenhausen, Dreieichstrasse 54 (tel: 613550). The Kommunale Kino in the Filmmuseum, Schaumainkai 41 (tel: 212-38840) does a good job of presenting older films and international movies in their original. The experimental cinema "mal seh'n" on Adlerflychtstrasse 6 (underground station Musterschule, tel: 5970845) is especially worth noting due to the number and variety of films shown here and to their habit of running debut films made by as yet unknown but promising film makers. There are drive-in movie theatres in Gravenbruch near Neu-Isenburg (tel: 06102/5500) and in the Main-Taunus-Zentrum (tel: 06196/23344).

NIGHTLIFE

The only problem with nightlife in Frankfurt is that much of it stops at 1am, on Fridays and Saturdays at 2am. But discotheques as well as some bars with "happy hours" (half price from 5 to 10pm), and even some restaurants, remain open longer.

The **Tigerpalast** is not only an unusual variety club with an international reputation, but also offers food of a quality one would never normally expect to get at such late hours. Heiligkreuzgasse 16–20, tel: 289691. Open Tuesday–Saturday 6pm–4am.

The **Nachtcafé** was never one of the Frankfurt scene institutions; perhaps that is why in its intergalactic cellar one meets people one would never expect to see here at all. Taubenstrasse 7, tel: 28941. Open daily 5pm–4am.

Jimmy's Bar has a distinctly British atmosphere. André, the barman, can remember what his customers like even if they haven't been in for years. In the Hessische Hof, Friedrich Ebert Anlage 40, tel: 7540-0. Open daily 8pm–4am.

The Taberna **Sevilla** has Spanish Flamenco. It is a very lively place indeed, particularly when they start dancing on the tables. Mainzer Landstrasse 243, tel: 735952. Open daily 8pm–4am.

John's Bar is the archetype of sophisticated Frankfurt bar culture. Based on the American model, there is good food until late and an easy-going atmosphere of jazz and Champagne. Steinweg 7, tel: 285477. Open Monday–Friday noon–3pm and 6pm–4am, Saturdays 6pm–4am.

Stylish bars with no last orders can be found in such elegant hotels as the Arabella Grand and the Frankfurter Hof (see hotels).

DISCOTHEQUES

Cooky's is known for the people who go as much as the music. Particularly popular with the international set, and a long-stayer in the Frankfurt scene. Am Salzhaus 4, tel: 287662.

The **Omen** is probably the best discotheque in Germany. Leading dancers show you how. Junghofstrasse 14, tel: 282233. Open Sunday–Thursday 10pm–4am, Friday and Saturday 6pm–6am.

The **Dorian Gray** is famous for its Techno Club that takes place every Friday. Also, there aren't many cities that have a top-class discotheque at the airport. Hall C, 0-Level, tel: 6902212. Open Monday–Thursday 9pm–4am, Friday 9pm–6am and Saturday 9pm– open end.

The **Jazzkeller** has been on the go for 40 years and is Germany's oldest jazz pub. There is dancing on Wednesdays and Saturdays. Kleine Bockenheimer Strase 18a, tel: 288537. Open Tuesday–Saturday 9pm–3am.

Sky Fantasy is located 222 metres (728 ft) up in the Television Tower and is well worth the ride up the lift, tel: 533077. Open Wednesday and Friday 10pm–4am, Saturday 10pm–5am.

The **Funkadelic** claims to have "the best funk in town". And it does. Brönnerstrasse 11, tel: 283808. Open Monday–Thursday 10pm–4am, Friday and Saturday 10pm–6am.

SHOPPING

Without a doubt the shopping mile with the highest turnover in all of Europe is the Zeil between Konstablerwache and Hauptwache. Perhaps a reason for its booming success is the fact that it's no luxury shopping street; here you'll find one department store after another; instead of small boutiques there are huge "megastores" for clothing, shoes and jewellery. Independent speciality shops do exist, but they're mostly to be found along the smaller side streets. If you continue along the Zeil from Hauptwache in the direction of the Alte Oper (Old Opera House), you'll come to the beginning of the "Fressgass" (Eaters' Alley), aptly named for the abundance of gourmet shops and delicatessens alternating with restaurants and high-class boutiques. The shops along Goethestrasse (running south and parallel to Fressgass) are more expensive, exclusive and of international repute. The boutiques here attract an affluent clientele and are frequently represented in Düsseldorf and Paris as well. Most of the shops along the way from the Hauptwache in the direction of the Theaterplatz cater to well-to-do tourists.

On Theaterplatz itself the cafés, boutiques, bookshops and delicatessens laid out on three floors of the BfG building provide a peaceful and relaxing shopping atmosphere. Frankfurt's trendy boutiques are located in the area between Hauptwache and Eschersheimer Gate. Here you'll find contemporary clothes and outfits supremely suited to disco-hopping at prices you can actually afford. Popular arcades are the B level of the Hauptwache, which is a whole shopping centre in itself, the Hauptbahnhof with its shops with extended opening hours (6am–10pm at weekends) and the Sandhof arcade for those ambling from the Hauptwache to the Paulskirche. With its boutiques, hi-fi shops and two cafés, the latter is is primarily geared to the young.

To the right of the Zeil, if you follow the Neue Kräme or the Hasengasse, you'll come to the Kleinmarkthalle – the small covered market, an exotic world of international tastes and fragrances. The countless stands sell fruit and meat, spices and vegetables from all over the world. Alongside Japanese tea and Moroccan lamb, you'll find Italian pasta and Korean soups.

Frankfurters who don't live right in the middle of the city prefer to do their shopping along the boulevards in their own districts. In Bornheim the main shopping drag is Berger Strasse (take the U 4) in Bochenheim it's Leipziger Strasse (U 6 or U 7), in the Nordend the Oederweg (take the U 1, U 2, or U 3) and in Sachsenhausen is it's the elegant Schweizer Strasse (take the U 1, U 2, or U 3).

If you want something particular, whether it's books, CDs, bicycles or wine, you can generally assume that the city centre is going to have the greatest choice, while as a rule the districts provide better advice. Hugendubel, the giant bookshop at the Hauptwache, might have a lot of books, but if you are looking for more specific topics then you are probably better off rummaging through the shelves of a smaller bookshop away from the centre, for example in Bockenheim.

Some specialist shops are bunched together in the same street. Galleries and antique shops, for example, are located in Braubachstrasse which begins at the Römer (take the U 4). The reason for this is the proximity to the Museum of Modern Art and the Schirn Kunsthalle, each of which possesses an excellent art bookshop. There are also fine galleries to be found in the Westend:

Galerie ak, Gartenstrasse 47. Tel: 622104
Galerie der Künstler, Barckhausstrasse 1-3. Tel: 725526
Galerie L.A., Fahrgasse 87. Tel: 288687
Galerie Raphael, Domstrasse 6. Tel: 291338
Galerie Schwind, Fahrgasse 87. Tel: 287072
Galerie Tröster & Schlüter, Fahrgass 87. Tel: 288776
Galerie von Miller, Braubachstrasse 33. Tel: 292519
Galerie Wentzel, Fahrgasse 87. Tel: 280170

On the Mainzer Landstrasse in the west of the city there are a number of showrooms selling top makes of car from both home and abroad – these may be of interest to potential buyers from non-EC countries. On Hanauer Landstrasse you'll find shops selling avant-garde furniture design, as well as interior design firms, a large tile firm and carpet shops. For more elegant interiors you might prefer to browse along the Neue Mainzer Landstrasse in the city centre.

Most fur shops are situated in the district to the north of the main station around Düsseldorfer Strasse. The best photographic shops, believe it or not, are to be found in the red-light district of the Bahnhofsviertel.

There are three large shopping centres to be found on the outskirts of the city:

The **Main-Taunus-Zentrum** near Sulzbach (motorway towards Wiesbaden) has 83 shops, restaurants, cafés, a drive-in cinema, post office and a kindergarten for customers.

The **Hessen-Center** in Bergen-Enkheim (in the east) has more than 100 shops.

The **Nord-West-Zentrum** has 110 shops, a swimming pool and hotel, as well as restaurants and all kinds of special events.

Flea markets are held every Saturday. The best known is held on the Sachsenhausen side of the Main river – the Schaumainkai – every Saturday (9am–4pm). It is a popular place to browse for the modern, the antique and the abstract. Another flea market takes place in Offenbach and starts as early as 6am.

Weekly **markets** selling fresh produce alternate daily between the market places of the individual districts:

Tuesdays: in Höchst on the market square (also Friday and Saturday).

Wednesdays: in Bornheim beneath the clock tower.

Thursdays: in front of the Bockenheimer Warte at the university.

Fridays: in Sachsenhausen at Diesterwegplatz.

Saturdays: on the Konstablerwache (with specialities from the Vogelsberg region).

SPORTS

SPECTATOR SPORTS

The most prominent of the city's 158 sports grounds is the Waldstadion in the Riederwald in the south of the city. This is not only where open-air concerts take place, but it is also the home ground of Eintracht Frankfurt, the city's top football club and, latterly, one of the most successful clubs in Germany. In the summer, it is also the venue for the Tennis Federation Cup. The Velodrom directly adjacent is the centre for cycling championship races. The best-known cyling race in the city is the "round the Henningerturm" which is held every year on 1 May.

The Ballsporthalle Höchst is not only an architectural masterpiece; this is where the major handall, volleyball and basketball tournaments are held. An artifical wall for rock climbers is also occasionally installed. Details of sporting events are contained in the local press or the city magazines.

PARTICIPANT SPORTS

Ice-skating: The Eissporthalle (ice rink) at the Borheimer Hang is open all the year round, daily 9–11.30am, 3–5.30pm and 8–10.30pm. From the beginning of November to the end of February it is open 9am–10.30pm.

Swimming: A particular local favourite is the Rebstockbad. As well as the main indoor 50-metre pool there is also a wave pool, a heated outdoor pool, lounging area, sunbeds, saunas and a gym room. It is located behind the trade fair centre on August Auler Strasse 7; open Mondays 2–10pm, Tuesdays and Thursdays 9am–8pm, Wednesdays and Friday–Sunday 9am–10pm. Admission DM 9 (children DM 5).

The spa pool in Königstein with its panorama view is also well worth a visit: Le Canner Rocheville Strasse 1; open Mondays 4–10pm with nude bathing and sauna, Tuesday–Friday 7am–9.30pm, Saturday and Sunday 7am–8pm. Admission DM 12 (children DM 7). Those in search of a very special bathing experience, inclusive of sauna, are advised to head for the Taunus Thermal Baths in Bad Homburg: Seedammweg; open Sunday, Monday, Tuesday and Thursday 9am–11pm, Wednesday, Friday and Saturday 9am–midnight. Admission DM 20.

A number of less luxurious pools can also be recommended: Stadtbad Mitte, Hochstrasse 4–8; Höchst, Melchiorstrasse 21; Fechenheim, Konstanzer Strasse 16; Sachsenhausen, Textorstrasse 16; Nordweststadt, Nidaforum 4; Bornheim, Inheidener Strasse; Bergen-Enkheim, Fritz Schubert Ring.

More exotic sporting activities are possible in the environs of the city. For example, the **hanggliding** school on the Feldberg in the Taunus offers beginners courses (DM 575), as well as advice and equipment to experts. Contact: Drachenflugschule, 6204 Taunusstein 4, tel: 06128/8190.

Windsurfers can head for the Langener See (take the B 44 towards Gross Gerau and it's just after Zeppelinheim).

Canoeists who want to take to the waters of the Main can rent canoes from Supertramp (Jordanstrasse 30, tel: 777723). Canoes cost DM 90 for a weekend and Kayaks DM 50.

Golf is an expensive pastime in Germany, and the Frankfurt area is no exception. There are a number of attractive private golf courses in the Taunus, but the cost will be prohibitive for most people and you usually have to be a member of another club. For those who aren't, Golfomat simulators are available in Bad Homberg at the Taunus Therme (tel: 06172 40640) and in Kronberg-Oberhöchst (Steinbacher Strasse 42, tel: 06173 65999). A selection of golf clubs:

Frankfurter Golf Club e.V., Golfplatz Golfstrasse 41, 6000 Frankfurt 71. Tel: 6662318, Fax: 6667018.

Golf-Club Idstein-Wörsdorf Henriettenthal e.V, Postfach 1343, 6270 Idstein. Tel: 268866, Fax: 268833.

Golf und Land-Club Kronberg, Schloss Friedrichshof, 6242 Kronberg/Taunus. Tel: 06173/1426, Fax: 06173/5953.

Golf-Club Neuhof, Frankfurter Strasse 137, 6078 Neu-Isenburg. Tel: 06102/21050, Fax: 06102/3701-2.

Horseback Riding is available at Frankfurter Reit-und Fahrclub e.V, Hahnstrasse 85, 6000 Frankfurt 70. Tel: 6667585. DM 29 per hour; 10-hour ticket DM 280 for adults, DM 220 for youngsters.

Tennis and Squash is available at Tennisanlage Füssenich, Sigmund Freud Strasse, 6000 Frankfurt 50, tel: 542318; the Tennis & Squash Park Europa, Ginnheimer Landstrasse 49, 6000 Frankfurt 90, tel: 532040, with 3 indoor and 5 outdoor courts.

Special Information

TRADE FAIRS & CONVENTIONS

The Frankfurter Messe (Frankfurt Trade Fairs) have become internationally known especially due to the annual Buchmesse (Book Fair), the Herbstmesse (Autumn Fair), and the Automobilmesse IAA (Automobile Fair). Each year 2.6 million visitors come to see approximately 32,500 exhibitors spread out over the 400,000 sq. metres (478,400 sq. yds) which make up the fair site.

A TRADE FAIR CALENDAR

January: the Home Textile Fair and Premiere Fair (paper goods, gifts, perfume).

February: the Ambiente (household wares) and the Inter-Sat (satellites and cable television).

March: In-Cosmetics, the International Music Fair, Stage Art as Theatre Fair, Art Frankfurt and the Fur & Fashion Fair.

April: the Gardening Fair, the Interstoff and Infobase Fair (electrical equipment).

May: the Butcher Fair.

June: the Public Design Fair for Interiors and Objects.

August: The Frankfurt Autumn Fair for Consumer Goods.

September: the Automechanica Fair (car accessories) and the Plantec (horticulture).

October: the Frankfurt Book Fair, the Contact Fair (an exhibition of electronic technology), the Chefs' Olympiad, the Management and Marketing Services Fair, the Hifi-Video and Interstoff Fair.

November: the Interrace (motor sports), the Tourist Fair, the Expolingua Fair (translation and international communications), the Foodtec (food technology) and the Ars-Antique Fair (art and antiques).

For the so-called consumer fairs, visitors not belonging to the trade usually only have access at the weekends. If you refer to the above calendar, the **Ambiente** is one of the largest consumer trade fairs in the world. Here you can see everything that is going to be on the shelves of the boutiques and department stores the next winter. The **International Music Fair** displays vast quantities of musical instruments from all over the world as well as the very latest products in the field of electronics. At the same time interesting classical and pop concerts take place day and night not only at the fair but also at other venues, for example the Alte Oper.

Art Frankfurt is at the moment the best organised and most extensive of all art fairs. The atmosphere is a mixture of colourful parvenue, dandy and flaneur, as dealers come to judge the latest that the art world has to offer in the vast almost silent halls. Running parallel to Art Frankfurt, a number of events and exhibitions take place in Frankfurt's galleries. The **Frankfurt Book Fair** is the largest such fair in the world. At the same time, countless events take place in the city's bookshops, theatres, as well as in the Literaturhaus in the Westend. The opening parties of publishing companies in the cafés and pubs are legendary. The **IAA** (International Automobile Exhibition) was until now a major attraction for car enthusiasts. However, at the time of going to print it is not known exactly when the next one will be; indeed, it is not at all clear whether the IAA will remain in Frankfurt at all.

Trade fair visitors and exhibitors can make arrangements for overnight accommodation by calling either 7575-62 22 or 7575-62 89. Information regarding the exact dates of special events, exhibits and trade fairs is available on tel: 11516 (recorded message). It's possible to reach the Frankfurt Trade Fair itself by dialling 7575-0.

GETTING TO AND FROM THE MESSE

During all major international fairs a shuttle-bus service runs directly from the airport to the Messe area. A taxi from the airport to the Messe will take about 20 minutes. Otherwise, to reach the Messe from the airport take the suburban line S15 to the Hauptbahnhof (Main Station) and change onto trams 16 or 19. The total journey time should not be more than half an hour. To walk from the main station (in a northwesterly direction) will take about 10 minutes. Tickets are available from machines by all tram stops and on all railway station platforms.

The closest S-bahn station to the Messe is Westbahnhof. To reach the Messe from the station follow Emser Strasse in a southerly direction to the main road (Theodor-Heuss-Allee) and cross it. A few yards to the right is the Messe's Galleria entrance, or you can turn left in the direction of the immense Messeturm to the City entrance. Lines S3, S4, S5 and S6 serve the Westbahnhof; all run to the Main Station and the Hauptwache/Zeil or Konstabler-wache/Zeil. At Konstablerwache you can change onto bus line 36 which will take you directly south into Sachsenhausen (a good place for evening recreation).

Bus line 33 stops near the Galleria and the City entrances of the Messe, and connects with the restaurant and bar areas of the Westend (see also *Eating Out* chapter on page 98 and *Food Digest* below). Unfortunately there are very few such outlets within easy walking distance of the Messe.

Taxis wait outside both the City and the Galleria entrances.

If you arrive by car, simply follow the signs for "Messe" on the motorways. They will lead you directly to the Messe car parks near the Frankfurt West motorway interchange. There are over 20,000 parking spaces at the Rebstock Car Park, from where a free shuttle-bus service will whisk you to the Messe itself in a matter of minutes.

FOR THE DISABLED

A city guide for the disabled is available free of charge from: Arbeitskreis, Frankfurter Stadtführer für Behinderte, Kennedyallee 80, 6000 Frankfurt 70.

The city of Frankfurt provides (at a charge) facilities for the disabled; call 748090 or 748099. Taxi service for the disabled can be arranged by calling 230084. At the airport there are many special services for disabled travellers, details available from: Flughafen Frankfurt/Main AG, Communication and Information Department, 6000 Frankfurt 75, tel: 690-70554, fax: 690-5507.

USEFUL ADDRESSES

GENERAL

Information (telephone/telefax)
national: 1188
international: 00118
Airport (arrivals/departures): 690-3051
Tourist Information Office/Accommodation: 212-38708/09
Lost and Found: Mainzer Landstrasse 323, tel: 7500-2403 or 7500-2504
FVV (Frankfurt Transport Systems) Lost and Found: Hauptwache Level B, tel: 26940
German Federal Railways Lost and Found: 2650
Road Conditions: 1169
Frankfurt Animal Shelter (they also offer temporary shelter to pets): 423005
Mobile Animal Rescue: 08581/ 3666
Police: Emergency 110
Impounded Motor Vehicles: 419106, Uhlfelder Strasse 12
Taxi: 250001, 230001, 230033, 545011
Telephone Service for Telex, Telefax, Datex, Teletex: 1172; for TV, Radio and CB's: 1174
Telegram dispatch in German: 1131, in foreign languages: 1133

FRANKFURT CITY DEPARTMENTS

Police Headquarters, Friedrich-Ebert-Anlage 11. Tel: 2555-1
Sichergestellte Fahrzeuge, Uhlfelder Strasse 12. Tel: 419106
Department of Multicultural Affairs, Barckhausstr.1. Tel 212-38765
Adult Education/Volkshochschule, Hochstr.49. Tel: 212-38301
Department of Science and Arts, Brückenstr. 3. Tel: 212-34057
Housing Department, Adickesallee 67. Tel. 212-34742
City Library, Zeil 17/23. Tel: 212-38353
University Library, Bockenheimer Landstr. 134. Tel: 212-39256
Public Works Department, Störungsdienst, Kurt-Schumacher Str. 10. Tel: 213-0
Registry Office, Römer. Tel: 212-33328
Department of Transport, Kaiserstrasse 52. Tel: 212-38800

CAR RENTAL AGENCIES

All car rental agencies offer special weekend rates (beginning Friday at noon and lasting until 9am on Monday). As a rule there is no distance limit.

AK Autovermietung, airport, Arrival A. Tel: 692534, 6905514, Fax: 694569

Al Autohansa, Savignystrasse 71. Tel: 7561000, Fax: 749349

Atlantic, Karl-Benz-Strasse 27. Tel: 424010, Fax: 42098567

Autohansa Schuldt, Mörfelder Landstrasse 92. Tel: 610707; airport Arrival A. Tel: 6905575, 6902593, Fax: 692075

Avis, airport, Arrival A. Tel: 6902777, Fax: 1537241

AVM, Frankenallee 76. Tel: 730204, Fax: 7391337

DM, Wittelsbacherallee 118-120. Tel: 490777, Fax: 490770

Eurorent, airport, Arrival A. Tel: 6905250, Fax: 06104/7829

Goinar, Schulstrasse 7. Tel: 614004/05, Fax: 624070

Hertz, airport, Arrival A. Tel: 6905011

Herzog HC, Savignystrasse 28. Tel: 740466, Fax: 742644

Inter Rent, airport, Arrival A. Tel: 6905464, Fax: 694773

Mini rent, Eckenheimer Landstrasse 91. Tel: 596 20 35, Fax: 5962038

Raule, Hanauer Landstrasse 342. Tel: 414034, Fax: 414344

Sixt Budget, airport, Arrival A. Tel: 6905237, Fax: 6905638; Allerheiligenstrasse 52. Tel: 290066, Fax: 296328

Turtle rent, Gerbermühle 34. Tel: 621105, Fax: 620030

CHAUFFEUR SERVICES

Weingärtner, exclusive chauffeur limousines, Münchner Strasse 23. Tel: 239998.
The following aforementioned car rental agencies also offer chauffeur services: AL Autohansa, DM Autovermietung, Goinar, Hertz and Sixt Budget.

CAMPER VAN RENTAL AGENCIES

Autohaus Müller, Eschersheimer Landstr. 584, Homburger Landstrasse 455. Tel: 520166, Fax: 522092

Reisemobil Rutenkolk, Friedberger Landstrasse 434. Tel: 474545, Fax: 474207

Trueblood RV, Justinianstrasse 22. Tel: 345354

REPAIRS

Autoglas, Mainzer Landstrasse 262. Tel: 733626

Boschdienst, Sonnemannstrasse 39. Tel: 439355

Haertel, Homburer Landstrasse 211. Tel: 5481406

Hoffmann, Schmidtstrasse 65. Tel: 738557

Kempen, Schmidtstrasse 47. Tel: 73301

Marti-Oros Autodienst, Gartenstrasse 147. Tel: 637696

Müller, Eschersheimer Landstrasse 591. Tel: 51 63 93

Pit-Stop, Friedrich-Ebert-Anlage 32. Tel: 745367

Thiele, Keplerstrasse 15. Tel: 552102

Autodienst Windeckstrasse, Windeckstr. 42. Tel: 444060

TOWING SERVICES (DAY & NIGHT)

Central, tel: 517711

Dentz (underground garage service), tel: 542044

Henrich (recovery service), tel: 34312, 342622

Meyer, tel: 778090

Noss (ACE), tel: 341066

Petermann (AvD), tel: 459971

Preisler, tel: 635115

Safar (ADAC), tel: 544054

FOR BUSINESS PEOPLE

Industrie- und Handelskammer (Chamber of Commerce and Industry), tel: 2197-0

Frankfurt Stock Exchange:
Foreign Exchange Market, tel: 29977-0
Stock Exchange hall, tel: 281918, 285073
Administration, tel: 29977-398
Frankfurt Grain & Commodity Exchange, tel: 2197-0
Official broker chamber, tel: 2173-0
Collective securities deposit, tel: 1302-0
Stock Exchange news: at home, tel: 1168; abroad, tel: 11608

BANKS (A SELECTION)

Deutsche Bundesbank (Central Bank) Telephone information: 19710, switchboard: 158-1; National Central Bank, tel: 2388-1

ADCA Bank, Solmsstrasse 2-26. Tel: 7906-0

Algemene Bank Nederland, Mainzer Landstrasse 39. Tel: 2553-0

Allgemeine Hypothekenbank, Bockenheimer Landstrasse 25. Tel: 7179-0

Allied Irish Banks, Oberlindau 5. Tel: 728458

American Express Bank, Theodor-Heuss-Allee 80. Tel: 793010

Amro AG, Hochstrasse 2. Tel: 290002-0

Arab Banking Corp., Niedenau 13. Tel: 714030

Australia & New Zealand Banking, Mainzer Landstrasse 46. Tel: 7100080

Banca Commerciale Italiana, Bockenheimer Landstrasse 23. Tel: 71701-0

Banco Bilbao Vizcaya, Ulmenstr. 18. Tel: 714009-0

Banco de Santander, Zeppelinallee 35. Tel: 794060

Banco di Roma, Wilhelm-Leuschner-Strasse 41. Tel: 271006-0

Banco Exterieur, Grosse Gallusstr. 1. Tel: 1330-0

Banco Hispano Americano, Bockenheimer Landstrasse 47. Tel: 714000-0

Banco di Napoli, Guiolettstrasse 54. Tel: 714008-0

Banco di Sicilia, Bockenheimer Landstrasse 13. Tel: 7122-0

Bank of America, Mainzer Landstrasse 46. Tel: 7128-00

Bank of China, Bockenheimer Landstrasse 61. Tel: 170090-0

Bank of Seoul, Mainzer Landstr. 27. Tel: 27107-0

Bankers Trust, Bockenheimer Landstrasse 39. Tel: 7132-0

Bankhaus Bethmann, Bethmannstr. 7. Tel: 2177-0

Banque Nationale de Paris, Bockenheimer Landstrasse 22. Tel: 7193-0

Barclays Bank, Bockenheimer Landstrasse 38. Tel: 71408-0

Bayerische Vereinsbank, Bleidenstr. 12. Tel: 2174-1

Berliner Bank, Bockenheimer Anlage 2. Tel: 1506-1

Bank für Gemeinwirtschaft, Theaterplatz 2. Tel: 258-0

BHF Bank, Bockenheimer Landstr. 10. Tel: 718-0

Cassa di Risparmio (Firenze, Genova etc), Rossmarkt 21. Tel: 20541

CC-Bank, Taunusanlage 21. Tel: 170006-0

Chase, Alexanderstrasse 57. Tel: 24789-0

Citibank, Neue Mainzer Strasse 75. Tel: 1366-0

Commerzbank, Neue Mainzer Str. 32. Tel: 1362-0

Continental Bank, Mainzer Landstrasse 46. Tel: 71001-0

Crédit Commercial de France, Niedenau 45. Tel: 7118-0

Credito Italiano, Westendstrasse 24. Tel: 7160-0

Dellbrück & Co, Neue Mainzer Strasse 75. Tel: 1331-0

Deutsche Bank, Taunusanlage 12. Tel: 7150-0

Deutsche Bau- und Bodenbank, Taunusanlage 8. Tel: 2557-0

Deutsche Hypothekenbank, Taunusanlage 9. Tel: 2548-0

DEVK, Untermainkai 23. Tel: 2648-0

Deutscher Kassenverein, Börsenplatz 7. Tel: 1302-0

DG Bank, Platz der Republik. Tel: 7447-01

Dresdner Bank, Jürgen-Ponto-Platz 1. Tel: 263-0

Frankfurter Sparkasse 1822, Neue Mainzer Strasse 47-53. Tel: 2641-0

Frankfurter Volksbank, Börsenstrasse 1. Tel: 2172-0

Hauck & Sohn, Kaiserstrasse 24. Tel: 2161-1

Hessische Landesbank, Junghofstrasse 26. Tel: 132-01

Hypo Bank, Bockenheimer Landstrasse 33-35. Tel: 7138-0

Korea Exchange Bank, Bockenheimer Landstrasse 5. Tel: 7129-0

Merck Finck, Neue Mainzer Strasse 55. Tel: 2564-0

Merrill Lynch, Neue Mainzer Strasse 75. Tel: 299868-0

National Westminster Bank, Feldbergstrasse 35. Tel: 17006-0

Nationalbank von Griechenland, Gutleutstrasse 5. Tel: 2550-0

New Japan Bank, Mainzer Landstrasse 46. Tel: 17098-0

Norddeutsche Landesbank, Bockenheimer Landstrasse 39. Tel: 714007-0

Ökobank, Brönnerstrasse 9. Tel: 299870-0

Oppenheim Sal, Bockenheimer Landstrasse 20. Tel: 7134-0

Ost-West Handelsbank, Stephanstr. 1. Tel: 2168-0

Prager Handelsbank, Gutleutstr. 32. Tel: 27304-0

Rothschild, Ulmenstrasse 22. Tel: 971017-0

Royal Bank of Canada, Lyoner Strasse 15. Tel: 66905-0

Salomon Brothers, Wiesenhüttenstrasse 10. Tel: 2607-0

Schweizerische Bankgesellschaft, Bleichstrasse 52. Tel: 1369-0

Schweizerische Kreditanstalt, Kaiserstrasse 30. Tel: 2691-0

Security Pacific Bank, Ulmenstr. 30. Tel: 7156-0

SGZ Bank, Bockenheimer Anlage 46. Tel: 7139-0

Skandinaviska Enskilda, Alte Rothofstrasse 8. Tel: 2983-0

Société Générale, Mainzer Landstrasse 36. Tel: 7174-0

Sparda Bank, Güterstrasse 1. Tel: 7537-0

Südwestdeutsche Landesbank, Grüneburgweg 102. Tel. 15304-0

Svenska, Wiesenau 43. Tel: 17001-0

T.C. Zirat Bankasi, Hochstrasse 50, 29805-0

The Bank of New York, Niedenau 61. Tel: 7141-0

The Bank of Tokyo, Wiesenhüttenstrasse 10. Tel: 2576-0

The Ind. Bank of Japan, Niedenau 13-19. Tel: 71405-0

UBAE Arab German Bank, Neue Mainzer Strasse 57. Tel: 2715-0

Union Investment, Mainzer Landstrasse 47a. Tel: 2567-01

Westdeutsche Landesbank, Taunusanlage 3. Tel: 2579-01

ADVERTISING AGENCIES (SELECTION)

Baginski und Muth, Hamburger Allee 45. Tel: 795008-0

CDC, Bachstelzenweg 14 (Höchst). Tel: 309066

GGK, Kennedyallee 111. Tel: 633008-0

HEAD's Communication, Hedderichstrasse 108/110. Tel: 605099-0

imago, Ginnheimer Landstrasse 1. Tel: 247714-0

Lintas, Zeppelinallee 77. Tel: 79202-0

Lowe Lürzer, Hamburger Allee 45. Tel: 79404-0

McCann, Hedderichstrasse 108. Tel: 605093-0

McCann-Erickson, Ulmenstrasse 39. Tel 7131-0

Michael Conrad + Leo Burnett, Alexanderstrasse 65. Tel: 78077-0

Ogilvy & Mather, Hainer Weg 44. Tel: 6051-0

Reporter Public Relations, Schwarzburgstrasse 10. Tel: 152000-0

Saatchi & Saatchi, Wiesenau 38. Tel:7142-0

Schell und Partner, Walter-Kolb-Strasse 13. Tel. 60909-0

Sudler & Hennessey, Lersnerstr. 23. Tel: 15301-0

J.W. Thompson, Bockenheimer Landstrasse 104. Tel: 7436-0

Young & Rubicam, Bleichstrasse 64. Tel: 2192-0

TRAVEL AGENCIES (IATA)

American Express Reise-Service, Kaiserstrasse 8. Tel: 2105-1

Thomas Cook, Kaiserstrasse 11. Tel: 1347-33

DER, Eschersheimer Landstrasse 25. Tel: 5962017

German Tourist Board, Beethovenstrasse 69. Tel: 7572-0

Euro-Lloyd, Oskar-Sommer-Strasse 15. Tel: 6316-0

Hapag-Lloyd, Kaiserstrasse 14. Tel: 2162-0

Manta, Opernplatz 6. Tel: 281286

Reisebüro Wessel, Theaterplatz 2. Tel: 238514-22

CONSULATES & MISSIONS

Argentina, Consulate General, Wiesenhüttenplatz 26, 6000 Frankfurt 1. Tel: 233644

Australia, Consulate General, Gutleutstrasse 85, 6000 Frankfurt 1. Tel: 2739090

Austria, Consulate General, Am Weingarten 25, 6000 Frankfurt 90. Tel: 7072558

Belgium, Consulate General, Fellnerstrasse 5, 6000 Frankfurt 1. Tel: 590578

Brazil, Consulate General, Stephanstrasse 3, 6000 Frankfurt 1. Tel: 290708

Cameroon, Honorary Consulate, Mainzer Landstrasse 41, 6000 Frankfurt 1. Tel: 2542311

Chile, Consulate General, Humboldtstrasse 64, 6000 Frankfurt 1. Tel: 550194

Colombia, Consulate General, Rudolfstrasse 13–17, 6000 Frankfurt 1. Tel: 251650

Cyprus, Consulate General, Theaterplatz 2, 6000 Frankfurt 1. Tel: 232821

Denmark, Consulate General, Am Leonhardsbrunn 20, 6000 Frankfurt 90. Tel: 773091

Dominican Republic, Consulate General, Fuchshol 59, 6000 Frankfurt 50. Tel: 521035

Ecuador, Honorary Consulate, Berliner Strasse 56–58, 6000 Frankfurt 1. Tel: 1332295

Egypt, Consulate General, Eysseneckstrasse 52, 6000 Frankfurt 1. Tel: 590557

El Salvador, Consulate, Stresemannallee 35–37, 6000 Frankfurt 70. Tel: 638511

Finland, Consulate General, Lessingstrasse 5, 6000 Frankfurt 1. Tel: 728148

France, Consulate General, Ludolfusstrasse 13, 6000 Frankfurt 90. Tel: 7950960

Greece, Consulate General, Cronstettenstrasse 64, 6000 Frankfurt 1. Tel: 595750

Iceland, Consulate General, Schmidtstrasse 12, 6000 Frankfurt 1. Tel: 731646

India, Consulate General, Wilhelm Leuschner Str. 93, 6000 Frankfurt 1. Tel: 271040

Iran, Consulate General, Guilettstrasse 56, 6000 Frankfurt 1. Tel: 71400 50

Italy, Consulate General, Beethovenstrasse 17, 6000 Frankfurt 1. Tel: 75310

Japan, Consulate General, Hamburger Allee 2, 6000 Frankfurt 90. Tel: 770351

Kenya, Consulate General, Hochstrasse 53, 6000 Frankfurt 1. Tel: 282551

Korea, Consulate General, Eschersheimer Landstrasse 327, 6000 Frankfurt 1. Tel: 563051

Liberia, Honorary Consulate General, Bernusstrasse 7, 6000 Frankfurt 90. Tel: 457075

Luxembourg, Consulate, Jürgen-Ponto-Platz 2, 6000 Frankfurt 1. Tel: 236611

Mexico, Consulate, Neue Mainzer Strasse 57, 6000 Frankfurt 1. Tel: 235709, 230514

Morocco, Consulate General, Wiesenhüttenplatz 26, 6000 Frankfurt 1. Tel: 231737

Nepal, Royal, Consulate, Flinschstrasse 63, 6000 Frankfurt 60. Tel: 40871

Netherlands, Consulate General, Beethovenstrasse 5, 6000 Frankfurt 1. Tel: 752021

Norway, Royal Consulate, Hanauer Landstrasse 330, 6000 Frankfurt 1. Tel: 411040

Oman Sultanate, Honorary Consulate, Mainzer Landstrasse 46, 6000 Frankfurt 1. Tel: 721036

Pakistan, Consulate, Börsenstrasse 14, 6000 Frankfurt 1. Tel: 287489

Peru, Consulate General, Rossmarkt 14, 6000 Frankfurt 1. Tel: 20301

Philippines, Consulate, Dreieichstrasse 59, 6000 Frankfurt 70. Tel: 627538

Portuguese, Consulate General, Zeppelinallee 15, 6000 Frankfurt 1. Tel: 702066

Senegal, Consulate, Grosse Bockenheimer Strasse 41, 6000 Frankfurt 1. Tel: 288187

Sierra Leone, Consulate, Melsunger Strasse 5, 6000 Frankfurt 60. Tel: 476707

South Africa, Consulate, Ulmenstrasse 37, 6000 Frankfurt 1. Tel: 7191130

Spain, Consulate General, Steinlestrasse 6, 6000 Frankfurt 1. Tel: 638071

St. Lucia, Consulate, Steinberger Frankfurter Hof, Am Kaiserplatz 1, 6000 Frankfurt 1. Tel: 21580-0

Sweden, Consulate General, Gutleutstrasse 45, 6000 Frankfurt 1. Tel: 230479

Switzerland, Consulate General, Bockenheimer Landstr. 2, 6000 Frankfurt 1. Tel: 725941

Tanzania, Consulate, Bettinaplatz 2, 6000 Frankfurt 1. Tel: 745989

Thailand, Honorary Consulate, Rossmarkt 14, 6000 Frankfurt 1. Tel: 20110

Turkey, Consulate General, Baseler Str. 37, 6000 Frankfurt 1. Tel: 7950030

United Kingdom, Consulate General, Bockenheimer Landstr. 42, 6000 Frankfurt 1. Tel: 1700020

United States of America, Consulate General, Sismayerstrasse 21, 6000 Frankfurt 1. Tel: 7535-0

Uruguay, Consulate, Eschersheimer Landstrasse 532, 6000 Frankfurt 50. Tel: 518510

Venezuela, Consulate, Brönnerstrasse 17, 6000 Frankfurt 1. Tel: 287284

ART/PHOTO CREDITS

INDEX

INSIGHT *POCKET* GUIDES

● ●

United States: **Houghton Mifflin Company, Boston MA 02108**
Tel: (800) 2253362 Fax: (800) 4589501

Canada: **Thomas Allen & Son, 390 Steelcase Road East**
Markham, Ontario L3R 1G2
Tel: (416) 4759126 Fax: (416) 4756747

Great Britain: **GeoCenter UK, Hampshire RG22 4BJ**
Tel: (256) 817987 Fax: (256) 817988

Worldwide: **Höfer Communications Singapore 2262**
Tel: (65) 8612755 Fax: (65) 8616438

"I was first drawn to the Insight Guides by the excellent "Nepal" volume. I can think of no book which so effectively captures the essence of a country. Out of these pages leaped the Nepal I know – the captivating charm of a people and their culture. I've since discovered and enjoyed the entire Insight Guide Series. Each volume deals with a country or city in the same sensitive depth, which is nowhere more evident than in the superb photography. **"**

Sir Edmund Hillary